ROSEMARY J.
STEVENSON
University of Durham, UK

Language,
Thought
and
Representation

JOHN WILEY & SONS
Chichester · New York · Brisbane · Toronto · Singapore

Copyright © 1993 by John Wiley & Sons Ltd,
Baffins Lane, Chichester,
West Sussex PO19 1UD, England

Other Wiley Editorial Offices

John Wiley & Sons, Inc., 605 Third Avenue,
New York, NY 10158-0012, USA

Jacaranda Wiley Ltd, G.P.O. Box 859, Brisbane,
Queensland 4001, Australia

John Wiley & Sons (Canada) Ltd, 22 Worcester Road,
Rexdale, Ontario M9W 1L1, Canada

John Wiley & Sons (SEA) Pte Ltd, 37 Jalan Pemimpin #05-04,
Block B, Union Industrial Building, Singapore 2057

Library of Congress Cataloging-in-Publication Data

Stevenson, Rosemary J.
  Language, thought and representation / Rosemary J. Stevenson.
    p.   cm.
  Includes bibliographical references and index.
  ISBN 0-471-93629-4 (pbk.)
  1. Psychlinguistics.   2. Cognitive psychology.   3. Performance.   4. Thought
and thinking.   5. Mental representation.   I.Title.
  BF455.S7148   1993
  153—dc20   92–18679
                                                                  CIP

British Library Cataloguing in Publication Data

A catalogue record for this book is available from the British Library

ISBN 0-471-93629-4

Typeset in 10.5/13pt Palatino from author's disks by Text Processing Department,
John Wiley & Sons Ltd, Chichester
Printed and bound in Great Britain by Biddles Ltd, Guildford, Surrey

Language,
Thought
and
Representation

CONTENTS

PREFACE

In this book, I have tried to convey the enormous progress that has been made in our understanding of cognitive processes since the early days of cognitive psychology. I have also tried to convey my belief that theories are rarely wrong. Instead they focus on different parts of the total phenomenon. While such focusing is necessary to reveal the intricacies of each component part, I firmly believe that an overall picture of cognition must show how the component parts combine and interact. Furthermore, a serious answer to the questions posed by psychology, which acknowledges the value of different points of view, must explain why each view is useful and how the different proposed processes operate together. That is what I have tried to do. Not in any specific part, but in the book as a whole. I have tried, that is, to paint an integrated picture of language and thinking that respects both their interrelatedness and the features that make them distinct.

I have been helped in this endeavour by a number of people who have kindly given their time to read and comment on one or more chapters. My thanks to them all. They are Robin Cooper, Jonathan Evans, Phil Johnson-Laird, David Kleinman, David Over, Martin Pickering, Tony Sanford, Keith Stenning, Agnieszka Urbanowicz, and Henk Zeevat. David Kleinman's contribution extended far beyond his views on some of the chapters. John Wiley's reviewer read and commented upon all the chapters and successfully encouraged me to include a final chapter, which resulted in Chapter 12. Thanks are also due to Peter Whewell, who might be surprised to learn that he is probably responsible for both the structure and the content of the final chapter. I also thank Ros Crawley with whom I have shared my thoughts over a number of years. Two generations of students in my final year Cognitive Science option at Durham University have been subjected to earlier versions of the book. Their insightful comments and their willingness to say when something was not clear have been inestimable. Wendy Hudlass at John Wiley maintained just the right balance between urgency and patience throughout. Thanks also to Malcolm Rolling for preparing the figures, to Noa Kleinman for preparing the index, and to Ros Crawley for letting me use a bibliography she had compiled. It has been my good fortune, while writing the book, to be part of the Human Communication Research Centre at Edinburgh, Glasgow and Durham Universities, where the opportunity to talk about language and thinking in an interdisciplinary environment has been invaluable. Finally, my thanks to the Psychology Department at Durham, where my almost total retreat behind the closed doors of my office while the writing was in progress seems to have been regarded with bemused tolerance.

The book starts from the point where perceptual processes have identified the individual words of a sentence and focuses on the processes of language that combine the words to yield an interpretation of the sentence. This means that none of the work on word recognition has been included. Instead, I have concentrated on those aspects of language comprehension that seem to require the use of linguistic processing rather than perceptual processing. This has enabled me to focus on the processes of language on the one hand and the processes of thought on the other. The first chapter sets the scene for the subsequent chapters. It presents an historical overview of the way that ideas about language and thinking have developed from the early days of cognitive psychology to the present time. Chapter 2 discusses representation and introduces symbolic, connectionist and hybrid representational systems, which are frequently referred to in the rest of the book. There follow four chapters dealing with basic topics in language: syntactic processing, semantic processing, and the processing of texts and of discourse; and five chapters that deal with basic topics in thinking: reasoning, concepts, problem solving, expertise and creativity, hypothesis testing and decision making. The final chapter is an attempt to make explicit the way in which an integrated account of cognition can be developed. I discuss language, thought and representation in relation to some common themes that recur in the book and use those themes to show how an integrated model of language and thinking is possible.

Lastly, a word on gender neutral language. For the most part, either I have used the phrase 'he or she' where the generic pronoun is required, or I have avoided using a pronoun altogether by choosing a different construction. Where this second option proved difficult and the use of the above phrase resulted in clumsy prose (because of repeated repetition for example), I have used the pronoun 'she' instead. I am aware that the British Psychological Society requires that in the interests of neutrality neither 'he' nor 'she' should be used in isolation. However, in the combined interests of producing readable prose and of redressing the imbalance resulting from centuries of texts containing 'he', I felt that 'she' was surely appropriate.

Rosemary Stevenson

Durham, April 1992

CHAPTER 1   Language and thought

Most people would agree that language and thinking are central human activities. They are certainly major components of human cognition. Among other things, thinking guides our actions in the world and language guides our communications with others. What is much harder to agree upon is the nature of these two systems and how they relate to each other. Take language, for example. Behaviourists believed language to be exactly the same as any other learned behaviour, subject to similar rules and principles (e.g. Skinner, 1957). By contrast, Chomsky (1959) argued forcefully that language was a specific cognitive skill governed by its own rules of grammar and that it defied analysis in terms of conditioning and learning.

Views of thinking are equally divergent. They range from views that propose a set of general purpose rules that are applied in any domain to highly specific rules that are domain specific. General purpose rules have been proposed in problem solving (Newell and Simon, 1972), decision making (Kahneman and Tversky, 1972a, b), deduction (Braine, 1978; Johnson-Laird, 1983; Rips, 1983), cognitive development (Bruner, Olver, Greenfield et al., 1966; Piaget, 1950; Vygotsky, 1934) and concept formation (Medin and Smith, 1984; Rosch, 1973). Domain-specific rules have been proposed in problem solving (Chi, Glaser and Farr, 1988), deduction (Cheng and Holyoak, 1985; Cosmides, 1989), cognitive development (Carey, 1985; Gelman, 1990; Keil, 1989; Markman, 1989), and concept formation (Murphy and Medin, 1985; Murphy, 1988, 1990).

In a similar vein, the nature of the relationship between language and thought has been hotly debated. Some behaviourists believe that they are the same thing (e.g. Watson, 1925), while Chomsky and his followers believe that language and thought are distinct (Chomsky, 1957, 1965, 1980). People who have studied other languages (frequently exotic ones) have believed that thought is determined by language (e.g. Sapir, 1944; Whorf, 1941), while Piaget (1950) believed that language is determined by thought.

This chapter comments on the nature of language and thought and on the relationship between them. First, a description is given of language on the one hand and thought on the other. Second, the way in which the two abilities have been discussed in cognitive psychology is traced from Chomsky's influence in the early 1960s up to the present day. Assumptions about the relationship between language and thought, which underlie these discussions, are pointed out. In particular, two dominant views can be discerned, which have recently led to a third combined view. One (influenced by Chomsky) sees language and thought as distinct and independent abilities. The other sees language and thought as components of a single integrated system. The third, combined view holds that language and thought are distinct but interrelated systems. The independence view was prevalent in the early days of cognitive psychology, while the integrationist view was most prominent in the 1970s. The 1980s saw the emergence of the combined view. However, before tracing the development of these views, it is necessary to define language and thinking.

LANGUAGE AND THOUGHT DEFINED

Language

Language is very difficult to pin down. It is used as a basis for communication, but we need to go beyond its communicative function if we wish to establish what makes it unique. We need to consider its structure, the component abilities that contribute to successful language use. Regardless of the particular stand that is taken on the relation between language and thought, it is possible to distinguish between linguistic and non-linguistic abilities. Linguistic abilities consist of syntactic, semantic and phonological operations, while non-linguistic abilities consist of our general cognitive abilities, that is, thinking. Consider first, syntax and semantics.

Syntax is concerned with the structure of language. For example, in the following sentence:

John loves Mary.   (1.1)

John is the subject of the verb and *Mary* is the object. In English, this syntactic, or structural, information is conveyed by word order: the first noun in an active sentence is the subject, as in the above example. Other languages code syntactic information in different ways, by inflections for example. In every language, though, syntactic information plays an important role in specifying the relations that hold between the words in the sentence.

In 1965 Chomsky made an important distinction between two levels of language, which he called a deep structure and a surface structure. The deep structure of language characterized the basic semantic relations of a sentence, the proposition it expresses, while the surface structure carried all the information that is actually spoken. In Chomsky's view at that time, active and passive sentences were said to have the same deep structure. Thus, the passive sentence, shown in (1.2), that corresponds to the active in (1.1) expresses the same grammatical relations as (1.1).

Mary is loved by John.   (1.2)

In both the active and the passive, *John* is the subject of the verb *to love* and *Mary* is the object. The first noun in the passive sentence, *Mary*, is sometimes said to be the subject of the sentence. However, in Chomsky's theory, *Mary* is the surface subject, that is, it is only the subject at the level of surface structure. At the level of deep structure, *John* is the subject and *Mary* the object. To clarify which subject is being referred to in a sentence where the surface and the deep subject are different, the term logical subject is often used to refer to the deep subject.

Both (1.1) and (1.2) are surface structures: the final string of words in the sentence, although (1.1) retains the deep structure word order. To convert a deep structure into a surface structure, transformational rules were used. Minimal transformational rules were required to convert a deep structure to an active surface form. Thus, in (1.1), for example, a transformational rule would ensure that the present tense ending -*s* was added to the verb *love*. To derive the surface word order in the passive sentence, transformations such as the following were proposed:

1.   transpose the two noun phrases (*John* and *Mary*);
2.   add the preposition *by*;
3.   add the auxiliary verb *be*;
4.   add inflections to the verb (e.g. *is loved*).

Since the 1960s, Chomsky's model of grammar has undergone considerable revision (e.g. Chomsky, 1981), and in the current theory, active and passive sentences are assumed to have different deep structures (now called d-structures). Nevertheless, the distinction between deep and surface structures had considerable impact on psychology, and the notion that there is a basic meaning to a sentence, the proposition it expresses, that can be determined by referring to deep grammatical relations, remains a core notion in much psychological theorizing about language. (See Greene (1986) for a clear account of Chomsky's (1957, 1965) views, and Stevenson (1988) for an account of the changes to the theory in recent years.)

Semantics is concerned with meaning. To know the meaning of a sentence is to know what the world would have to be like for the sentence to be true. Thus, if you know what the following sentence means:

Anthony Hopkins will open the new theatre.   (1.3)

you are in position to complain if you turn up to the opening ceremony and the mayor opens the theatre instead. Because you know what the sentence means, you know what situations make it true or false.

Syntax and semantics, together with phonology, which specifies the sounds associated with the words of a language, make up the grammar of the language. The grammar is logically sufficient to describe the sentences that people use, and many linguists are preoccupied with spelling out the rules that underlie grammar. However, as far as psychology is concerned, grammar alone is not enough. For successful communication we need to take account of non-linguistic knowledge, or pragmatics.

Pragmatics concerns those aspects of comprehension that depend on inferences based on non-linguistic general knowledge. For example, if someone were to say, *I'm going to the pub*, then no amount of linguistic knowledge will enable you to find the pub in question, unless you have non-linguistic knowledge of their drinking habits. Then you can infer that the person means *The Victoria pub*. Of course, the sentence itself is very simple, its syntax and semantics are straightforward and so the linguistic meaning is easy to discern. Pragmatics is concerned with the information over and above the linguistic meaning and it consists of inferences based on non-linguistic world knowledge.

Thought

Thinking enables us to derive conclusions on the basis of what we already know. To derive a conclusion is to make an inference, which can informally be defined as something that has not been explicitly stated but that follows from the explicit information. Inferences can be categorized into two broad classes: deductive and inductive. Deductive inferences are logical inferences; they necessarily follow from the premises (the explicit information). The syllogism in (1.4) is a an example of a deductive argument:

All authors are human.   (1.4)
All humans are mortal.

Therefore, All authors are mortal.

The relationship between *authors* and *mortal* in the conclusion has been inferred from the information in the premises. Inductive inferences, on the other hand, are non-logical inferences, they do not necessarily follow from the premises. In general, the inference that is accepted is the one that is deemed the most plausible. Consider the example in (1.5):

Twenty witnesses saw Joe leave the library with a knife.   (1.5)
The victim was stabbed through the heart in the library.

Therefore, Joe committed the murder.

Although things look bad for Joe, the case is not watertight, and other conclusions are possible. Joe may only have discovered the murder, for example, or the victim may have been killed before being stabbed. The inference is not deductively valid, but the truth of the premises renders it plausible. Inductive inferences do not depend on explicit premises in the way that deductions do. Thus, if you read a text that contains the following sentence:

John watched the bird pecking at the ice.   (1.6)

you may well infer that the bird flies. In this case you have supplied, by induction, additional information based on a knowledge of birds. As with the previous example, though, the inference is not watertight. It is based on default information: that in the absence of any information to the contrary, birds normally have wings. Thus, it may turn out to be wrong. The bird may be injured so that it cannot fly, or it might be a flightless bird, such as a penguin.

Overall, however, in both forms of thinking, a conclusion that was not explicitly stated must be inferred. The two types of thinking differ in the nature of the inference. Deductions depend on the rules of logic. As long as the rules have been correctly followed, a deductive argument guarantees that the conclusion is correct. But with induction, no such guarantee is possible. Inductions are best guesses or hunches based on whatever information is available. Induction has been studied in a number of different ways: in problem solving and creativity, in concept formation, and in hypothesis testing, although deduction is generally involved as well in these cases. Such breadth of coverage reflects the fact that induction is at stake whenever new knowledge about the world is acquired. The inferences that are made are conclusions about the state of the world. By contrast, deduction does not involve learning something new, since the conclusion that is arrived at by deduction is already contained in the premises and only needs to be made explicit. Armed with these brief definitions of language and thought, we can now turn our attention to the relationship between them. This requires a consideration of the way that the two have been discussed in cognitive psychology.

LANGUAGE AND THINKING: A BRIEF REVIEW

This discussion is divided into three sections, one that considers developments in the 1960s; one that considers developments in the 1970s; and one that considers developments in the 1980s. These time bands are very approximate and are used only to distinguish between early, later, and current work. In actual fact, the developments to be discussed occurred gradually over the entire period. Nevertheless, each decade seems to have distinctive characteristics, and it is these characteristics that are emphasized below.

The Early Days of Cognitive Psychology: the 1960s

Language and the influence of Chomsky

In the 1960s, Chomsky's ideas focused the attention of many psychologists on syntax. According to Chomsky (1957, 1965), syntax explained the creativity of language: the fact that we routinely produce and comprehend sentences that we have never encountered before. Such creativity is possible because syntactic rules enable words to be combined in novel ways. The distinction between deep and surface structures, which has already been described, was crucial to Chomsky's account of creativity. Transformational rules acting upon a limited number of deep structures could generate an infinite number of surface structures. Chomsky's work is that of a linguist, it explains people's underlying competence, that is, the tacit knowledge of the rules of language. Competence is distinct from performance, which is the subject matter of psychology. Performance is concerned with the processes that underlie comprehension and production where constraints on memory, for example, may mask the underlying competence. Overall, Chomsky's major contributions to psychology have been the deep and surface structure distinction, the competence/performance distinction, and the emphasis on the importance of syntax.

In 1962, the psychologist, George Miller suggested that the rules of competence proposed by Chomsky might also be used to characterize performance. Miller put forward the kernelization hypothesis. This stated that when sentences are remembered, they are mentally 'detransformed' (the transformations are run backwards) and stored in their kernel (deep structure) form, together with a set of transformational footnotes that indicate the transformations that are needed to restore the original sentence. There followed a flurry of experimentation testing Miller's hypothesis, which resulted in a number of positive results (e.g. Savin and Perchonock, 1965). However, much of the work turned out to be flawed in one way or another, and attention subsequently turned elsewhere. Nevertheless, the interest in syntax has been maintained and it reflects a view of language and thinking that holds that they are distinct abilities. As Chomsky argued, the rules of syntax are very specific and so cannot be reduced to general laws of thought. Language and thought, therefore, are seen as independent, and this view was predominant in the 1960s.

Thinking

The study of thinking during this period seemed to take longer to emerge from the Behaviourist doldrums, and focused on the factors that affected thinking rather than trying to study the thinking process itself. However, Piaget's work (e.g. Piaget, 1926) on cognitive development continued throughout the behaviourist era, and his ideas were widely accepted in the 1960s. Some notable cognitive psychologists went beyond behaviourist thinking in the 1960s and the work of these individuals can be seen as precursors to the independence view on the one hand (e.g. Newell and Simon, 1972) and the integrationist view on the other (e.g. Wason, 1960, 1968).

Studies of induction in problem solving being conducted during this period had enormous significance for later developments and continue to be very influential today. In 1958, Newell, Shaw and Simon produced a computer program called the Logic Theorist, which was capable of proving 38 of the theorems from Whitehead and Russell's (1910–1913) *Principia Mathematica*. That is, it was capable of simulating logical thinking. More importantly, Newell et al. (Newell, Shaw and Simon, 1958) claimed that they were not merely demonstrating a 'thinking machine', rather they were demonstrating thinking of the kind carried out by humans. The program, therefore, was a full-blown simulation of the kinds of processes they thought responsible for human thinking. Thus began a programme of experimentation by Newell and Simon and their colleagues that was to result in the information processing view of problem solving. Newell and Simon demonstrated that most simple problems consisted of a vast number of possible solutions, and that each solution could be broken down into a series of discrete steps. They called the range of possible solutions the problem space (Newell and Simon, 1972) and argued that successful problem solving was the result of a search for a route through this problem space. They also distinguished between algorithmic processes, which are deductive and guarantee that the correct route will be found, and heuristic processes, which are inductive 'best guesses' at choosing a route to a solution and do not guarantee success. According to Newell and Simon (1972), most problem solving is inductive and makes use of heuristic strategies.

This work was reviewed by Newell and Simon in 1972, and an influential aspect of it was the proposal that there is a small number of general purpose heuristics that are used to solve a wide range of problems. Working backwards from something that has already been proved to something that needs to be proved is an example of such general purpose heuristics. Newell and Simon, therefore, laid the groundwork for an independence view of language and thinking by stressing the use of general purpose rules. They also put forward a view of thinking that emphasized the serial, deliberate nature of analytic thought, thus highlighting even more the dissociation of thinking from language comprehension, which is fast, automatic and not amenable to conscious reflection.

A specific version of general purpose rules was propounded by Piaget, namely, that people possess a mental logic. That is, the mind uses rules that are the mental equivalent of the rules of logic and these rules are applied to any logical problem. According to this view, the mental rules of logic will automatically be applied to a problem to yield the correct solution. This view remained virtually unchallenged until some dramatic demonstrations by Wason showed that people deviate from logical principles in consistent ways. Wason showed, for example, that in trying to test a hypothesis, people persistently try to confirm their hypothesis when logical rules dictate that falsification should be used (Wason, 1960). More significantly, Wason showed that the ease with which people conform to logical principles when testing a hypothesis, depends crucially on the content of the problem (e.g. Wason, 1968; Wason and Shapiro, 1971). People readily solve problems that have a familiar content, but they have extreme difficulty with abstract problems, even when the two kinds of problem have identical logical structures. Wason's work, therefore, undermined the view that there are general purpose rules of thought that are applied to any problem.

Thus, Wason's work emphasized the importance of specific knowledge for thinking, and as such it can be seen as an early influence on integrationist views, in which domain-specific knowledge supports inferences in both language and thinking. However, the studies that were carried out in the 1960s, on both deduction and induction, studied phenomena that were very different from linguistic phenomena, or more specifically, syntax. Work on thinking, in other words, also reflected an assumption that language and thought are distinct.

Meaning and Inference: Cognitive Psychology in the 1970s

Language

The preoccupation with syntax in the early 1960s soon gave way to an alternative view of linguistic performance, a view that recognized the importance of semantics rather than syntax and of non-linguistic world knowledge (pragmatics) rather than linguistic knowledge.

First, a study by Sachs (1967) cast doubt on Miller's idea that transformational footnotes are stored along with the kernel sentence. Previous workers (e.g. Savin and Perchonock, 1965) had argued that the more transformational footnotes that need to be stored, the greater will be the memory load and so the more likely it is that they are forgotten. If this were the case, then passive sentences should be forgotten more readily than active sentences, since they require more transformations than do actives. However, Sachs found that active sentences were forgotten just as readily as passive sentences. In particular, when given a recognition test, subjects confused an active with its passive equivalent just as frequently as they confused an original passive with its active equivalent. This should not happen according to Miller's hypothesis. Transformations can be forgotten, which is what happened with passive sentences, but they should not be added, yet this is what happened with the active sentences. Thus, the part of Miller's hypothesis concerning the storage of transformational footnotes was disconfirmed.

However, Sachs' results were still consistent with the part of Miller's hypothesis that stated that the sentence was stored in its kernel form. Subjects never confused the original sentence with one of a different meaning, and in Sachs' study meaning was perfectly correlated with the deep structure of the sentence. A study by Johnson-Laird and Stevenson (1970) tested this part of Miller's view. They found that subjects did confuse sentences with different deep structures as long as they were not informed of the subsequent memory test. Thus, when subjects were presented with the sentence:

John liked the painting and he bought it from the duchess. (1.7)

at recognition, they frequently said that they had actually heard the following sentence:

The painting pleased John and he bought it from the duchess. (1.8)

While similar in meaning, these two sentences differ in their deep structure. In (1.7) *John* is the subject of the verb and *the painting* is the object. In (1.8) the grammatical roles are reversed: *the duchess* is the subject and *John* is the object. Thus it appears that the meaning of a sentence is remembered, but not its deep structure syntax.

If sentences are not remembered as deep structures, how are they remembered? Two proposals became popular in the early 1970s. One was that a sentence is stored as a set of propositions that encode the linguistic meaning of the sentence (e.g. Fodor, Bever and Garrett, 1974; Fodor, Fodor and Garrett, 1975; Kintsch, 1974). The other was that people forget the linguistic information altogether and store an abstract conceptual representation of the ideas expressed in the sentence. This latter proposal was due to Bransford and his colleagues (e.g. Johnson, Bransford and Solomon, 1973; Barclay, 1973; Bransford and Franks, 1971; Bransford and Johnson, 1972). Its basic claim was that the underlying ideas are abstracted from the linguistic input and it is the underlying ideas that are stored in memory, not the linguistic structure. Thus, the two opposing views of the relationship between language and thought are represented, the dependence view and the integrationist views respectively. For Fodor et al. and for Kintsch, language and thinking were distinct and separable processes, while for Bransford and his colleagues, comprehension invariably involved the use of inferences, both deductive and inductive. That is, language comprehension involved thinking.

To highlight the issues involved in this debate, consider the following sentence:

John killed Mary.   (1.9)

On hearing sentence (1.9) there are a number of other things that can be inferred from it. First, the fact that Mary died can be inferred. This inference is necessarily true if the sentence is true. It is therefore a logical (or deductive) inference. However, there are other inferences that can be made after hearing sentence (1.9). These additional inferences are not necessarily true but they are plausible given the information in the sentence, together with a context. Thus, if there is much blood at the scene of the crime together with a blood-stained knife, then it might be plausible to infer that John stabbed Mary. Of course, this inference may be unwarranted. It is inductive rather than deductive. Nevertheless, if you want to construct a representation of the situation described by the sentence, then a number of these inferences must be made. For example, to represent the sentence above in such a way requires knowledge of (or an inductive guess at) the scene of the murder, the manner in which the murder was carried out, the consequences for Mary, and so on. In short, it requires both inductive and deductive inferences. Bransford and his colleagues argued that these inferences are made during comprehension so that a non-linguistic conceptual representation of the information is constructed. Fodor et al., on the other hand, argued that inferences are not involved in comprehension and only a propositional representation of the sentence is constructed. These contrasting views received a lot of attention in the 1970s and their developments are discussed below, first with respect to language and then with respect to thinking.

The independence view of language Fodor et al. and Kintsch argued that the end-product of language comprehension is the linguistic meaning of the sentence, devoid of any inferences. A non-linguistic representation may require the use of such inferences, but these are not part of comprehension. Instead, they are part of a separate optional inference process that may be used to construct a non-linguistic representation if necessary. Linguistic meaning is usually expressed in the form of propositions. These consist of a relation (or predicate) and one or more arguments. For example, the propositional representation of the sentence above consists of the predicate *kill*, and two arguments, *John* and *Mary*, as shown below:

KILL (JOHN,MARY). (1.10)

The arguments of a proposition are ordered so that they express the syntactic relationships between them and the predicate. The first argument in the list is always the logical subject of the verb (or other predicate), while the second argument is the logical object.

Fodor and his colleagues spearheaded a research tradition that continues to this day (e.g. Frazier, 1990), a tradition that focuses on linguistic processes in comprehension. Fodor, Bever and Garrett (1974), for example, proposed that the propositions that are constructed during comprehension reflect deep structure relations. They therefore suggested that during comprehension, people use heuristic strategies to infer propositional structure. Such strategies do not guarantee that the correct deep structure will be found but they enable informed guesses to be made. The strategies proposed by Fodor et al. exploit syntactic knowledge. Thus, one strategy said: carry out a lexical analysis of the verb. This strategy assumes that part of the information that a person has about individual verbs concerns the deep structures that they can enter. For example, the verb *hit* is a pure transitive verb. It can occur only in a deep structure that contains a direct object. By contrast, a verb like *request* appears not only in sentences with a direct object (e.g. *Alice requested a raise.*) but also in a variety of other constructions, such as:

> Alice requested that Bill leave immediately.   (1.11)
> Alice requested Bill to leave the room.

Fodor et al. suggested that an early step in comprehension determines what deep structures are compatible with the verb in the sentence. Where there is more than one compatible deep structure, as with request, other information is needed to decide which is the right one. This means that sentences containing verbs like *request* should be harder to understand than sentences containing pure transitive verbs like *hit*. A study by Fodor, Garrett and Bever (1968) confirmed this expectation.

Numerous studies suggested that comprehension involved a wide range of possible strategies, many of which were enumerated by Kimball (1973). Semantic strategies have also been proposed, as can be seen in the extensive review by Clark and Clark (1977). For example, Bever (1970) proposed the following semantic strategy: *Using content words alone, build propositions that make sense and analyse the sentence accordingly.*

Thus, both syntactic and semantic knowledge were seen to guide the construction of a propositional representation of the sentence. The merit of this approach is that it has enabled a detailed picture of linguistic (particularly syntactic) processes to be painted (see Chapter 3). However, its drawback is its failure to address the issue of how non-linguistic processes might contribute to language comprehension. Indeed, the syntactic theorists denied the possibility of such a contribution. However, in the 1970s, this issue was confronted head-on by Bransford and his colleagues.

The integrationist view of language Bransford et al. carried out a number of studies that revealed the role of non-linguistic inferences in language comprehension. First, they showed that people make both logical (deductive) and non-logical (inductive) inferences in order to integrate information from different sentences. This results in a single integrated representation of a set of sentences (Barclay, 1973; Bransford and Franks, 1971). Second, they showed that people make inferences based on what they hear in conjunction with general knowledge of the world and so remember more than is explicitly expressed in a sentence (Johnson, Bransford and Solomon, 1973).

Barclay (1973) showed that people use deductive inferences to construct an integrated representation of a text. He used texts that supported transitive inferences, based on the logical properties of relations such as *to the right of*. Subjects were presented with a series of 11 sentences, each of which described a spatial relationship between two animals. Some examples are the following:

> The giraffe is to the right of the lion.   (1.12)
> The bear is to the left of the moose.
> The moose is to the right of the lion.
> The moose is to the left of the cow.
> The lion is to the left of the bear.

The complete set of sentences described an array of animals as in:

> lion   bear   moose   giraffe   cow

Subjects were told either to memorize the sentences or to figure out the array. In a subsequent recognition test, the memorizers tended to be accurate in their performance, recognizing the sentences they had actually heard and rejecting those they had not. However, the array subjects not only correctly recognized the original sentences, they also said that they had heard sentences that described the array but that had not been originally presented. For example, given the sentences above, they might say that they had actually heard the sentence: *The bear is to the left of the giraffe*, which correctly describes the final array but was not one of the original sentences. These subjects, therefore, seemed to remember the situation described by the sentences, the final array, not the sentences themselves.

Bransford and Franks (1971) demonstrated a similar phenomenon with non-logical inductive inferences. They presented subjects with a list of sentences that described four different ideas. For example, one idea was:

> The scared cat, running from the barking dog, jumped   (1.13)
> on the table.

Another was:

> The girl who lives next door broke the large window   (1.14)
> on the porch.

Each idea consisted of four propositions. The propositions in (1.13) above are:

> The cat was scared.   (1.15)
> The dog was barking.
> The cat was running from the dog.
> The cat jumped on the table.

In the presentation list, subjects heard sentences containing one, two or three propositions, but they never heard the complete idea, a sentence that contained all four propositions. Further, sentences from each of the four ideas were randomly interspersed throughout the list, so that the sentences containing propositions from a single idea were not presented together. After hearing the presentation list, the subjects were given an unexpected recognition test, which consisted completely of new sentences. Some of them were clearly wrong since they combined propositions from two different ideas, e.g.:

> The scared cat which broke the window on the porch   (1.16)
> jumped on the table.

Subjects correctly rejected these sentences. Others presented new combinations of two or three propositions in an idea, while yet others contained all four propositions. Subjects generally said that they had heard these before. Moreover, the more propositions a sentence contained, the more confident were the subjects that they had heard it before. The highest confidence ratings were given for sentences containing all four propositions, even though no sentences in the presentation list had contained all four. Thus, the more closely a recognition sentence matched the underlying idea the more likely were the subjects to say they had heard it before. These results suggest that, on hearing the sentences, subjects integrate the information about each idea and the underlying idea is remembered, not the original sentences. Subjects, therefore, used induction to infer that different sentences described a single event and so a single integrated representation of the event (the idea) could be stored in memory.

Subjects also make inferences from what they hear to 'flesh out' the linguistic input and they remember the inferred information as well as the explicit information in the sentence. Johnson, Bransford and Solomon (1973) presented subjects with a series of short texts such as the following:

> The farmer must be warned of the oncoming flood,   (1.17)
> the sheriff cried. He mounted as quickly as possible
> since he knew that it would take quite a while to spread
> all the news.

In a subsequent recognition memory test, sentences containing inferences that were not explicitly stated were included, e.g.:

> He mounted his horse as quickly as possible since   (1.18)
> he knew that it would take quite a while to spread
> all the news.

Subjects were just as likely to say that they had heard an inference sentence before as they were to say they had heard the original sentence. In other words, subjects made inductive inferences based on general knowledge to fill in the details that were not explicitly stated and that is what is remembered: the original information together with the inferred details.

These studies by Bransford and his colleagues point to one conclusion: Linguistic processes are insufficient to account for the way we comprehend and remember sentences. Thinking, the ability to make inferences, is needed. Bransford et al. claimed, therefore, that an abstract conceptual representation is held in memory, not a linguistic representation. Thus they proposed a full-blown integrationist view, which contrasted with the view of Fodor and his colleagues that language and thinking are independent.

Thinking

At the same time that the experiments described above were being carried out, work on thinking, both deductive and inductive, was also developing in new ways. In particular, the role of language in thinking was gaining a sharper focus.

As far as deduction was concerned, studies of transitive inference focused on a debate that mirrored the one between Fodor et al. and Bransford et al. in studies of language (Clark, 1969; DeSoto, London and Handel, 1965; Huttenlocher, 1968). One thing that was beginning to emerge from the work on deduction, for instance, was that the way in which a problem is phrased affects the ease with which a conclusion can be derived. Consider transitive inference as an example. The debate between Clark (1969) and Huttenlocher (1968) focused on the way that people solve transitive inference problems, and it concerned the relationship between language and thinking. Clark adopted what might be called a linguistic view of deduction, which was rooted in ideas derived from Chomsky's model of language and which was consistent with the views of Fodor et al. and of Kintsch on the distinction between language and thought. Clark argued that each premise of a transitive inference problem such as the following:

John is taller than Bill.   (1.19)
Bill is taller than Pete.

Therefore, John is taller than Pete.

is represented as a proposition corresponding to the deep structure of the sentence. Thus the representation of the first premise above is something like:

John is more tall.   (1.20)
Bill is less tall.

The representation of the second premise is something like:

Bill is more tall.   (1.21)
Pete is less tall.

Then the two representations for the common item about Bill are amalgamated and the final propositional representation for the two premises is:

John is most tall.   (1.22)
Bill is middle.
Pete is least tall.

Thus the representation is a linguistic representation of the premises. No thinking is involved at all. No inferences are made. Thinking, inferencing, only occurs when a question about the premises is presented, e.g.:

Who is tallest?   (1.23)

However, here too the linguistic form of the question has a great influence. Specifically, the propositional representation of the question must be congruent with the propositional representation of the premises to enable an inference to be made. The representation of the question above, therefore, must be converted to *Who is most tall?* to enable a match to be made with the representation of the premises.

Clark proposed a number of linguistic features that influenced the ease with which inferences could be made. But the main point of his proposal for present purposes is that it represents the view that language and thought are distinct. Language comprehension involves the construction of a propositional representation. Thinking has nothing to do with this process and only occurs at a later stage if it is required to answer a question.

This view was challenged by Huttenlocher (1968). She extended a proposal by DeSoto, London and Handel (1965) which held that the information in the premises of a transitive inference problem is represented in a spatial array. That is, people construct a spatial array of the situation described by the premises and the original linguistic information is discarded. This view, therefore, corresponds to Barclay's (1973) view of language comprehension: transitive inferences are made during comprehension in order to construct the spatial array. What Huttenlocher added to this view was that the linguistic form of the premises affects the ease with which a spatial representation can be constructed. She suggested that the construction of a representation was relatively straightforward if the end term was the surface subject of the premise, as it is in the example above. However, if the end term is not the surface subject, then the construction of the representation is difficult, perhaps because the premise must be reordered. This would be the case if the first premise in the example above were:

Bill is shorter than John.   (1.24)

Thus Huttenlocher's ideas converge with Barclay's in that language comprehension is seen to include a non-linguistic inferential component. In addition, Huttenlocher indicated the way that linguistic information itself, the structure of the sentence, affects the ease with which these inferential processes can be implemented. This debate between Clark and Huttenlocher was never really resolved. As will be seen in the next section, it evolved into a more detailed debate about processes and representations in language and thinking. However, its most interesting feature was the way that the protagonists, whatever their point of view, envisaged the relationship between language and thinking. For Clark they were distinct and separable processes. For Huttenlocher, linguistic and inferential processes were part of a single integrated system.

In addition to this work on transitive inferences, the work pioneered by Wason in the 1960s was developing rapidly. As a direct consequence of Wason's work, investigations began into the principles responsible for the facilitation of reasoning with familiar materials (e.g. Johnson-Laird, Legrenzi and Legrenzi, 1972), and into the role of linguistic factors in reasoning (e.g. Evans, 1972; Wason and Johnson-Laird, 1972). Together with the studies by Tversky (1972) on decision making, much of this work concentrated on biases in reasoning. The net result of these developments was an even greater move away from the Piagetian view of general purpose principles of thought and towards a view of the importance of specific knowledge for making inferences and a view in which language and thought are integrated. (See Evans (1982) for a review of the work on deductive reasoning that took place during this period.)

Turning to induction, Newell and Simon and their colleagues continued their pioneering studies of problem solving. Their early work had concentrated on investigations into the heuristic processes used in problem solving. Now they turned their attention to other aspects of the cognitive system that needed to be understood as part of a general theory of problem solving. In particular, they started to investigate the processes responsible for constructing an initial internal representation of a problem, that is, of the ways in which comprehension (or perception) is used to construct a representation. These early studies produced ideas about induction that reflected the two views of transitive inference described above, corresponding to the independence view and the integrationist view.

The importance of comprehension, or perception, in problem solving was first brought home to people in a situation that did not involve language at all. Instead it involved the way that chess experts perceive chess positions on the board. It became clear that chess experts represented the board positions differently from novices and that this was due to the way that they perceived patterns rather than individual pieces. Similar observations began to emerge from studies of verbal problems. For example, Hayes and Simon (1974) presented subjects with the Tower of Hanoi problem, in which three disks must be moved from one peg to a different peg according to certain rules. By presenting different versions of the problem, they found that subjects represented each version in a way that was close to its surface linguistic form. Similar results were obtained when other problems were used (Hayes and Simon, 1977) and taken together, the results suggest a view of problem solving that is close to Clark's linguistic view of deductive thinking.

Other studies of problem solving come closer to Huttenlocher's view of deduction. Mayer and Greeno (1972) for example, investigated the way that statistical problems are solved as a function of instruction. Subjects who were given the formulae only after they had been introduced to everyday concepts of probability, such as batting averages or the probability of rain, were very good at solving new problems and at recognizing impossible problems, although they were less good at calculation. By contrast, a group that was given the formulae before they were presented with the conceptual information were very good at calculation but less good at solving novel problems or at recognizing impossible problems. Mayer and Greeno argued that the two groups of subjects constructed different representations of the problem that depended not on its linguistic form but on the nature of the general knowledge that could be used to support inferences. Thus, like Huttenlocher, Mayer and Greeno viewed thinking, in this case problem solving, as dependent on the ease with which inferences could be made during comprehension.

Overall, therefore, the work on thinking began to converge on views that were prevalent in studies of language. One view is that processes of comprehension and processes of inferencing are distinct. The other is that they are integrated in a single system. With these developments came a greater preoccupation with the nature of the representations that are used. Thus Clark (1969) spelled out the propositional representations that underpinned his view of transitive inference, and DeSoto, London and Handel (1965) and Huttenlocher (1968) spelled out the nature of their proposed spatial representations. Newell and

Simon and their colleagues investigated the representations that might support problem solving. These ranged from propositional representations (e.g. Hayes and Simon, 1977) through integrated conceptual representations (e.g. Mayer and Greeno, 1972), to highly specialized production rules (e.g. Simon and Gilmartin, 1973). The scene was set, therefore, for full-blown accounts of the way that linguistic and inferential processes and representations are used in language and in thinking.

Levels of Representation: Cognitive Psychology in the 1980s

The distinction between an independence view and an integrationist view remains a concern in current thinking on the topic. However, in the 1980s a third, combined view also emerged. The independence view holds that input and output systems (such as vision and language) are autonomous and informationally encapsulated (e.g. Fodor, 1983). As such they are distinct from the general cognitive system, which is responsible for thinking. Thus language, which is autonomous and modular, is distinct from thought, which is not. The integrationist view emphasizes the importance of inferences in language comprehension and sees these inferences as the crucial ingredient of language use (e.g. Sanford, 1990). The combined view holds that there are levels of representation for linguistic information on the one hand and non-linguistic information on the other. These levels of representation may coexist but they have different functions and different rates of decay in memory (e.g. Johnson-Laird, 1983; Kintsch, Welsch, Schmalhofer and Zimny, 1990). In general, the integrationist view does not deny the role of linguistic processes in comprehension (Sanford, 1987). Instead, it assumes that inferences based on general knowledge may override the linguistic information or even bypass it altogether. Rather than discuss the details of how such a view differs from the combined view, the discussion is confined to the independent and combined views.

Language

The independence view People who hold the independence view have spelled out the processes involved in constructing a linguistic representation of a sentence (e.g. Frazier and Fodor, 1978; Frazier, 1987). This view is an extension and elaboration of the strategies approach to sentence comprehension that was described in the last section. Frazier and her colleagues have conducted numerous studies investigating the proposition that all the strategies that were previously listed independently by people such as Fodor et al. and Kimball can be collapsed into two general strategies: minimal attachment and late closure. These two strategies are used to construct the simplest possible structure of a sentence that is consistent with the input. The strategy of minimal attachment holds that wherever possible people construct a syntactic representation of a sentence that involves the minimum number of choices. The strategy of late closure holds that wherever possible people assume that incoming information belongs with the phrase that is currently being processed.

This view assumes that the processing of syntactic input takes place in a module that is independent of other modules. Further, while the output of processing in the linguistic module feeds into higher-level pragmatic processes, it is not itself influenced by those higher-level processes. Finally, the cognitive system itself, the vehicle for thought, is not modular, since it is influenced by lower-level processing and is subject to the influences of general knowledge of the world. This assumption of strict autonomy of processing has been contested (e.g. Altmann and Stedman, 1988; Crain and Stedman, 1985; Taraban and McClelland, 1988). Nevertheless, the work of Frazier and her colleagues gives a comprehensive account of syntactic processing, and it reflects the view that language and thought are distinct.

The combined view A combination of the independence view and the integrationist view can be found in Johnson-Laird's (1983) notion of a mental model. This is a non-linguistic representation of the situation described by the sentence that is derived from a propositional representation by means of inferences based on general knowledge. Thus, it assumes linguistic processes that construct propositions, consistent with the ideas of Fodor, Bever and Garrett (1974) and of Kintsch (1974), and inferential processes that construct a mental model from these propositions, consistent with the ideas of Bransford and his colleagues. Van Dijk and Kintsch (1983) have adopted a similar view, except that they also propose that there is an initial representation of the surface structure of the sentence from which a propositional representation is constructed. The notion of a mental model or situation model (van Dijk and Kintsch, 1983) reflects the view that both linguistic and non-linguistic processes contribute to comprehension. Further, the notion of a mental model makes precise the ideas of Bransford et al. that the end-product of language comprehension is an abstract conceptual representation. This abstract conceptual representation can be thought of as a mental model.

Thinking

The independence view and the combined view are evident in the work on deduction as well as in work on language. The independence view characterizes what has come to be called the syntactic approach to deduction and was prefigured in Clark's (1969) linguistic model of transitive inference. The combined view characterizes what has come to be called the semantic approach to deduction and was prefigured in Huttenlocher's (1968) spatial model of transitive inference.

The syntactic view of deduction argues that people construct a propositional representation of the premises and apply the rules of logic to those premises in order to derive a conclusion. This view, which is rooted in Piagetian notions of logical thought, is espoused by Braine (1978) and Rips (1983). According to this view, any errors that are made in reasoning are due to errors in comprehension; that is, to errors in the construction of a propositional representation. This represents a syntactic view because the inferences are made on the basis of the form of the premises, not their content. The semantic view argues that people construct a mental model of the premises, which yields a potential conclusion (Johnson-Laird, 1983; Johnson-Laird and Byrne, 1991). This potential conclusion is then tested for its validity, that is, alternative mental models consistent with the premises are constructed. If the potential conclusion is true in all of them, then the conclusion is valid. If the potential conclusion is not true in all the alternative models of the premises, then it is invalid and a search is made for another potential conclusion which is tested in the same way. This represents a semantic view because the inferences are made on the basis of the content of the premises: the conclusion must be true in all the situations in which the premises are true.

As far as induction is concerned, an important development of the 1980s was the realization that domain-specific knowledge is a major determinant of the way that people solve problems. Observations of expert problem solvers (Anderson, 1983; Larkin, 1983) led Newell and Simon and their colleagues to propose that general purpose heuristic strategies are primarily used by novices in a domain. Experts, on the other hand, use very powerful, domain-specific rules. Indeed, when solving difficult problems in a given domain, novices appear to use a propositional representation and apply rules or strategies to that representation, while experts appear to manipulate mental models (e.g. Kintsch et al., 1990). This is probably because experts have the relevant knowledge that enables them to construct a mental model of the problem while novices do not. Thus, the work on problem solving shows how both views of the relationship between language and thought might have arisen, the independence view in the context of novice performance and the integrationist view in the context of expert performance. The nature of expertise and its acquisition, therefore, is clearly an important feature of both language and thinking and it has become a focus of study in its own right. Both Anderson (1983) and Gick and Holyoak (1980) propose specific solutions to the way in which knowledge and expertise contribute to problem solving. Indeed, the ideas of Gick and Holyoak on analogical thinking have had far-reaching effects, extending beyond the scope of a discussion on the relationship between language and thinking and reaching into other important issues, such as conscious versus unconscious processing and serial versus parallel processing.

SUMMARY

This chapter has given a 'whirlwind tour' of work on language and thinking from the early days of cognitive psychology to the present. Of necessity, the tour has been very sketchy: it has ignored many differences of detail between people holding similar views, and it has ignored the way in which different views spell out the processes and representations that explain performance. Nevertheless, the aim was to convey how the work in cognitive psychology reflects underlying assumptions about the nature of the relationship between language and thought. In particular, three main views of this relationship seem to underlie much of the work that has been done: an independence view, which holds that language and thought reflect distinct and dissociable processes; an integrationist view, which holds that language and thought are subject to similar inferential processes; and a combined view, which holds that both linguistic and non-linguistic processes contribute to comprehension. All of these views are implicit in the literature, and have their roots in the early ideas of cognitive psychologists. Some of these roots have been traced in the present chapter. However, the richness of the current views has been ignored in an attempt to convey some of the major issues at stake. A more complete picture of these views, particularly the independence view and the combined view, is presented in the rest of this book.

CHAPTER 2   The representation of knowledge

Vast amounts of general knowledge are stored in long-term memory, knowledge of concepts and knowledge of specific things and events. Systems of knowledge representation are designed to explain how such knowledge is stored so that it can quickly and easily be retrieved when needed. Two different kinds of knowledge are represented in such systems, usually called *knowing that* and *knowing how*. *Knowing that* is declarative knowledge and refers to knowledge of facts, such as knowledge of concepts and knowledge of individuals and events in the world. *Knowing how* is procedural knowledge and refers to knowledge of how to do things, such as multiplying two numbers or driving a car. Two broad classes of model can be distinguished, serial symbolic models and parallel distributed models.

Serial symbolic models represent the traditional (or 'classical') approach to representation and assume that cognition involves the manipulation of symbols. Thus, representational systems have symbols as units and explicit logical rules which operate on these units. According to this view, thinking is a conscious, deliberate, rule-governed process, which is severely limited by capacity constraints in short-term memory. Hence it takes place one step at a time, in a sequential manner.

By contrast, parallel distributed models assume that the units in the system are extremely simple and not symbolic at all. According to this view, the explicit representation of symbols and rules is unnecessary and knowledge is best captured by patterns of activation across a large number of units. Thus, the representation of a concept is distributed over the system and is not localized in discrete symbols. This view assumes that the activation of units occurs in parallel and that much thinking occurs in long-term memory as a result of changes in patterns of activation. Thus, thinking is not a conscious sequential manipulation of symbols in short-term memory. Instead it is a rapid, non-logical parallel activation of many interconnected units.

A third hybrid connectionist model has emerged, which combines features of symbolic systems with features of distributed systems. These models try to account for the symbolic nature of cognition and for the way that retrieval is determined by the satisfaction of multiple constraints. Rule-governed behaviour is captured by symbolic propositional representations, while multiple constraint satisfaction is captured by the parallel activation of relevant propositions.

SEQUENTIAL SYMBOLIC REPRESENTATIONS

The most articulate account of the classical view of representation is given by Fodor and Pylyshyn (1988) in their critique of parallel distributed processing. They point out that speakers who know how to say *John loves the girl* generally also know how to say *The girl loves John*. Thus native speakers of a language can take the meanings of individual words and combine them in new ways according to the rules of syntax to produce meaningful utterances. This ability is made possible by the fact that sentences have a structure (a syntax) that allows words, or their meanings, to be combined in systematic ways.

Fodor and Pylyshyn propose an exactly analogous argument for thought. They point out that creatures who can think that *John loves the girl* can typically also think that *The girl loves John*. This, they argue, is because thoughts, like sentences, have structure. Thinking that *John loves the girl* involves an internal representation with discrete units for *John*, *loves*, *the*, and *girl*, and a system of rules that operate on these representations to combine the units in allowable ways. Thus, the units can be combined to produce the thought that *John loves the girl* or the thought that *The girl loves John*. Each of these thoughts is produced from the same elements combined in different but systematic ways. Fodor and Pylyshyn argue, therefore, that mental representations, like sentences, have internal structure that is characterized by symbols that can be combined in systematic ways. In other words, mental representations are rule governed. Serial symbolic representations are designed to describe such representations. Four main types of symbolic representations have been proposed: (1) logic-based systems (2) semantic networks (3) frames and scripts, and (4) production rules. The first three characterize declarative knowledge, the last one procedural knowledge.

Logic-based Systems

Logic-based systems make explicit the views of Fodor and Pylyshyn and assume that thoughts are composed of the propositions of the predicate calculus. What better way to characterize the language of thought than to use the language of logic? The predicate calculus is a logical system that was invented by Frege (1879), and it allows logical inferences to be derived from propositions. In logic-based systems, therefore, concepts are stored in long-term memory as unordered lists of propositions.

A simple proposition consists of a predicate and one or more arguments, that stand for individuals. Thus, the assertion *John loves Mary* expresses a proposition which contains a predicate and two arguments standing for individuals as follows:

LOVES(john, mary)   (2.1)

To represent statements about classes of individuals, the universal and existential quantifiers are used. A universal statement like *All authors read novels* is represented by a variable, x, and the universal quantifier, which allows the variable to range over the set of all authors. This can be written as follows:

For all x, if x is an author then x reads novels.   (2.2)

Similarly, the existential statement, *Some authors read novels* can be written as follows:

For some x, if x is an author then x reads novels.   (2.3)

In these quantified examples, the logical connective *if* was used to combine the two propositions, *x is an author* and *x reads novels*. Other logical connectives are *and, not* and *or*.

Propositions, or expressions in the predicate calculus, are often called well-formed formulae (WFFs), and there are rules for their formation. However, perhaps the most important rules are those that derive new WFFs from other WFFs. These rules allow the deduction of new assertions from existing ones. That is, they allow a conclusion to be drawn from a set of premises. Moreover, if the premise are true, then so too will be the conclusions. Thus, one of the most powerful uses of logic in representational systems is to use WFFs to represent assertions about a domain (that is, premises), and a theorem prover to deduce new facts that will be certain to be true. For example, the predicate calculus can formally express cases of the logical rule known as *modus ponens* (see Chapter 7) that involves general assertions about a set of objects:

All birds can fly.   (2.4)
Robins are birds.

Therefore, Robins can fly.

A logic-based system, then, consists of lists of concepts represented as propositions to which rules of inference are applied. One of its drawbacks as an account of cognitive functioning is that it does not reflect the ease with which people retrieve the relevant concepts when, say, solving a problem or understanding a text. An unordered list of propositions would need to be searched through until the relevant one was found and could be retrieved. But a simple search through a list seems unable to account for the ease with which relevant and related concepts are retrieved. Furthermore, logic-based systems ignore the fact that we need to be able to represent our knowledge of the world and not just conceptual knowledge. Semantic networks try to address both of these issues of how related concepts are retrieved so rapidly and of how world knowledge might be represented.

Semantic Networks

Semantic networks (e.g. Quillian, 1968) are directed graphs that enable all the information about a particular concept to be stored together. A directed graph consists of nodes connected by (directed) links where the nodes stand for concepts and the links stand for the relations between them. Two important types of links are class inclusion links and attribute or feature links. For example, the node for cat is linked to the mammal node to indicate class inclusion, and is also linked to the attributes *is fluffy* and *has claws*. Networks are also used to represent individuals and the relations between individuals. Thus, they can represent facts about the world and not just concepts. For example, they can represent the fact that Jake, the cat, is large and chases butterflies. Attempts have been made to provide an explicit semantics for these networks (e.g. Brachman, 1979, 1983).

Knowledge of concepts

Figure 2.1 shows a semantic hierarchy that was proposed by Collins and Quillian (1969). Each node is connected upwards to its superset and downwards to its subsets. The links sideways from each node state attributes that are true of the node – that fish can swim, for example, or that a shark is dangerous. A node and its configuration of links represents the meaning of a concept. In the model, properties of higher nodes are inherited by the lower nodes to which they are connected unless there is an attribute attached to the lower node that specifically overrides it. Thus we can infer from the network that robins can fly because birds in general can fly, but we cannot make the same inference about ostriches because there is an explicit statement at the ostrich node that it cannot fly.

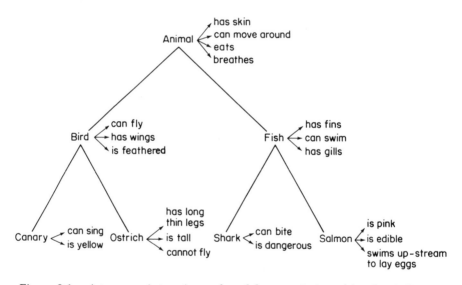

Figure 2.1.   A taxonomic tree (reproduced, by permission of Academic Press, from Collins and Quillian, 1969)

Whereas logic-based systems use the rules of the predicate calculus to make inferences, semantic networks use links between nodes. Thus, the inference that robins can fly is equivalent to the following deductive inference:

All birds can fly.
Robins are birds.

Therefore, Robins can fly.

Networks, therefore, are equivalent to logic-based systems in their ability to allow deductive inferences. Where they differ is in the way that information about a particular concept is gathered together at the node representing that concept. In the predicate calculus, information about a particular concept is asserted in a series of independent propositions. Searching through these propositions for those that describe a particular concept is a laborious process. The use of semantic networks to group together all the information about a concept enables the information to be retrieved very quickly once the relevant part of the network is accessed. Thus, one difference between logic and semantic networks lies in the ease with which information can be retrieved.

Early experimental work on the speed with which people make semantic judgements indicated that a network like that in Figure 2.1. has psychological plausibility (Collins and Quillian, 1969). However, the empirical data turned out to be more complicated than was at first envisaged. The frequency of the link was found to affect decision latencies (Conrad, 1972), and Smith, Shoben and Rips (1974) argued that prototypical information also influences decision latencies. This latter finding reflects the fact that category judgements are not as logical as symbolic systems suppose. Category statements are not simply true or false; their acceptability also depends on the similarity between the individual instance and the category. For example, the statement *A robin is a bird* is more acceptable than is *A penguin is a bird* (Rosch, 1973).

Collins and Loftus (1975) revised the original hierarchical model to take account of these difficulties. They emphasized the notion of *spreading activation*. At all times, each node in a network is at some level of activation, that spreads among nodes along the links. If the level of activation reaches a high enough value in some portion of the network, that portion of the network is accessible to conscious attention. A number of assumptions need to be made to ensure that spreading activation does not get out of control. First it is assumed that activation at a node is divided among the links that lead from it. Thus, as activation spreads through the network, it is rapidly weakened by successive divisions as it reaches successive nodes. Second, it is assumed that activation at a node fades rapidly with time. If these two assumptions, or similar ones, are not made, then a single thought would rapidly activate the entire knowledge base and bring about total confusion. Third, it is often assumed that nodes and links can have different activation capacities. For example, links might be assumed to differ in the proportion of available activation they receive, where the higher capacity links are the ones that have been more frequently activated in the past, and so are more easily accessible. In this way, prototypical information can be used to influence semantic decisions.

Knowledge of individuals

To represent facts about the world, it is necessary to have nodes for individuals, such as *Jake* and *Ginger*, and not just nodes for sets of individuals, such as *cats*. It is also necessary to represent the variety of relations that can hold between individuals, for example the relation of chasing expressed by the utterance: *Jake chases Ginger*. Nodes for individuals are connected to other nodes by set membership links; relations between individuals are represented by nodes standing for propositions.

The inclusion of individuals in a network creates difficulties for inheritance, that is, for the way that instances inherit the characteristics of the category. For example, Jake and Ginger are my cats. If they are represented as instances of cats in my semantic network, then they will inherit all the characteristics of cats, such as being furry, having claws and chasing mice. However, facts that are true of cats in general may not be true of my cats. Jake and Ginger do not chase mice, for example, they chase butterflies instead. Thus, the inherited characteristics may not be true of specific individuals, and so individuals and classes of individuals need to be distinguished in the network. Indeed, incorrect inferences (such as that Jake chases mice) are problematic for semantic networks, since their correction requires complex computations. This is because semantic networks (and symbolic systems in general) are logical systems. They yield 'correct' conclusions and so do not readily allow for the fact that inferences based on knowledge of the world are inductive and error-prone.

However, there is evidence to support the idea that people use semantic networks to represent knowledge of individuals. One prediction that differs from a prediction derived from logic is that information about an individual is clustered round a single node in the knowledge base. Thus people should recall related information just as readily as the original information. A number of studies support this prediction. For example, Anderson and Bower (1973) showed that people could not remember whether they had heard:

> George Washington had good health. (2.5)

or

> The first president of the United States had good health. (2.6)

This finding is compatible with the view that all information about George Washington is organized around a single node.

The semantics of semantic networks

In many programmes using semantic networks, the meaning of nodes and links has been interpreted intuitively rather than described rigorously and systematically, a problem that was first highlighted by Woods (1975) and has since been tackled by Brachman (1979, 1983).

One way to interpret generic nodes (ones that refer to a general class or concept) is as sets. Thus the relation holding between a node at one level of a hierarchy and that at a higher level is that of subset to superset. If, for example, the network indicates that a canary is a bird, it is in effect stating that the set of all canaries is a subset of the set of all birds. Further, if the generic concept is interpreted as a set, then the relation of nodes representing individuals to generic nodes in the network is one of set membership. A second possible interpretation of generic nodes is as prototypes, and of instance nodes as individuals for whom the generic nodes provide a prototypic description. Rather than describing an individual or picking out a class of individuals, a prototype describes what the typical exemplar of the class is like. Individuals will then be more or less like the prototype.

Johnson-Laird, Herrman and Chaffin (1984) argue that such semantic interpretations are inadequate on a number of grounds. In particular, the interpretations only specify intensional relations, that is, the relations between the meanings of words. They give no account of extensional relations, that is, what each word refers to in the world. To capture extensional relations, it is necessary to show how the concepts and propositions refer to elements and situations in a model of the world so that their truth value can be determined (see Chapter 4). Johnson-Laird et al. therefore argue that semantic networks (and by implication, logic-based systems) are unable to give an adequate account of knowledge representation, since they are unable to show how concepts (or word meanings) relate to things in the world. Johnson-Laird et al.'s preferred alternative is the use of mental models (Johnson-Laird, 1983). Mental models can also be expressed as propositions but they differ from other symbolic systems in that they have an explicit semantics for extensional as well as intensional relations.

Frames and Scripts

The ease and flexibility with which people retrieve relevant information from memory suggests that a simple semantic network is not sufficient to capture important elements of knowledge representation. Indeed, general knowledge goes considerably beyond having concepts for discrete objects and events such as *cat* or *cats chase mice* and involves a complex network of domain-specific knowledge. Frames and scripts were developed to represent this complex knowledge. They can be viewed as attempts to make the notion of a schema more precise. Schemas were first discussed by Bartlett (1932), who proposed that our interactions with the world are mediated by large-scale memory schemas, each of which encapsulates our knowledge about everything connected with an object or event. These schemas were said to guide the interpretation of events, utterances and written texts. However, Bartlett's notion of schemas leaves the unresolved difficulty of defining how particular schemas are represented and accessed when needed.

Frames and scripts are attempts by computer modellers to define the schema concept more precisely. They are elaborate semantic networks that are grouped together into knowledge structures. Frames characterize a knowledge of concepts while scripts characterize knowledge of typical events. They both explicitly attempt to represent general knowledge of the world and not just knowledge of concepts.

Frames

Consider knowledge of a simple concept like dog. (This example is modified from Greene, 1986.) As well as knowing its superset (animal), its subset (different types of dogs) and its attributes (e.g. has four legs), all of which would be encoded in a semantic network, we also know the kinds of situations where we are likely to find dogs (in parks, houses, shops), the sorts of things that owners do with dogs (walk them, feed them), the sorts of people that dogs do not like (post-people, intruders), and much more besides. Frames (Minsky, 1977) are designed to represent such a cluster of complex knowledge. Activating a frame means activating the complete cluster so that it can be manipulated as a whole. It is similar to the psychological notion of chunking that has long been recognized in work on memory. For example, when reading a text and encountering the word *dog*, the activation of a frame would activate the complete cluster of knowledge that is associated with dogs. This allows information that is not in the text to be added to the memory for that text and so is consistent with the findings in work on memory for sentences showing that people frequently remember more information than was explicitly expressed in the sentences (e.g. Johnson, Bransford and Solomon, 1973).

A frame is a collection of slots and slot fillers that describe a stereotypical item. The slot structure is a way to capture the interrelational structure of a concept. For example, just to list the facts associated with dogs does not reflect their organization. The basic insight of frames is that concepts like dog are defined by a configuration of attributes, and each of these attributes involves specifying a value the object has on some attribute. Thus, the concept of dog has the following partial representation:

DOG

Slot:		Value:
superset:		animal
number of legs:	default:	four
subset:	optional values:	collie, spaniel
situations:	optional values:	park, house, shop ...
owner's actions:	optional values:	walk, feed, buy ... etc.

In this list, terms like *superset* or *situations* are the attributes or slots, and terms like *animal* or *park* are the values. Each pair of a slot and a value amounts to a proposition about a dog. Slots can be filled in a number of ways including a default value, an optional value, or another frame. A default value is a value that we assume to be true unless told otherwise and it allows frames to represent stereotypical information. A special slot in each frame is its superset, which is, in fact, another frame higher up in the hierarchy. Similarly, the subset slot points to alternative frames lower down in the hierarchy. This allows a frame representing a specific object to be derived from one representing a type of object. Thus the frame for a specific dog, for example, a collie, makes a copy of the information in the dog frame. Some slots will already be filled in the collie frame, that its size is big and its colour is black, for example. However, other slots will be empty and these will be filled in from the information in the dog frame. Thus frames are organized into inheritance hierarchies in the same way as semantic networks. The structure of a frame, therefore, is intended to mirror the important aspects of the structure of an object, and frames themselves are organized into systems that are intended to reflect higher-order structures in the world.

Scripts

Some stereotypical knowledge is episodic or sequential in nature and is represented by scripts (Schank and Abelson, 1977). A script is an elaborate causal chain about a stereotypical event. It can be thought of as a kind of frame where the slots represent events that are typically ordered in a particular sequence. For instance, there are scripts for going to a restaurant, going to a party and going to a lecture. Scripts contain the following sorts of information: an identifying name or

Table 2.1.   Restaurant script

Name: Restaurant

Props:	Tables	*Roles*:	Customer
	Menu		Waiter/waitress
	Food		Cook
	Bill		Cashier
	Money		Owner

| *Entry conditions*: | Customer is hungry
Customer has money | *Results*: | Customer has less money
Owner has more money
Customer is not hungry |

Scene 1:	*Entering* Customer enters restaurant Customer looks for table Customer decides where to sit Customer goes to table Customer sits down
Scene 2:	*Ordering* Customer requests menu Waitress brings menu Customer reads menu Customer decides on food Customer orders food Waitress gives food order to cook Cook prepares food
Scene 3:	*Eating* Cook gives food to waitress Waitress brings food to customer Customer eats food
Scene 4:	*Exiting* Customer asks for bill Waitress gives bill to customer Customer gives tip to waitress Customer goes to cashier Customer gives money to cashier Customer leaves restaurant

Source: Greene (1986). Reproduced by permission of Open University Press.

theme (such as eating in a restaurant), typical roles (customer, waiter, cook ...), entry conditions (customer is hungry and has money), a sequence of goal-directed scenes (entering and getting a table, ordering ...) and a sequence of actions within each scene. Schank's restaurant script is shown in Table 2.1.

Schank and Abelson developed a computer program that used scripts, like the one in Table 1.1, to understand natural language. They presented the computer with stories like the following:

> John went to a restaurant. The waiter gave John a menu. The waiter came to the table. John ordered the lobster. John was served quickly. John left a large tip.

The computer could answer questions about the text that required inferences to be made about information not explicitly stated. For example, in answer to the question *Why did John get a menu?* the computer responded *So he could order*. In answer to the question *Why did John give the waiter a large tip?* the computer responded *Because he was served quickly*. Like frames, scripts enable all the stereotypical information about events to be activated as a unit so that it is available for understanding the rest of the story, for resolving ambiguities, and for making inferences to fill in gaps in the story.

Schank (1982) has revised his notion of scripts to make the knowledge structure more flexible and to allow learning to take place. He suggests that actions which are common to a number of scripts, such as entering buildings, asking for services and making appointments are organized at a more abstract level into what he calls Memory Organization Packets or MOPs. For example, information about paying bills would be stored as a separate MOP that can be used to reconstruct many different superscripts. Scripts like the restaurant script are now much smaller because the general actions common to many scripts are extracted as MOPs for storage elsewhere.

One problem with frames and scripts and, to a lesser extent, MOPs, is that they are inflexible. They encode large packages of information that are retrieved as complete units. However, such large packages can be very unwieldy, and in many cases, people do not seem to infer all the additional information that would be expected if a complete script had been retrieved (see Chapter 5).

Another problem arises with frame or script (or MOP) selection. When stored knowledge is used to understand natural language, some method must be employed for accessing the information. One possibility is to have a word access its corresponding frame or script, for example, the word restaurant for the restaurant script,. But in many cases the name of the script itself will not be mentioned in a text. Another possibility is to use the keyword method whereby a script is activated by keywords such as *waiter* or *menu*. However, even this method does not completely solve the problem. Garnham (1985) gives the following example:

The five-hour journey from London to New York.   (2.7)

This phrase suggests a plane flight, but no single word in it should. If it did, the plane flight script would be activated in numerous inappropriate contexts (whenever the word *journey* occurred, for example) as would scripts for train journeys and for other kinds of journeys.

The problems of inflexibility and of knowledge activation, then, are difficult ones for complex knowledge structures, like scripts. This is not the case with semantic networks, which can be entered at any point in the hierarchy. Thus if a word matches a concept in the hierarchy, that concept will be activated and will cause the spread of activation to related concepts.

Production rules

The representational systems discussed so far all account for declarative knowledge, that is, knowledge of concepts and facts about the world. However, we also need to represent procedural knowledge. This is our knowledge of how to do things, such as solving a problem or driving a car. Procedural knowledge is represented by production rules.

A set of production rules make up a production system. Each rule consists of a condition and an action and is expressed in an if–then form: If the condition is met, then the action is executed, for example:

IF the goal is to drive a car
        and the car is in first gear
        and the car is going more than 10 miles an hour
    THEN go into second gear.

In psychological models that use productions (e.g. Anderson, 1983; Newell and Simon, 1972), it is assumed that the rules are stored in long-term memory as part of our stored knowledge about the world. They are triggered by the conditions specified in the IF part of the rule. These conditions are held in short-term memory, which has a limited capacity. There are, therefore, limitations on the number of conditions that can be considered at one time, and on the actions that can be performed.

In general, all of these symbolic systems make a number of assumptions. First, they assume that the processes governing learning, memory and interpretation depend on rules. Thus the networks and rules have to be explicitly represented. Second, they all assume that cognitive processing occurs in short-term memory and so memory limitations place constraints on what can be computed at any moment. Hence they subscribe to the view that cognitive processes are serial. Third, they are committed to explaining mental life in symbolic terms. Hence concepts are represented as symbolic units. Doubts about this set of assumptions lie behind the alternative conception of representations as parallel and distributed. In addition, because symbolic systems are logical, they derive a correct conclusion from a set of premises, and they have difficulty in recovering from errors. The emphasis on logic also produces difficulties in representing knowledge about the world, where inductive error-prone inferences are used. The developments from logic-based systems through semantic networks to frames and scripts represent successive attempts to deal with the problem of world knowledge and inductive processes. Parallel Distributed Processing PDP) systems explicitly address these issues.

PARALLEL DISTRIBUTED REPRESENTATIONS

Parallel distributed representations (McClelland and Rumelhart, 1986) or 'connectionism' systems (Feldman and Ballard, 1982) differ from symbolic representations in three main respects. First, they are not rule based. Hence they generate incorrect as well as correct solutions. Second, they are parallel systems that are not subject to the capacity constraints of short-term memory, and third, the units are simple elements, not symbols. A concept, therefore, is represented by a distributed network of simple elements whose pattern of activation corresponds to the activation of the concept.

Connectionist models explain the way that memory retrieval requires the satisfaction of multiple constraints. Word recognition is one example of this and it has been modelled by McClelland and Rumelhart in a partially parallel system. There are a number of other cognitive phenomena that are easily explained by a fully parallel connectionist system. One is content-addressable memory, the ability to retrieve a fact when presented with incomplete information. Another is graceful degradation. This refers to the ability to act on incorrect or inconsistent information, and to the ability to act even when part of the system has been damaged, through ageing or injury, for example. In addition, people working with connectionist systems have been at pains to show that their systems can explain the same things that symbolic systems explain. Thus, connectionist simulations have been produced that infer stereotypical or default information, schemas, and stereotypes.

Multiple Constraint Satisfaction in Word Recognition

In word recognition, a letter is detected more quickly when it occurs in a word than when it occurs in a nonsense string (Wheeler, 1970). Thus people can more readily detect the *t* in *hate* than the *t* in *hote*. In

Figure 2.2 Ambiguous letter displays. Each letter in the first word is ambiguous, as shown by the alternative possibilities in the lower three words (from McClelland, Rumelhart and Hinton (1986); copyright 1986 MIT Press

addition, the identification of one letter in a word can influence the identity of another letter. McClelland, Rumelhart and Hinton (1986) give the example shown in Figure 2.2.

Each letter in the word RED is partially masked by inkblots but it is immediately recognizable as RED, even though the first letter could be P or R, the second letter F or E, and the third letter B or D. At first glance, these examples may seem paradoxical. The identity of each letter is constrained by the identities of each of the other letters. But we cannot in general know the identities of any of the letters until we have established the identities of the others. So how can we get the process started? According to McClelland and Rumelhart (1981), the resolution of the paradox is simple. Only one of the different possible letters in each position fits together with the others. Apparently our perceptual system is capable of exploring all of these possibilities without committing itself to one until all the constraints are taken into account.

McClelland and Rumelhart (1981) proposed an interactive model of word recognition to account for these observations. In the model, processing is partially distributed and so resembles a connectionist system, but the representations are not distributed, since the nodes stand for symbols not simple units. A simplified illustration of how the model might work is shown in Figure 2.3.

The reader's knowledge consists of the direct visual input, and information in long-term memory about the letters and words of English. The letters and words (and also features, such as lines and angles) are represented by nodes, with connecting arrows that capture the interactions among them. The solid arrows represent positive support (e.g. the arrow connecting the node R in the first position with the node RED). The broken arrows represent negative counter evidence (e.g. the nodes R and P in the first letter position are mutually incompatible).

The network can recognize the word RED in Figure 2.2 by parallel constraint satisfaction. The unit representing the word RED will be excited by those units representing R in the first position, E in the second position, and D in the third position. Although other words will be slightly excited by units for other plausible letters (e.g. OFF by F in the second position), no word will receive as much activation as RED. In turn, the node for RED will feed activation back to the units representing the individual letters that excite it, and so on, until the word unit is sufficiently active to reach a threshold corresponding to recognition.

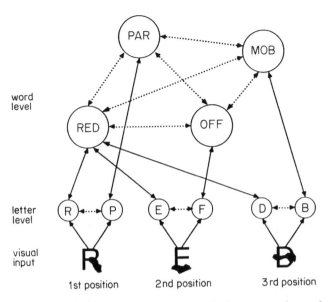

Figure 2.3   An illustration of part of the knowledge network needed to recognize the top word in Figure 2.2 using parallel constraint satisfaction (from Holyoak (1990); copyright 1990 MIT Press)

This interactive model of word recognition, however, is still partially serial because the activation of higher level units (such as word units) depends upon receiving activation from lower level units (such as letter units). Its partial parallelism is due to the fact that activation is not confined to a single direction: higher level units can feed activation back down the hierarchy to lower level units. In a fully parallel system (sometimes called massively parallel systems, e.g. Waltz and Pollack, 1985) many different units may be activated at the same time without being dependent on the prior activation of other units. McClelland and Rumelhart's interactive model would thus be a fully parallel model if, on encountering a word such as RED, all the relevant units, including those at the feature level, the letter level and the word level, were activated directly by the visual stimulus. While McClelland and Rumelhart's model of word recognition helps to illustrate a parallel system, it is not itself fully parallel and so is not a true connectionist (or PPD) system. Connectionist models are fully parallel in the way just described and it is such fully parallel models that are the focus of the discussion that follows.

Content Addressable Memory

Human memory has the remarkable ability to recall an item when presented with partial cues. Thus partly obliterated letters, as shown in Figure 2.2, are readily identified. This ability is known as content addressability: each cue (or feature) contains the address of the total memory (or concept) which enables the concept to be retrieved.

How might a symbolic system encode content addressability? One way is to search sequentially through memory to find the memory that includes the content specified by the cue. But it was to avoid such a time-consuming serial search that semantic nets included the grouping of information at a node. The problem with this though, and also with scripts and frames, is that the links are directional. This can be

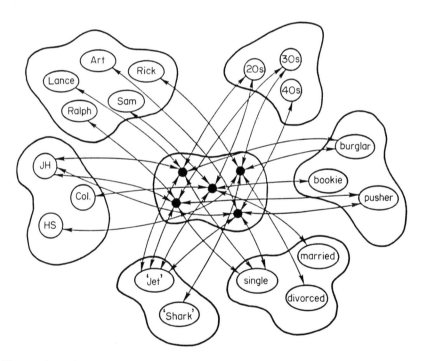

Figure 2.4   Some of the units and interconnections needed to represent knowledge of the Jets and the Sharks. *Notes.* Units connected with double-headed arrows are mutually excitatory. All units within the same cloud are mutually inhibitory. The left-hand cloud contains features for level of education. JH = Junior High; HS = High School; Col = College (from McClelland (1981) reproduced by permission of J. L. McClelland)

rectified by including additional indexes (like the index in a library for locating a book) which point in the opposite direction along a link. In general, though, encoding content addressability in a symbolic representation is very laborious.

By contrast, a distributed model accounts for the phenomenon in a direct and simple manner. This can be illustrated with McClelland's model of the Jets and the Sharks (McClelland, 1981). The model encodes information about the members of two gangs, the Jets and the Sharks, and is illustrated in Figure 2.4.

In this network there is an instance unit for each of the characters, Lance, Art, Rick and so on. Each instance unit is linked by mutually excitatory connections to all of the units for that person's properties. In the figure, the 'clouds' indicate that the units inside each cloud are mutually inhibitory, while the solid arrows represent excitatory connections. If you are told that someone is a Shark in his thirties, the *30s* and *Shark* units will be activated and these in turn will activate other units with which they have excitatory links. Thus, *Shark* will activate *High School, Rick, burglar*, and *divorced*, as well as *30s*; and *30s* will activate *Ralph, Junior High, single, pusher*, and *Jet*. This will result in a chain of excitation that spreads through the system along with a chain of inhibition due to the inhibitory links with these activated units. The final result is a pattern of activation involving units for *Shark, 30s, burglar, divorced*, a *high school education* and *Rick*. Furthermore, this same pattern of activation would result from any one of a number of partial descriptions, such as *a Shark who is divorced*. Thus, the final pattern of activation that results from the initial spread of activation can be achieved straightforwardly from a variety of incomplete inputs.

Graceful Degradation

Graceful degradation comes in two forms. The first says that the system must be capable of behaving in a sensible manner even if the data is incomplete or erroneous. The second says that the system must be able to continue to function even if some of the hardware has been damaged. The first of these forms is illustrated here. The previous discussion of content addressability has shown how partial data can prompt a full pattern of activation. An extension of this idea to include erroneous data is an example of graceful degradation. A cue which contains misleading features will most strongly activate the node that it matches best.

In McClelland's model of the Jets and the Sharks, the description, *a married Jet who is a bookie with a junior high school education* will most strongly activate *Sam* through activation of *bookie*, *married* and *Jet*. The misleading information about a junior high school education will initially activate *Rick* as well, but to a much lesser extent, due to the high level of inhibition from the *Sam* unit. The pattern of activation and inhibition ensures that misleading information is eventually inhibited and enables graceful degradation to occur. This contrasts with symbolic models where the ability to deal with erroneous cues requires enormous amounts of computation.

Default Assignment

Suppose you know that Lance is a Jet in his twenties with a junior high school education, but you do not know his occupation. That piece of information is missing (or has zero activation) in the representation. However, the information that you have will activate the *Lance*, *Jet*, *20s*, and *junior high school education* units. These units will cause other units to be activated too. The end product of this process is that the most highly activated unit for occupations is *burglar*, so a reasonable assumption (which of course may be wrong) is that Lance is a burglar too (McClelland, Rumelhart and Hinton, 1986). In this way, the *burglar* unit gets activated as a kind of default assignment to *Lance* without requiring the explicit representation of default features as in symbolic networks such as frames.

Schemas

Symbolic systems encode schemas through the use of scripts and MOPs. Rumelhart, Smolensky, McClelland and Hinton (1986) describe a PDP simulation which also acts 'as if' it were using schemas. Their demonstration shows how the properties of an explicitly stored schema may emerge from the activity of a parallel distributed network. In the model, schemas are not explicit representations but emerge at the moment they are needed from the interaction of large numbers of much simpler elements all working together.

Rumelhart et al.'s room system consists of a large number of units standing for microfeatures of rooms. The system works by having 'typical' kitchen microfeatures, such as cooker, or fridge linked together by excitatory connections and linked to 'untypical' microfeatures, such as bed, by inhibitory connections. Then, when a single unit for a prominent kitchen microfeature is activated, it will activate in a kind of chain all and only the units standing for items found in kitchens. Thus a kitchen schema emerges from activation of the network. In Rumelhart et al's simulation, if the oven unit is activated, then after a while all the kitchen microfeatures, such as ceiling, walls, window, telephone, coffee cup, and so on, are also activated and this total pattern of activation represents a typical kitchen. In contrast to symbolic models, therefore, a schema is not a permanent and explicit representation but a temporary and implicit representation brought about by the activation of many microfeatures.

Prototypes

In symbolic semantic networks, both generic nodes (e.g. the set of *cats*) and individual nodes (e.g. *Jake*) have to be explicitly represented. McClelland and Rumelhart (1986) propose a model of distributed memory that encodes specific experiences about individuals (such as Jake), from which a prototypical, non-specific understanding of the class emerges naturally, thus obviating the need for explicit and independent representations of specific individuals and general class information.

The system learns which properties are associated with a particular animal, such as Jake, via a learning rule (known as the delta rule because feedback is based on the difference, delta, between the observed activation and the desired activation). The system's main features can be described as follows. First, there is a set of units, say 16, which together encode the features of a prototypical cat, each unit standing for one feature. Next, each specific cat is represented by a unique set of eight units, none of which is identical to the prototype. The name of each cat is coded as a pattern of activation across the eight units. The network is then given a series of experiences of individual cats by activating the relevant units. After each exposure, a memory trace of the altered pattern of connections is laid down.

After 50 exposures, the system had never been exposed to the prototypical cat, but only to the instances. The system was then given a fragment of the prototype as input – not the pattern for a particular cat – and was able to activate the prototypical pattern. No name units became active because these were associated with particular cats and so inhibited each other. Instead, the network extracted the pattern that was common to all the instances, producing something like a proto-typical representation of the class. Of course, if the system is pre-sented with a distinctive cue for a particular cat, it will re-create the pattern for that cat, not the prototype.

In summary, PDP systems encode features as distributed units, and so remove the necessity to have a unit to represent a concept, such as *cat*, explicitly. The pattern of excitatory and inhibitory connections ensures that related units are activated together and it is this pattern of activation that represents a concept.

Second, knowledge is not encoded explicitly as it is in symbolic sys-tems. Instead, knowledge is stored implicitly in the connection strengths. In symbolic systems, retrieval of knowledge requires the retrieval of a stored pattern, such as a frame or script, from long-term memory and copying it into short-term memory. In PDP models, this is not the case, since the patterns themselves are not stored. Instead, the connection strengths between units are stored and these allow the patterns to be re-created. Rumelhart and his colleagues argue that this feature rules out the need for the explicit retrieval of relevant infor-mation from long-term memory. Instead, retrieval is an automatic consequence of the processing of an input.

Third, PDP models use parallel constraint satisfaction. McClelland and Rumelhart's model of word perception showed how the recogni-tion of a word is constrained by information about features, letters and words that is computed in parallel.

PDP models, therefore, exhibit a number of features that account for cognitive abilities in a simple and direct manner where symbolic sys-tems have only clumsy and inefficient accounts. A notable example is the way that parallel distributed representations can model the fast, automatic activation of general knowledge while symbolic models have to rely on unwieldy and relatively inflexible representations like scripts or frames. The fast retrieval of information from memory is subject to a number of constraints that have to be satisfied and PDP systems embody such constraints. PDP models also give straightforward accounts of content-addressable memory and graceful degradation, phenomena that are explained with difficulty in symbolic accounts. Finally, PDP models are good at using information about individuals to infer default information, schemas and prototypes. That is to say, they are good at inductive inferences, including the abstraction of general principles after exposure to a number of individuals. Such models, therefore, are good at learning. Nevertheless, PDP models have been severely criticized, particularly by people who focus on the rule-governed nature of language and thinking (e.g. Fodor and Pylyshyn, 1988; Pinker and Prince, 1988). Some of these criticisms are outlined in the next section.

A CRITIQUE OF PARALLEL DISTRIBUTED PROCESSING

Relational Information

Relational information cannot be represented in a connectionist network (Holyoak, 1991). For example, the sentence *Jake chases butterflies* must be represented in a form that captures the fact that *Jake* is the subject of the verb and *butterflies* is the object. But in a PDP network, all that would be stored is information about *Jake, chase* and *butterflies*, which would be indistinguishable from the stored information from the sentence *Butterflies chase Jake*, or even a word list consisting of *chase, Jake*, and *butterflies*. Quantified sentences pose even greater difficulties. Holyoak gives the following example: Suppose you know the rule *If a seller sells a possession to a buyer, then the buyer comes to own the possession*. You then find out that Bob sold a bicycle to Helen. You can easily infer from this that Bob is the seller, the bicycle is the possession, Helen is the buyer, and so Helen now owns the bicycle. But these inferences cannot be derived from a network of activated concepts. What is needed as well is a representation of the roles of seller, buyer and object and a way of 'binding' these roles to particular individuals, so that Bob ends up as the seller and not Helen. As Holyoak points out, there have been attempts to model relational knowledge, but they are not completely successful. The same arguments can be made about the relational structure of thought. As Fodor and Pylyshyn (1988) argue, thought is also structured and relational and this structure is not captured in a PDP system, only in a symbolic system by means of propositions.

The 'Blind' Activation of Units

The units of a PDP system are activated automatically by the relevant input. However, our ability to attend to salient features of the environment runs counter to the idea that distributed representations are 'blind'. People can easily override the automatic activation of perceptual features of an object if there is knowledge to indicate how they came about. Pinker and Prince give the example of an animal that looks like a skunk but is treated as a raccoon if prior information indicates that the stripe was painted on to a raccoon (see, for example, Keil, 1989). Thus, people are not invariably slaves to patterns of activation in a parallel network.

Planning, Sequencing and Organizing Information

The ability to plan, sequence and organize information is reflected in explicit and deliberate attempts to solve problems, such as finding a mathematical proof or solving a linear syllogism. Such deliberation is due to the fact that attentional capacity is limited to a single chain of thought and is best described by symbolic models that assume capacity limitations on short-term memory.

Learning

One advantage that is claimed for PDP models is their potential for learning. In particular, a fully distributed system enables learning 'from scratch' to occur. These models, therefore, circumvent a thorny question for symbolic models: how can learning get off the ground without assuming some prior knowledge? If the units are symbols, it is hard to see how they might be acquired from scratch. But if concepts are distributed, and learning involves the changes in connection strengths that make up the pattern of activation for a given concept, then prior knowledge does not have to be assumed. However, Pinker and Prince (1988) argue that this view of learning is too strong. PDP models assume that learning occurs gradually after a series of exposures to instances in the environment. But there is a wealth of evidence to suggest that both children (e.g. Nelson, 1974) and adults (e.g. Bruner, Goodnow and Austin, 1956) can learn a concept after encountering a single instance. This suggests a high degree of internal organization to make such learning possible. It is likely, therefore, that PDP models rely too heavily on the environment when learning occurs.

Symbolic models, therefore, seem to offer the best account of a number of cognitive phenomena. These include the way in which relational information is encoded, the ability to override automatic activation of perceptual features, and the planning, sequencing and organization of information in complex problem solving. These activities seem to be the outcome of conscious deliberations and are subject to severe attentional constraints.

PDP models, on the other hand, seem to offer the best account of retrieval, including the way retrieval is subject to multiple constraint satisfaction, and the ability to retrieve information from partial or incorrect cues. PDP models also try to explain induction, the ability to abstract general principles. It seems likely, though, that these accounts of induction will need to be supplemented by more powerful structural (symbolic) constraints that enable hypotheses to be formed after exposure to a single instance. Observations such as these have led to the development of 'hybrid' models, or symbolic connectionism (e.g. Holyoak, 1991; Kintsch, 1988).

HYBRID MODELS OF REPRESENTATION

Symbolic connectionism (Holyoak, 1991) combines standard symbolic representations with connectionist parallel constraint satisfaction procedures. Rule-based processes (that is, production rules) construct symbolic propositional representations while parallel processes produce an interpretation of the input. Examples are Kintsch's (1988) model of discourse comprehension (see Chapter 5) and Holyoak and Thagard's (1989, 1990) models of analogue retrieval and analogue mapping (see Chapter 9). Kintsch's model also has production rules for the processing of the syntactic structure of the sentence.

Kintsch's model of discourse comprehension accounts for the apparent ease with which we understand language despite the fact that it is fraught with lexical and syntactic ambiguities, and riddled with gaps that have to be filled in by inferencing. Symbolic models depend on the use of parsing and inference rules that are carefully tailored to produce 'correct' interpretations. Kintsch's model, by contrast, generates a number of possible interpretations, including incorrect ones. The 'correct' interpretation is the one that ends up with the highest activation level. Kintsch's model has four components: first, the initial parallel activation of concepts corresponding to the words in the text, together with the formation of propositions by parsing (that is, production) rules; second, the spreading of activation to a small number of close associates of the text concepts; third, the inferring of additional propositions by inference rules; and fourth, the complete set of concepts and propositions is connected by excitatory and inhibitory links that stabilize to produce a unique interpretation of a sentence. The central characteristic of the model is that it allows rule-based parsing and inferencing rules (production rules) to apply in a loose, error-prone fashion, over-generating inappropriate concepts and propositions that are subsequently discarded through the inhibitory links as a result of the discourse context.

Holyoak and Thagard's analogue retrieval model takes as input a symbolic propositional representation of a problem description and applies a small set of constraints (semantic and pragmatic) to build a network of units representing possible analogues of the problem, and then allowing parallel constraint satisfaction to settle the network into a stable state. The analogue with the highest activation level is consciously retrieved, while the others are discarded. Thus, multiple constraint satisfaction is carried out on a symbolic network. As in Kintsch's model of discourse comprehension, the model first over-generates a large pool of potential hypotheses, and then uses parallel constraint satisfaction to select a coherent subset. Holyoak and Thagard's analogue mapping model works in a similar manner, but includes syntactic constraints as well as semantic and pragmatic ones. There is some evidence to support the view that analogue mapping uses a parallel, automatic and relatively fast mapping mechanism (Novick and Holyoak, 1991). Verbal protocols collected from subjects searching for a correct mapping between an analogue and a problem revealed no overt signs of the mapping process, although they did reveal laborious attempts to work out the implications of the correspondences that were formed.

Overall, these models use highly general constraints, that are potentially applicable to an unlimited range of examples, on symbolic structures. Kintsch's model, for example, uses syntactic, semantic and pragmatic constraints. The resulting networks find a coherent interpretation that, if incorrect, is quickly discarded, and hence not available to conscious attention. The model also retains the use of production rules for processing relational information. Such symbolic connectionist models allow the construction of an over-general set of inconsistent hypotheses that are subsequently refined by the process of parallel constraint satisfaction. The interpretation that is finally accepted is the one that enters conscious awareness. Holyoak argues that this aspect of the models is an improvement on the brittleness and inflexibility of purely symbolic treatments of these tasks through the use of scripts or prespecified production systems. Holyoak also suggests that these parallel models account for the ease with which an intuitive solution (or insight) is reached in problem solving, as when an expert chess player finds the best moves without a serial search through alternative possibilities.

Symbolic connectionism, therefore, combines elements of connectionism with elements of symbolic representation in a way that gives a direct account of the use of both parallel and serial processes. Relational symbolic representations are constructed by means of production rules while retrieval is the result of parallel constraint satisfaction. Thus symbolic connectionism accounts both for the representation of relational information and for the way that insights are produced in problem solving (see Chapter 9). They occur when a single thought is sufficiently activated as a result of parallel constraint satisfaction to encroach on conscious awareness. Thus symbolic connectionism provides a way for a more satisfactory account of deduction and induction to be developed. Symbolic connectionism, therefore, has considerable appeal.

SUMMARY

Serial symbolic representations explain the rule-governed nature of cognition. They provide explicit representations of concepts and specify the logical rules that operate on those concepts to derive a conclusion. They are, therefore, deductive systems. In general, effort has concentrated on developing symbolic systems that are capable of explaining the ease with which general knowledge, including knowledge of the world, is retrieved from long-term memory, and the way in which inductive processes (based on default or stereotypical information) modify the derivation of logical conclusions. Frames and scripts are the result of these efforts. Scripts, for example, are retrieved as a unit, and they represent default information that may turn out to be incorrect. However, the inflexibility of scripts, the means by which they are accessed, and the difficulty of recovering from errors, remain problematic.

Parallel distributed systems offer solutions to these problems. They assume that representations are distributed so that a pattern of activation across several units represents a concept. PDP systems show how the rapid, automatic activation of units through parallel constraint satisfaction results in fast retrieval. They therefore give a better account of retrieval than do symbolic systems. In addition, PDP systems are inductive. They abstract general principles upon exposure to instances in the environment, and they are prone to error.

Symbolic connectionism exploits the positive features of the two types of model: the use of production rules to process relational information, the rapid retrieval of relevant general knowledge, including incorrect inductive guesses, by means of parallel constraint satisfaction; and the retrieval of symbolic information which is the basis of conscious thought. It thus provides a way of accounting for both deductive and inductive thinking.

CHAPTER 3   Syntactic processing

Syntactic information is clearly important for understanding language. The difficulties experienced by people with Broca's aphasia, an acquired language disorder, illustrate this point, since Broca's aphasics cannot use syntactic information. Caramazza and Zurif (1976) asked Broca's aphasic subjects to choose from a set of alternatives the picture which matched a sentence they had heard. When presented with a sentence like, *The bicycle that the boy is holding is broken*, the subjects had no difficulty choosing the correct picture. But when presented with a sentence like, *The man that the woman is hugging is happy*, the aphasic subjects rarely selected the correct picture. With the first sentence, a deficit in syntactic processing can be overcome by attending to the meanings of the content words, *bicycle, boy, holding, broken*. There is only one event that can plausibly be described by these four words; it must be the boy that is holding the bicycle and the bicycle that is broken. By contrast, the content words in the second sentence, *man, woman, hugging, happy*, can plausibly describe more than one event; either the man or the woman could be doing the hugging and either could be happy. It is only by understanding the syntactic structure of the sentence that the second sentence can be understood.

We comprehend sentences very rapidly and without any conscious awareness. This can make it seem as though comprehension is easy and involves no complex processing. However, an examination of what is required to parse a sentence (that is, to analyse syntactic structure) soon makes it clear that it is far from simple. There are a number of phenomena that need to be explained by a theory of parsing and that are not immediately apparent. These include the fact that many sentences contain syntactic ambiguities, although readers may not be aware of them; the fact that ambiguous sentences seem to have preferred interpretations; and the fact the syntactic information must be integrated with semantic and pragmatic information at some point during comprehension. The way that these phenomena are explained depends upon certain theoretical choices that are made concerning the operation of the syntactic processor. These choices require decisions about the nature of the relationship between syntactic and semantic or pragmatic processes; the nature of the representation that is constructed as a result of syntactic processing; and the way in which people can recover from parsing errors. The phenomena to be explained and the choices that need to be made are discussed in the next section, after which examples of three different models of parsing are discussed.

SOME PRELIMINARIES: SYNTACTIC PHENOMENA AND THEORETICAL ISSUES

Syntactic Phenomena

(1) Syntactic ambiguities

Consider the following sentence:

> The psychologist told the woman that he was   (3.1)
> having trouble with to leave.

Sentence (3.1) contains a local ambiguity at the word *that*. The sentence could continue with a relative clause, which restricts the identity of the woman to a particular one, as in (3.1), or it could continue with a complement clause, which says what the psychologist told the woman, as in (3.2):

> The psychologist told the woman that he was   (3.2)
> having trouble with her husband.

A psychological model of parsing must specify the syntactic processes that enable people to compute the intended interpretation. It must also show what happens when the wrong interpretation is selected and how people can correct such errors. In addition, there appear to be marked preferences for choosing one interpretation over another when a syntactic ambiguity is encountered. A parsing model must explain how such preferences arise.

(2) Preferred interpretations

In both of the sentences above, the preferred interpretation is that the word *that* introduces a complement not a relative pronoun. Thus sentence (3.2), which conforms to that interpretation, is easier to understand than sentence (3.1). One way to account for this preferred interpretation is to assume that people use heuristic strategies to construct the syntax of a sentence. Frazier (1987) proposes that people use a strategy that she calls minimal attachment. This says that, when parsing a sentence, the reader mentally constructs the phrase structure that has the minimum possible number of nodes. The tree structure in Figure 3.1 shows the phrase structure for sentence (3.1).

This is the structure that conforms to the relative clause (or non-minimal attachment) reading. According to this reading, the string *the woman that he was having trouble with* is interpreted as a relative clause.The phrase structure in Figure 3.2 shows the structure for sentence

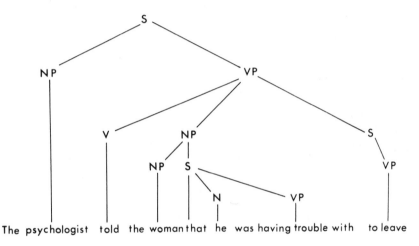

Figure 3.1   Phrase structure for sentence (3.1)

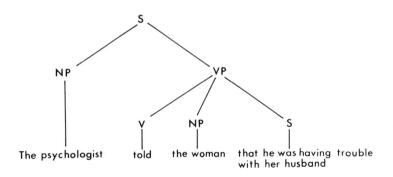

Figure 3.2   Phrase structure for sentence (3.2)

(3.2). This is the complement (or minimal attachment) reading in which the psychologist told the woman something. It is clear from Figures 3.1 and 3.2 that the phrase structure tree for the complement interpretation (Figure 3.2) has fewer nodes than does the phrase structure tree for the relative interpretation (Figure 3.1). Since the complement interpretation is the preferred one, the strategy of minimal attachment accounts for this preference.

(3) The relation between syntax, semantics and pragmatics

Sentences like (3.1) above are sometimes called garden path sentences, because they seem to lead the reader astray and into a wrong interpretation. What happens, though, if we precede (3.1) with a context sentence that makes a relative clause interpretation more plausible? This has been done in (3.3).

The psychologist saw two women.	(3.3.a)
He told the woman that he was having trouble with to leave.	(3.3.b)

Now the relative clause interpretation seems easy to construct and indeed it even seems to be the preferred interpretation. Compare (3.3) with (3.4), which contains the complement reading, when it is preceded by the same context sentence.

The psychologist saw two women.	(3.4.a)
He told the woman that he was having trouble with her husband.	(3.4.b)

Now the complement interpretation seems less likely. Thus, context can affect which syntactic structure is chosen when parsing an ambiguous sentence. A psychological model of processing needs to be able to show how context interacts with syntactic processing so that it can predict when one or the other interpretation is likely to be constructed.

Theoretical Issues

The autonomy of syntax and the modularity hypothesis

There is a tradition in work on syntactic parsing that proposes that syntax and semantics are autonomous, independent systems (e.g. Frazier, 1978). These 'autonomous' views assume that contextual and semantic information cannot influence the operation of the syntactic processor, which means that syntactic ambiguity is, as far as possible, resolved without the aid of context or non-linguistic knowledge. For example, the minimal attachment strategy of Frazier assumes that syntax is independent of semantics. Hence Frazier proposes that syntactic ambiguity is resolved by the application of this strategy and not by recourse to context. If it turns out that the minimal attachment interpretation is not compatible with the context, then the processor has to backtrack and reparse the sentence.

This notion of autonomous syntactic processing is embodied in Fodor's (1983) modularity hypothesis, which states that there are cognitive input systems, called modules, that are dedicated to specific tasks. For example, there are modules in the visual system that are dedicated to stereoscopic vision, colour vision and so on (Fodor, 1983). Fodor argues that there are also modules in the linguistic system. In particular, he argues that syntactic processing is modular. These input modules are distinct from the central processor, which is concerned with making inductive inferences on the basis of what the modules deliver. Modules have a number of characteristics that distinguish them from the central processor. These include:

1. Input modules are domain specific.
2. The operation of a module is obligatory.
3. Modules have limited access to the central processing system.
4. Modules are informationally encapsulated.

As far as domain specificity is concerned, the processes of the syntactic module are specific to language and are not used in other domains. The notion of obligatory operation means that the processes are not under conscious control. For example, we can't help hearing a word such as *money* as an English word, and we can't help interpreting its meaning. Limited access to central processing means that the end-product of processing is available to higher-level processing but the intermediate stages are not. Thus, higher-level (top-down) processes cannot penetrate the module and influence its operation. Another way to think about these latter two characteristics is to say that the processes within a module are unconscious and only the final output of the module is available to conscious thought. We are aware, for example, of the interpretation we have assigned to a sentence but not of how we arrived at the interpretation. Finally, informational encapsulation refers to the fact that the analysis performed by the module is shared with other systems only when processing is complete. This is a consequence of the fact that only the end-product of processing is available to higher-level processing.

According to Fodor, these characteristics of modularity guarantee the speed and automaticity of syntactic processing. However, not everyone agrees that modularity is necessary to account for such efficiency. This is because the effect of context on syntactic processing has led some people to propose that semantic and pragmatic factors *can* influence parsing decisions. These proposals have resulted in interactive models of parsing, which contrast with independent models. Independent models conform to the modularity hypothesis and assume that syntactic processing is serial (it takes place prior to semantic and pragmatic analyses), and that it is independent (its operations are not governed by what happens at higher levels). Interaction with higher levels occurs only when the output of the syntactic module is passed on to the semantic and pragmatic processors. Some interactive models also assume modularity, but others violate it. Crain and Steedman (1985) have distinguished between these two kinds of interactive models, which they call weakly interactive models and strongly interactive models respectively. Weakly interactive models assume that semantics may influence parsing to the extent of ruling out inappropriate analyses. That is, semantics operates on the output of the syntactic processor and hence maintains modularity. By contrast, strongly interactive models assume a much larger role for semantics and pragmatics, which may influence what syntactic analyses get proposed in the first place. Thus they violate modularity.

Do people construct syntactic representations?

Crain and Steedman (1985) have coined the term, representational autonomy to refer to the extent to which purely syntactic representations are constructed before translation into semantic representations (propositions). Frazier (1987) takes a strongly autonomous view of representation and proposes that each sentence is converted into an independent syntactic representation prior to semantic processing. This view is echoed by Kintsch (e.g. 1988) who proposes that a syntactic representation is constructed during sentence processing, prior to the construction of a propositional representation of the meaning of the sentence and an optional situational model of the situation described by the sentence. Others have argued for a modified version of representational autonomy and assume that clauses or phrases are converted into syntactic representations prior to semantic processing (e.g. Fodor, Bever and Garrett, 1974).

A more radical approach to representation is taken by Altmann and Steedman (1988), Crain and Steedman (1985) and Johnson-Laird (1983). They propose that a semantic (propositional) representation is constructed directly without any intervening syntactic representation. On this view, syntax is implicated in the processing of the sentence but there is no independent level of syntactic representation. The direct construction of a semantic representation is compatible with the notion of incremental parsing. This is an assumption held by most theories of semantics that each syntactic rule has a corresponding semantic rule, so that the semantic rule can be implemented as each syntactic rule is implemented. In other words, a semantic representation can be constructed as each syntactic constituent is parsed, thus rendering an independent syntactic representation unnecessary.

Recovering from garden paths

The existence of syntactically ambiguous sentences means that the sentence processor must be able to revise a syntactic decision if the wrong interpretation is constructed. For example, it is likely that most people need to revise their initial interpretation of sentence (3.1), repeated below:

> The psychologist told the woman that he was having trouble with to leave.

Work in artificial intelligence has revealed a number of ways in which the indeterminacy of syntax and its consequences for processing might be simulated. One way is to compute only one analysis and then backtrack if it turns out to be the wrong one. This strategy may be used when there are no contextual clues to interpretation, as in (3.1) above. This approach is adopted by people who use augmented transition networks in their simulations (e.g. Woods, 1970). It is also the approach used in serial independent models of parsing such as those of Frazier (1978, 1987) and Wanner and Maratsos (1978).

A second way is to compute all the possible analyses in parallel so that they are all available for as long as is necessary to determine the correct one. In artificial intelligence, one type of parser that computes parallel analyses is called a chart parser (e.g. Kay, 1973). Parallel computation is also used by parallel interactive models of parsing, such as those of Altmann and Steedman (1988) and Taraban and McClelland (1988). Both of these methods, backtracking and parallel analyses, build an element of uncertainty into syntactic processing. They allow for the fact that alternative analyses exist and that the wrong one may be chosen. These methods, therefore, are non-deterministic. They do not assume a single, fixed end-product of syntactic analysis.

By contrast, a deterministic parser does not allow such flexibility; once an analysis is initiated, it is not revised. A parser of this type, therefore, will need to simulate non-determinism in some other way; for example, by building in a look-ahead component that allows the parser to inspect words later in the text so that the correct analysis can be chosen. This approach is adopted by Marcus (1980) in his computer simulation of syntactic processing based on Chomsky's model of language. Some strongly interactive models, such those of Winograd (1972) and Schank and Abelson (1977), use semantic and pragmatic information to select the correct interpretation. They therefore assume a form of determinism since they assume that by bringing semantics and pragmatics to bear on the choice of analysis the likelihood of selecting an incorrect interpretation is greatly reduced.

Now that some preliminary issues have been aired, the rest of this chapter will review models of parsing that espouse the views of either serial independence, weak interaction or strong interaction. Connectionist models will also be discussed. The serial independent view is held by Frazier and her colleagues (e.g. Frazier, 1978; Frazier and Rayner, 1982; Rayner, Carlson and Frazier, 1983), while weak interaction is illustrated by Altmann and Steedman's (1988) model. Two computer simulations, those of Winograd (1972) and of Schank (e.g. Schank and Abelson, 1977), are used to illustrate strong interaction, and the experiments of Taraban and McClelland (1988) are also discussed. Finally, Waltz and Pollack's (1985) connectionist system is described. Connectionist models are massively parallel systems with many interconnections between the parallel processes. However, in many connectionist models, including the case of Waltz and Pollack's (1985) model, modularity is maintained. In fact, connectionist models do not fit easily into any of the categories used above but it will be suggested that they are best thought of as weakly interactive models. However, the major emphasis in connectionist systems is on parallel processing, regardless of whether or not modularity is maintained.

MODELS OF PARSING

Serial Independence: the Use of Heuristic Strategies

The use of heuristic strategies to compute the syntactic structure of a sentence was first proposed by Fodor, Bever and Garrett (1974). They argued that the end-product of syntactic processing was a syntactic representation. In fact, they held that this representation was the deep structure of the sentence as described by Chomsky (1965). They therefore believed that the goal of the parser was to recover the linguistic deep structure, and that the linguistic representations that are described by linguists are psychologically real. Work by people such as Sachs (1967) has shown that we do not use processes that mirror linguistic rules when interpreting sentences. So, unlike linguistic representations, the rules proposed by linguists are not psychologically real. Fodor et al. proposed, therefore, that we use heuristic strategies to recover the syntactic structure of a sentence. Unlike linguistic rules, which are algorithmic and thus provide a systematic procedure for parsing, heuristic strategies are rules of thumb. These are generally effective but may occasionally fail.

Fodor et al.'s model was the first of several that held to the importance of linguistic theory for psychological performance, and it was developed in different ways by Kimball (1973) and by Frazier and Fodor (1978; Frazier, 1978, 1987). Fodor et al. proposed a number of strategies that people might use to determine the deep structure of a sentence, and Kimball extended this list quite considerably, although he assumed that it was sufficient to analyse the surface structure of the sentence. One of the achievements of Frazier's work was that she successfully combined a number of these different strategies into two basic strategies, thus removing problems associated with a proliferation of proposed strategies.

Frazier's two strategies for recovering underlying syntax are:

1. *The late closure strategy*: If grammatically permissible, each new incoming term is attached to the clause or phrase currently being processed.
2. *The minimal attachment strategy*: Each new incoming item is added to the phrase structure in a way that requires the minimum additional nodes.

According to Frazier, sentence (3.5), produces a garden path because people are using the Late Closure strategy.

> Since Jay always jogs a mile and a half seems like   (3.5)
> a short distance.

At the word *jogs*, which is a constituent of a verb phrase, the new input is a noun phrase (*a mile and a half*) and late closure says attach the new input to the verb phrase that is currently being processed. This results in the incorrect interpretation in which the noun phrase (*a mile and a half*) is the object of the verb *jogs*. In order to retrieve the correct analysis, Frazier and Rayner (1982) suggest that people backtrack to the point of ambiguity (*jogs*) and compute the alternative analysis. Frazier and Rayner base this proposal on the results of eye movement studies in which they presented subjects with sentences like (3.5) and recorded their eye movements during reading. They found that fixation durations increased in the part of the sentence following the point of ambiguity (e.g. at *seems* in the example above) and also that regressive fixations returned to the region of ambiguity (e.g. at *jogs* in the example above).

Similarly, according to Frazier, sentence (3.6) produces a garden path because people are using the minimal attachment strategy:

> The performer sent the flowers was very pleased.   (3.6)

When the word *sent* is encountered, a verb phrase is attached to the sentence node, as shown on the left in Figure 3.3.

If the relative clause analysis were constructed instead, the resulting phrase structure of the string, *the performer sent the flowers*, would be as shown on the right in Figure 3.3. The minimal attachment construction requires only the addition of a verb phrase node. By contrast, the

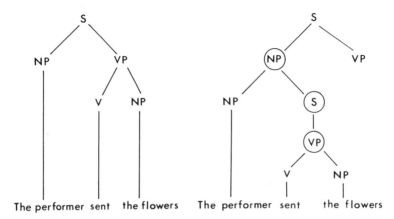

Figure 3.3   Phrase structures for the string the florist sent the flowers...... The left-hand panel shows the minimal attachment interpretation, and the right-hand panel shows the relative clause interpretation.

non-minimal attachment construction requires the three additional nodes circled in the right-hand panel of Figure 3.3. Thus, Frazier argues that people construct the simpler, minimal attachment analysis and this accounts for the garden path effect in sentences like (3.6). Rayner, Carlson and Frazier (1983) tested this view by comparing sentences like (3.6) with sentences like (3.7).

The florist sent the flowers was very pleased.   (3.7)

They argued that the minimal attachment reading is more pragmatically plausible in (3.6) than (3.7) because it is more likely that a performer will be sent flowers than that a florist will be sent flowers. As before, they recorded eye movements while subjects read the sentences, and they found that the garden path effect was equally strong in both kinds of sentence. Pragmatic plausibility had no effect. Subjects spent longer inspecting the words, *was very*, in both (3.6) and (3.7) compared to inspection times for the same phrase in an unambiguous sentence, such as *The performer who was sent the flowers was very pleased*. This supports a serial, independent view, in which syntactic processing is completed without regard to context, rather than an interactive view, in which pragmatic knowledge influences the choice of syntactic analysis.

It could be argued that these sentences do not provide a very strong test of the independence of syntax and pragmatics, since sentences like (3.7) can be disambiguated only after the initial syntactic analysis has been made: *flowers* is not read until the after the minimal attachment interpretation has occurred (see Figure 3.3). However, there are sentences where two (or more) syntactic analyses are grammatically possible but where prior pragmatic information renders one of them pragmatically implausible. Sentence (3.8) is an example: it is not possible to interpret the sentence to mean that the spy used the revolver to see the cop. By contrast, sentence (3.9), which has the same syntactic structure, is not pragmatically implausible on either of the syntactic analyses. Hence two interpretations of the sentence are possible: that the spy used the binoculars to see the cop with, or that the cop had the binoculars.

> The spy saw the cop with a revolver but the cop   (3.8)
> didn't see him.

> The spy saw the cop with binoculars but the cop   (3.9)
> didn't see him.

Rayner et al. examined subjects' eye movements while reading sentences like (3.8) and (3.9). According to Frazier, minimal attachment in each case should lead the parser to attach the preposition phrase *with a revolver* or *with binoculars* to the verb phrase. This is a pragmatically implausible reading in (3.8) but a plausible one in (3.9) (see Figure 3.4). Rayner et al. found that subjects paused on revolver in (3.8) but not on binoculars in (3.9). Thus, when pragmatic plausibility was consistent with minimal attachment, as in (3.9), comprehension flowed smoothly. By contrast, when pragmatic plausibility was inconsistent with minimal attachment, as in (3.8), comprehension was impeded. While these results support the notion of minimal attachment, they suggest, in addition, that plausibility may affect the syntactic reanalysis at an early stage in comprehension: subjects paused on the word *revolver*, indicating that they were aware of the pragmatic anomaly immediately the word was encountered. To account for this, Rayner et al. suggested that a thematic processor operates independently of, but in parallel with, the syntactic processor to produce the plausible thematic relations between the verb in the sentence and potential thematic (semantic) roles. If the thematic processor produces a more plausible set of relations than those consistent with the syntactic processor, then the analysis is revised. However, as Norris (1987) points out, it is hard to see how Rayner et al.'s thematic processor could be distinguished from a plausibility monitoring process which simply discards implausible analyses such as the one in (3.8). In fact, Frazier (1987) has suggested that the parser may indeed be weakly interactive in this respect.

However, the main features of Frazier's model are that a single analysis is pursued, that backtracking occurs when an error is corrected, that the syntactic analysis occurs without any involvement of semantic or pragmatic processes, and that a syntactic representation of the sentence is constructed prior to semantic or pragmatic involvement. It is the last feature that needs to be modified to allow a thematic processor to discard an improbable analysis when a pragmatically implausible word is encountered: syntactic representations need to be passed to higher level processors before the end of the sentence.

The major difficulty with Frazier's model is that a model based on heuristic strategies can never give a complete account of sentence processing. In particular, we need to know how backtracking and reanalysis are possible, but there is as yet no detailed account of the processes underlying these achievements. On the other hand, it can be argued that strategies yield the correct analysis most of the time and so give a good account of the speed with which syntactic processing is carried out, and also of the surprise that can be experienced when this rapid process is disrupted because a wrong analysis was pursued. In addition, the model encompasses a wide range of evidence and an array of garden path phenomena. If comprehensiveness is the criterion for a successful parsing model, then Frazier's is successful.

Weak Interaction

A weakly interactive model is one in which the syntactic component is independent of the semantic and pragmatic components but in which the semantic component rules out the least plausible syntactic analyses. Weakly interactive models assume that all possible syntactic analyses are computed in parallel by the syntactic component. This assumption is necessary if the semantic interpretation is to rule out the least plausible analyses. Such models provide a more explicit account of sentence processing than do strategy models. Because they do not propose the use of strategies, they do not have the problem of specifying what happens when strategies fail. They also provide an account of the processes involved when reanalysis is required: an earlier, discarded partial analysis is retrieved; it does not have to be computed from scratch as is the case in the strategies view.

The weakly interactive model to be described has been proposed by Crain and Steedman (1985) and by Altmann and Steedman (1988). The emphasis here will be on the most recent version of the model, the one presented by Altmann and Steedman. The model is based on the notion of referential failure, and it accounts for the parsing of the second sentence in examples such as (3.10).

> The psychologist saw a man and a woman.   (3.10.a)
> He told the woman that he was having trouble   (3.10.b)
> with to leave.

Sentence (3.10b) produces a garden path: Readers prefer to interpret the string *the woman*, as a simple noun phrase, not as a complex noun phrase that contains a relative clause (*the woman that he was having trouble with*). Frazier would argue that the simple noun phrase interpretation is preferred because people use the strategy of minimal attachment. However, Altmann and Steedman argue that people only garden path on sentences like (3.10b) when the context fails to support the relative clause interpretation, as is the case in (3.10). They point out that a relative clause presupposes that one entity must be selected out of several similar entities in the discourse model. If, therefore, the current discourse model (derived from preceding context) contains only one entity for *woman*, as in (3.10), the presuppositions of the relative clause are violated. This results in referential failure, because the relative clause is unable to fulfil its role of identifying a unique referent in a discourse model containing several referents. Consequently, the relative clause interpretation will be discarded leaving only the simple noun phrase interpretation. Conversely, if the current discourse model contains representations of two women, as would be the case for (3.11), then the presuppositions of the relative clause are met, and so the relative clause interpretation will not be discarded.

> The psychologist saw two women.   (3.11.a)
> He told the woman that he was having trouble   (3.11.b)
> with to leave.

However, the presence in (3.11) of two entities in the discourse model violates the presuppositions of the simple noun phrase interpretation, which assume that only one entity exists which fits the description in the noun phrase. This also results in referential failure, since the noun phrase is unable to pick out a unique referent in the discourse model. The simple noun phrase interpretation is therefore discarded, leaving only the relative clause interpretation. Thus, whenever the presuppositions of a noun phrase, simple or complex, are violated by the contents of the discourse model, referential failure ensues and the offending interpretation is discarded.

To recapitulate, according to Altmann and Steedman, sentence (3.10a) introduces one entity standing for the woman into the discourse model. So the relative clause interpretation is not supported and is therefore discarded, leaving the simple noun phrase interpretation to be pursued. By contrast, sentence (3.11a) introduces two women into the discourse model. So the relative clause interpretation is supported because it will pick out one of the two women. On the other hand, the simple noun phrase interpretation is not supported because the noun phrase *the woman* is unable to pick out a specific woman from the two available in the discourse model. Consequently, the simple noun phrase interpretation is discarded.

To test their weakly interactive model, Altmann and Steedman presented subjects with sentence pairs like those in (3.10) and (3.11) and sentence pairs like those in (3.12) and (3.13).

The psychologist saw a man and a woman.	(3.12.a)
He told the woman that he was having trouble with her husband.	(3.12.b)
The psychologist saw two women.	(3.13.a)
He told the woman that he was having trouble with her husband.	(3.13.b)

Sentences (3.12b) and (3.13b) allow only the simple noun phrase interpretation of the string *the woman*, but the context rules out this interpretation in (3.13), since the simple noun phrase interpretation fails to identify a unique woman. Altmann and Steedman found that reading times for the simple noun phrase analysis were faster in the context of (3.12a) than in the context of (3.13a). By contrast, reading times for the relative clause analysis were faster in the context of (3.11a) than in the context of (3.10a). Thus the results supported the idea that referential failure rules out an inappropriate parse.

The findings of Frazier and Rayner (1982) seem to contradict Altmann and Steedman's model. Frazier and Rayner found no effect of the plausibility of sentences on the extent of the garden path in sentences like *The florist sent the flowers was very pleased* versus *The performer sent the flowers was very pleased,* where it is more plausible to assume that a performer will be sent flowers than that a florist will be. However, their sentences were not preceded by context sentences and Altmann and Steedman argue that the noun phrase *the florist* or the relative *the florist sent the flowers* carry presuppositions even in the absence of a context. The simple noun phrase presupposes that there is a unique entity in the discourse model, the relative presupposes that there are several similar entities in the discourse model and that one of them will be picked out by the relative. Thus the noun phrase carries fewer presuppositions about the contents of the discourse model than does the relative and Crain and Steedman (1985) argue that in the absence of context, the interpretation carrying the fewest presuppositions is the one selected. Thus, the preferred interpretation in the absence of context will be the simple noun phrase interpretation. Since the simple noun phrase interpretation is consistent with minimal attachment, the findings of Frazier and Rayner are consistent with weak interaction.

Ferreira and Clifton (1986) also obtained results that appear to contradict those of Altmann and Steedman. Despite the presence of a context, they obtained a clear effect of the use of a minimal attachment strategy. They used passages like the following.

Non-minimal attachment context–Non-minimal (3.14) attachment target:

John worked as a reporter for a big city newspaper. He sensed that a major story was brewing over the city hall scandal, and he obtained some evidence that he believed pretty much established the mayor's guilt. He went to his editors with a tape and some photos because he needed their approval before he could go ahead with the story. He ran a tape for one of his editors and he showed some photos to the other. *The editor played the tape agreed the story was a big one.*

Minimal attachment context–Minimal attachment   (3.15)
target:

John worked as a reporter for a big city newspaper. He sensed that a major story was brewing over the city hall scandal, and he obtained some evidence that he believed pretty much established the mayor's guilt. He went to his editors with a tape and some photos because he needed their approval before he could go ahead with the story. He gave a tape to his editor and told him to listen to it. *The editor played the tape and agreed the story was a big one.*

They measured subjects' eye movements while reading passages such as these and found that the target sentence in passages like (3.14) produced longer reading times per character than the target sentence in passages like (3.15). However, as Altmann and Steedman (1988) point out, the crucial comparison for the parallel view cannot be made in this experiment because the type of context was not varied independently of type of target. So differences due to the nature of the target sentence cannot be isolated and the critical interaction between type of target (relative or non-relative) and type of context, that is predicted by the parallel model, cannot be tested.

Overall then, the weakly interactive view assumes that all analyses are constructed in parallel and inappropriate ones are discarded on semantic grounds. The analysis that remains yields the interpretation of the sentence. If it turns out to be wrong, analysis does not have to start again from the beginning, only from the point where a previous analysis was discarded. This model, therefore, also accounts for the speed and efficiency of syntactic processing. However, it has yet to be shown conclusively that people do not have to backtrack and reanalyse a sentence when an error is made. Often the effects of misanalysis are quite marked and people even find it difficult to construct an alternative analysis at all. Such observations are consistent with the serial view but less consistent with a parallel view. The eye movement data of Frazier and Rayner (1982) also indicates that backtracking occurs. However, some backtracking would be necessary to retrieve a partial analysis even on a parallel view, so the issue is not clear-cut. It is also the case though, that referential failure accounts for a much narrower range of cases than do Frazier's strategies. It remains to be shown that referential failure, or some other feature of weak interaction, can give as good an account of the full range of sentences as it does for noun phrase ambiguities.

Strong Interaction

The main feature of strongly interactive models is that the syntactic component is regarded as less important than the semantic or pragmatic components. In strongly interactive models, semantics and pragmatic context can specify courses of action for the syntactic processor and hence actively restrict the search space within which the processor operates.

Two computer models will be described in this section those of Winograd (1972) and of Schank and Abelson (1977). Both are also serial models in that they assume that only a single analysis is pursued. To ensure that the correct analysis is chosen, these models bring semantic and pragmatic processes into play very early so that they can be used to select the correct interpretation. Taraban and McClelland (1988) propose a parallel interactive system rather than a serial one and their work is also discussed below.

Winograd's SHRDLU

Winograd's comprehension system consists of three components: a syntactic component, a semantic component and an inference mechanism. SHRDLU lives in a world inhabited by blocks of different colours, shapes and sizes, a 'blocks world'. The inference mechanism relies on general knowledge about the blocks world and on knowledge about the current state of the array. SHRDLU moves blocks around in this world in response to sentences that refer to the blocks world. For example, SHRDLU might be asked to:

Put the red cube in the box on the block.   (3.16)

This sentence contains an ambiguous noun phrase which can be interpreted in two different ways. Either the red cube is to be put in the box that is on the block, or the red cube in the box is to be put on to the block. Winograd's way of resolving this ambiguity is to use knowledge about the blocks world to identify a unique referent. SHRDLU inspects the array and if there is a unique referent for *red cube* (only one red cube in the array), then the first interpretation is selected. However, if there is more than one red cube in the array, SHRDLU will select the second interpretation. Thus, syntactic processing is determined by referential success: SHRDLU selects an interpretation if the referent for that interpretation is present in the blocks world. This contrasts with Altmann and Steedman's weakly interactive model which uses referential failure to *rule out* an interpretation when the presupposed number of referents is absent.

Schank's script-based strongly interactive model

Schank and his colleagues (e.g. Schank and Abelson, 1977) have developed computer models of language comprehension that allow the general knowledge component to carry the main burden of interpretation. Specifically, Schank claims that there is no autonomous syntactic processing since he argues that semantics and general knowledge can carry out the task just as well. The model contrasts with Winograd's, therefore, since Winograd does assume that an independent syntactic component is necessary to provide a structural analysis of the sentence. Garnham (1985) argues quite convincingly that Schank's semantic processor is largely concerned with the computation of structural analyses, and so syntax plays a larger role in the model than Schank acknowledges. Nevertheless, Schank maintains the view that general knowledge guides both syntactic and semantic processing.

The general knowledge component consists of well-defined knowledge frames or scripts that characterize the specific information that we know about particular events or situations, such as visiting a restaurant or going to a birthday party. A script can be thought of as an elaborate semantic network that describes what we know about a stereotypical sequence of events, for example, a restaurant script might contain information about the way people are shown to a table, given a menu, place an order, eat the food, and pay the bill. A script, therefore, enables a reader to infer typical information when reading a text that refers to a restaurant. On encountering a word such as *restaurant*, the complete script is activated and the reader assumes by default that the typical events take place.

Schank argues that once a script becomes activated, it can be used to predict what people and events will be mentioned in subsequent sentences and what roles they will play. These proposals clearly assume that higher-level processes influence and direct parsing and so illustrate strong interaction. However, the evidence reviewed in this chapter indicates that people have difficulty in comprehending sentences containing syntactic ambiguities. Despite these ambiguities, people are able to construct a unique representation of a sentence, but to do so requires specifically syntactic processing. Schank, however, has nothing to say about how people interpret such sentences. He circumvents the problem in his simulations by using texts that are composed of very simple sentences with minimal syntactic ambiguity. Thus a model such as Schank's is unable to account for the garden path phenomena that were discussed earlier.

Taraban and McClelland's experiments

Taraban and McClelland (1988) focus on the results of Rayner, Carlson and Frazier's (1983) experiment that was described above. Rayner et al. proposed a thematic processor to account for the finding that people pause on encountering the word *revolver* in (3.17) but not on encountering the word *binoculars* in (3.18).

> The spy saw the cop with a revolver but the cop   (3.17)
> didn't see him.

> The spy saw the cop with binoculars but the cop   (3.18)
> didn't see him.

Rayner et al. propose that the thematic processor can veto a syntactic analysis that has been constructed, hence the preferred minimal attachment reading is discarded in (3.17). This results in backtracking so that the alternative analysis can be constructed instead. Taraban and McClelland dispute this account of the phenomenon. They argue instead for a parallel account: subjects use syntactic, semantic and pragmatic processes to construct all possible analyses of the sentence and the pragmatically preferred interpretation becomes highly activated as soon pragmatic information is available. Taraban and McClelland argue that in the examples above pragmatic information is available in the content of the sentence even before the ambiguous word *with* is encountered. The ambiguity is shown in Figure 3.4.

In theory, once *with* is encountered, readers can either attach the preposition phrase to the verb phrase (VP) node, as in the top panel of

Figure 3.4, or to the noun phrase (NP) node, as shown in the bottom panel of Figure 3.4. Attachment to the verb phrase yields the minimal attachment reading, while attachment to the noun phrase yields the non-minimal attachment reading. (An additional node is required for the non-minimal attachment reading.)

Taraban and McClelland propose that the content of the sentence, particularly the verb, will favour either verb phrase attachment or noun phrase attachment. As long as the sentence is consistent with the favoured interpretation, comprehension flows smoothly. If the sentence turns out to be inconsistent with the favoured interpretation, then comprehension is disrupted. Taraban and McClelland argue that in the sentence above, the verb *see* favours the interpretation in which

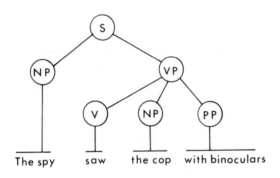

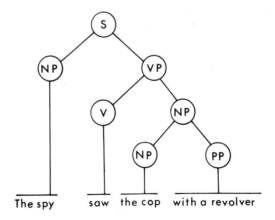

Figure 3.4   Phrase structures for the strings, The spy saw the cop with the binoculars (top panel) and The spy saw the cop with the revolver (bottom panel)

the prepositional phrase which begins with the word *with* will mention an instrument – what the actor used to see the object. In other words, the pragmatic constraints based on content select verb phrase attachment (the minimal attachment reading), not noun phrase attachment (the non-minimal attachment reading). Thus Taraban and McClelland argue that the content of the materials used by Rayner et al., favoured minimal attachment, and so they claim that pragmatic constraints based on content, not minimal attachment, may explain Rayner et al.'s results.

Taraban and McClelland present evidence to support this view. They presented subjects with sentences like (3.17) and (3.18) and asked them to rate the critical noun (*binoculars* or *revolver*) for how much it was expected. They found that all of Rayner et al.'s minimal attachment sentences had a higher expectancy rating than did their non-minimal attachment sentences, thus supporting the view that Rayner et al.'s sentences favoured minimal attachment readings.

In a subsequent experiment, Taraban and McClelland obtained reading times for each word in the sentence when the sentence contained one of the following: the expected noun in the critical position, a less expected noun but one with the same role (e.g. instrument), a noun with a less expected role, or a noun with the less expected attachment. The sentence in (3.19) contains a verb which leads to the expectation that an instrument will be mentioned in the prepositional phrase. This is shown in (a). A less expected instrument is shown in (b), a less expected role is shown in (c), and the less expected attachment (noun phrase attachment) is shown in (d). The examples in (3.20) show the same conditions when the verb leads to the expectation that the preposition phrase will contain a modifier of the object noun (that is, the content favours noun phrase attachment).

The janitor cleaned the storage area with the   (3.19)
    (a) broom
    (b) solvent
    (c) manager
    (d) odour
because of many complaints.

The hospital admitted the patient with   (3.20)
    (a) cancer
    (b) amnesia

(c) bodyguards

(d) apologies

while the other incoming patients waited calmly.

The results showed that there was a marked increase in reading times for the word following the critical noun when it was either an unexpected role or an unexpected attachment. Taraban and McClelland conclude from these results that content not syntax determines the choice of analysis, since an unexpected role is present in both of these conditions. That is, the slow reading times in (3.19) (c) and (3.19) (d) can both be explained by the presence of an unexpected roles regardless of whether the attachment is expected, as in (3.19) (c) or unexpected, as in (3.19) (d).

Taraban and McClelland argue, therefore, for a parallel model of parsing and suggest that a connectionist system of parallel constraint satisfaction can best describe the processes involved. Frazier (1990), however, contests this view. In particular she contests the idea that any semantic bias, however slight, determines on a word-by-word basis the structural analysis that is pursued. She argues that Taraban and McClelland's results may apply only to the sentences they used and that they are due to the fact that a parallel thematic processor (Rayner, Carlson and Frazier, 1983) evaluates the arguments of a verb on a word-by-word basis. That is, the thematic processor carries out a partial semantic analysis of each word and may reject an inappropriate analysis but not select an appropriate one. Frazier argues that this account is consistent with the whole range of data on minimal attachment while Taraban and McClelland's account is consistent only with data from sentences with ambiguous preposition phrase attachments.

A slightly different proposal in support of the strategies view has been made by Clifton (1990). He argues that the first rapid analysis of a sentence is purely syntactic and follows the principles of minimal attachment and late closure. This first pass analysis accounts for the evidence of Frazier and her colleagues. However, a subsequent, more leisurely, second pass analysis takes account of semantic and pragmatic factors, and this second pass analysis accounts for the evidence of people like Altmann and Steedman. Clifton reviews a range of evidence favouring this view, which clearly defends the spirit of a serial system, since the first rapid analysis is purely syntactic and serial. Nevertheless, it is clear that semantic and pragmatic processes work very quickly in comprehension, and so a connectionist model which uses multiple cues in parallel to jointly specify a set of constraints (Taraban and McClelland, 1988) is a feasible proposition.

A Connectionist Model of Parsing

Waltz and Pollack (1985) propose a connectionist model that has an independent syntactic parser that analyses the input in parallel with a semantic and a contextual processor. The units in each processor are nodes in a connectionist network. The syntactic parser constructs parallel analyses that are subject to excitation and inhibition. Elements within a constituent have excitatory links, while elements in separate constituents have inhibitory links. For example, the link between a verb and a verb phrase is an excitatory link, while the link between a verb and an adjective is an inhibitory one. The units in the syntactic component are syntactic categories, such as verb, verb phrase, noun, noun phrase, and so on.

The semantic component is based on a spreading activation model of semantic priming (e.g. Collins and Loftus, 1975), in which the units are different senses of a word. There are excitatory links between related words and inhibitory links between different senses of a word, for example the 'performer' and 'terrestrial body' senses of *star*. The units in the contextual component consist of features that both define a concept and associate a concept with others sharing the same features. The resulting interconnections simulate the observation that sentence contexts are much more general than the specific word associations of the semantic component, so that there may not be any explicit word in the context that triggers the contextual excitation.

The feature that makes the model a strongly parallel one is that it contains both excitatory and inhibitory links between word senses, syntactic categories and semantic context. For example, the link between the word sense *tired* and the syntactic category *adjective* is excitatory, but the link between *tired* and *noun* is inhibitory. Thus, each component constructs parallel analyses that are then either excited or inhibited by the analyses constructed by other components. The units that result in the highest activation level are the ones that constitute the final interpretation. Waltz and Pollack show how a sentence like (3.21) is analysed:

John ate up the street. (3.21)

There are two possible networks for this sentence, one that (correctly) analyses *up the street* as a preposition phrase, and one that analyses *the street* as the object of *ate up*. The syntactic analysis initially chooses the second, incorrect, interpretation since it selects the shortest tree it can find. (This is consistent with minimal attachment.) However, semantic information overrides this selection very rapidly. In this way, Waltz and Pollack argue that the network simulates the garden path phenomena associated with minimal attachment, without building in a minimal attachment heuristic as part of the architecture.

The syntactic component constructs units that are sentence constituents, such as verb, verb phrase and so on, not complete sentences. Thus the syntactic units are comparable to those in Altmann and Steedman's weakly interactive model. In addition, the units are subject to excitation or inhibition from semantics and context only after they have been activated. That is, inhibition from the semantic and contextual components acts in the same way as in Altmann and Steedman's model: it is used to discard (or reduce the activation level of) inappropriate analyses. Since syntactic processes are confined to an independent component and since semantic and contextual processes are used to discard inappropriate analyses, the model can best be characterized, therefore, as weakly interactive. Indeed, we saw in Chapter 2 that connectionist models in general have serious difficulties in representing relational (that is, syntactic) information. It is not surprising therefore that Waltz and Pollack's model relies on an independent component for the processing and representation of syntactic relations.

SUMMARY

Models of syntactic parsing are either modular or non-modular. Modular accounts include the serial independent model of Frazier, the weakly interactive model of Altmann and Steedman and the connectionist model of Waltz and Pollack. Non-modular accounts include the computer simulations of Schank and Winograd. The major differences between the models reside in whether or not a syntactic representation is constructed and the point at which semantic and pragmatic processes are brought to bear. Frazier's model is the most extreme modular account, assuming as it does a serial processor that constructs a single syntactic representation of a sentence without any involvement of semantic and pragmatic processes. However, Rayner, Carlson and Frazier's (1983) proposal that a thematic processor may be used to rule out inappropriate parses reduces the size of the syntactic constituent that is constructed from the complete sentence to smaller categories, such as *verb* or *noun*. The proposal still assumes that only one analysis is pursued at a time, but the analysis that is pursued may be subjected to a plausibility check as each word is encountered rather than at the end of the sentence.

Altmann and Steedman propose a parallel weakly interactive model, in which a propositional representation is constructed, not a syntactic one. The model pursues all possible analyses at once and context is used to rule out the inappropriate analyses. In this way, they remove the problem of having to reanalyse the sentence after a garden path. However, the presence of backward regressions in eye movement records (e.g. Frazier and Rayner, 1982) suggests that recovery from garden paths is not as straightforward as Altmann and Steedman imply. Waltz and Pollack's connectionist model is similar to Altmann and Steedman's. It constructs syntactic representations that are then subject to excitation or inhibition from the semantic and contextual processes.

Strongly interactive models dispute the assumption that syntactic processing is modular, and semantic and pragmatic processes enjoy a much more intrusive role. They are able to penetrate the syntactic module and influence the choice of interpretation that is made. The strongly interactive models of Winograd and Schank are also serial models since they pursue only one analysis at a time. By contrast, Taraban and McClelland propose a strongly interactive model that is parallel rather than serial and they argue for a connectionist view of parsing. Certainly, Waltz and Pollack's connectionist model simulates the findings of Frazier and her colleagues on minimal attachment. Hence it gives a better account of the syntactic phenomena than do strongly interactive serial models. However, the connectionist model seems to be weakly rather than strongly interactive, since it assumes a modular structure for syntactic, semantic and pragmatic processes.

One way to reconcile the differences between serial models and weakly interactive models is to argue, as does Clifton, that an initial rapid analysis of a sentence is primarily structural while a second pass analysis involves semantic and pragmatic processes. The evidence of

Altmann and Steedman may well reflect the outcome of the second pass analysis, especially if structural representations are constructed at the word or phrase level. However, it is also the case that the serial nature of Frazier's model can be simulated in Waltz and Pollack's parallel system. This suggests that the most important distinction between models of parsing is whether or not they preserve modularity. It also suggests that the decision concerning serial versus parallel systems will have to be made on other grounds, grounds such as whether or not connectionist systems can explain the intricacies of linguistic processing. Such issues have received a lot of discussion in recent years and they were reviewed in Chapter 2 on representation. Studies that investigate the nature of syntactic processing will continue to clarify the kinds of processes, like minimal attachment or referential failure, that need to be accounted for in a model of syntactic processing.

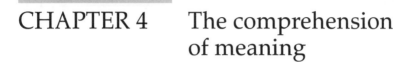

CHAPTER 4   The comprehension of meaning

How might the meaning of an expression be grasped in comprehension? This chapter will examine formal semantic theories and consider how the insights about language that they have revealed might be used in a psychological theory. The theory of mental models is then discussed and this is followed by a discussion of the way in which word meanings contribute to the overall meaning of a sentence. The discussion of word meaning allows the theory of mental models to be examined alongside a view that favours the use of meaning postulates to construct a linguistic representation of the meaning of a sentence (e.g. Fodor, Fodor and Garrett, 1975).

WHAT IS SEMANTICS?

Knowledge of semantics reveals itself in certain abilities that we possess. One is the ability to judge that various relations hold among sentences. These relations include the recognition that one sentence can entail another, that two sentences can be synonymous, and that a sentence can be ambiguous. The relation of entailment is shown in (4.1) where the (a) sentence entails the (b) sentence.

>   John is a bachelor.   (4.1.a)
>   John is unmarried.   (4.1.b)

Two synonymous sentences are shown in (4.2), and an ambiguous sentence is shown in (4.3), where the word *light* is ambiguous, having a 'light in weight' sense and a 'light in colour' sense.

>   John bought a car from Mary.   (4.2)
>   Mary sold a car to John.

>   The man wore a light suit.   (4.3)

A second ability that we can attribute to a knowledge of semantics is our ability to judge the relations between language and the world. For example, if someone says, *The sun is shining*, then as speakers of English we know that the utterance is a true description of the world if the sky is clear, and that it is false if the sky is clouded over. A knowledge of meaning, therefore, provides the link between language and the world.

These two kinds of knowledge – of the relations among sentences in the language, and of the relations between language and the world – have often been regarded as distinct and have been thought of as indicating a knowledge of meaning in the first case and a knowledge of reference in the second. Semantic theories known as truth conditional theories are concerned with both sense and reference (that is, with both intensional and extensional relations). Thus, truth-conditional theories distinguish between sense on the one hand and reference on the other. However, they differ in whether they use the term 'reference' to refer to the truth conditions of a sentence (e.g. Frege, 1879) or to the specific situation described by the sentence (e.g. Barwise and Perry, 1983).

Language and the World

What is it that we know when we say that we know what a sentence means? The key to answering this question lies in the notion of truth: to know the meaning of a sentence is to know what the world would have to be like for the sentence to be true. In other words, to know the meaning of a sentence is to be able to specify its truth conditions. This definition lies at the heart of truth-conditional theories of meaning.

Of course, there are other things that we know (or believe) when we comprehend a sentence, other than what it is that would make the sentence true. We may know the intentions of the speaker, or what 'speech act' he or she is trying to convey, as when someone makes a promise for example. These non-truth conditional aspects of meaning are not normally regarded as part of semantics but of pragmatics, and they are discussed in Chapter 6 on discourse. The distinction between semantics and pragmatics is supported by many linguists (e.g. Chierchia and McConnell-Ginet, 1990; Gazdar, 1979), although it is sometimes difficult to maintain, as we will see in Chapter 6. However, the present chapter is concerned with truth-conditional aspects of meaning, that is, with semantics.

Truth-conditional Semantics

To amplify on the notion of truth that was discussed above, consider a situation in which you are asked to look after a visitor to Britain who is not a native speaker of English. How would you decide whether or not the visitor could grasp the meaning of what she heard? One obvious way to do this would be to find out whether or not she understood the situations that made a sentence true and that made it false. Thus on hearing the sentence, *The sun is shining*, you might feel confident that the visitor knew what it meant if she could successfully say when she was in situations that made the sentence true and when she was in situations that made the sentence false. From such observations you might reasonably infer that the visitor knew the meaning of the sentence: she could be presented with any possible situation that might occur in the world and correctly judge the truth or falsity of the sentence. Such a procedure is the essence of truth-conditional semantics, which specifies that the meaning of an expression – what proposition it expresses – is characterized by a division of situations into those that make the sentence true and those that make it false.

Meaning, reference and truth

Truth-conditional semantics is concerned with three aspects of meaning: what the sentence means, the truth value of the sentence, and what the sentence refers to in the world. The logician Frege used the terms 'sense' and 'reference' to distinguish between the first two aspects of meaning. For Frege, the reference of a sentence was its truth value and the sense was the conditions that must hold for the sentence to be true. Consider for example, the two noun phrases in (4.4).

the tallest man in the room   (4.4)
the heaviest man in the room.

The way you would discover what makes the noun phrase true would be different in the two cases. In the first case you would concentrate on height but in the second case you would concentrate on weight.

The meanings therefore are different in the two cases. However, the sentence would have the same truth value in both cases, since in both cases the noun phrase would be a true description. Thus the sense of an expression can be distinguished from its reference.

Frege's notion of reference, that is, the truth value of a sentence, is important in formal semantic theories because the truth value of an expression is needed to evaluate the validity of logical inferences (see Chapter 7). Since work on formal semantics originally developed to give a semantic interpretation to logical languages, the notion of logical validity (and hence truth) is important. However, when semantic theories are used to give a semantic interpretation to real language, rather than to logic, then the specific situation that is referred to by an expression is crucial for determining its truth value and for understanding its full meaning. For example, to know the sense or meaning of the noun phrase *the man*, is to be able to identify all those situations that contain just one man. There are, of course, indefinitely many such situations. The meaning, therefore, simply tells you to check that one of these situations holds, but it does not tell you the particular situation (that is, the particular man) that is being described. Nor does Frege's notion of reference, or truth value, help in this respect, since all the situations that contain a unique man will make the sentence true.

It is only fairly recently that semantic theories have been proposed that address the question of who or what is being referred to (e.g. Barwise and Perry, 1983; Heim, 1983; Kamp, 1981). These developments have arisen as a result of attempts by linguists and philosophers (e.g. Montague, 1974) to develop a rigorous semantic theory for explaining the way that real language is interpreted. As Barwise and Perry (1983) point out, the sense or meaning of an utterance places constraints on the described situation: the sentence will be true in all those situations in which the described situation is true. This is the standard assumption of truth conditional semantics. However, Barwise and Perry go on to argue that constraints that the meaning places on the utterances, such as who is being referred to, are equally important. Barwise and Perry, therefore, use the term 'reference' to refer to this aspect of meaning: the situation described by the sentence, not the sentence's truth value.

Since knowing what specific situation an expression refers to in the world is such a crucial ingredient of comprehension, we will adopt Barwise and Perry's terminology in this chapter and use the term 'reference' in its more everyday sense to refer to the specific situation in the world that the sentence describes. We will retain the term 'truth value' for Frege's notion of reference. Current semantic theories use the terms 'intension' and 'extension' to refer to meaning and truth value respectively. In this chapter, however, the term 'extension' will be synonymous with the everyday notion of reference; that is, the specific situation being referred to.

Model-theoretic Semantics

Truth conditional semantic theories discuss meaning in relation to a model not in relation to the world. For example, imagine a model of a world that contains two men (George and Peter) who are both writers, and three women (Sue, Jan, and Rosa) who are all politicians. In this model, the sentence *A man writes* will be true. The noun man picks out the set of men, George and Peter, the verb *writes* picks out the set of writers, and the word *a* says that an element in the set of men is also in the set of writers. There is, therefore, at least one man in the set of writers, and so the sentence is true in the model. By contrast, the sentence *A woman writes* will be false with respect to the model, since none of the women is in the set of writers. The notion of truth with respect to a model is due to the logician Tarski (1931) who was thereby able to give a rigorous account of the truth of sentences in a specialized language such as logic.

A model-theoretic account such as the one above gives a precise account of the intension of a sentence: it is the set of entities in the model that make the sentence true, and of the truth value of a sentence: it is truth with respect to the model. What is not accounted for in this model is the reference of a sentence: the particular situation or person in the model that is being referred to by the expression. For example, the meaning of the definite noun phrase *the chair*, is the set of all chairs in the model (or in the context of the utterance). On hearing the sentence, *Move the chair away*, uttered in a room containing several chairs, the meaning of *the chair* will not identify the specific chair that is to be moved. To identify the specific chair, we need to know the referent of the noun phrase and not just its meaning. Solutions to this aspect of semantics have been proposed by Barwise and Perry (1983) and by Kamp (1981), who also attempt to provide a semantics for fragments of natural language rather than for logic.

Barwise and Perry have introduced a semantic theory known as situation semantics. Situation theory adopts many of the insights of model-theoretic semantics. However, it differs from model-theoretic semantics in that it tries to show how the meaning of an utterance determines not only the set of things that make the utterance true (the traditional domain of model-theoretic semantics), but also how the meaning determines who or what is being referred to by the utterance. Thus, in situation semantics, definite descriptions, such as *the man*, and *the boy who cried* identify unique individuals as well as the sets of individuals that make the descriptions true.

In order to identify the reference of a sentence, Barwise and Perry propose that contextual constraints are applied to the meaning of an expression to yield a unique individual. Context, for Barwise and Perry includes the discourse situation, such as who the speaker is, and the time and location of the utterance. Thus *the Prime Minister* when uttered by a character in a 1980s British novel is likely to be interpreted as Mrs Thatcher. Context also includes speaker connections, that is, connections between the speaker and objects, properties, places and times. For example, when using a name like *Peter*, the speaker exploits a connection with an individual in the world, and this constrains the situations being described to those that contain the Peters connected to the speaker. Finally, context includes the resource situation, that is, the ability on the part of the speaker to exploit one state of affairs to convey information about another. For example, if someone says, *Let's go to the pub that we used last time*, the speaker can exploit the fact that people went to a particular pub on the previous occasion to identify the pub that she wishes to refer to now. Barwise and Perry have developed a formal specification of the ways in which these contextual constraints yield a unique referent for an expression.

Kamp (1981) and Heim (1983) have also attempted to show how a specific individual can be referred to by a definite expression. They both proposed the idea of a discourse model that contains entities that have been introduced into a discourse. Any subsequent definite references are then taken to refer to entities that are in the discourse model. Consider the short text in (4.5):

A man came in. He was very late.   (4.5)

Both Kamp and Heim propose that the meaning of such a discourse depends on the construction of a discourse model. Traditional semantic theories would describe the meaning of the first sentence as saying that the set of individuals that are men and that came in is not empty. By contrast, Kamp and Heim suggest that the meaning says that a novel entity that is a man and that came in must be introduced into a discourse model. Thus they argue that the meaning of *a* is to indicate that somebody new is being talked about and so must be added to the discourse model. The definite pronoun *he* in the second sentence indicates that the person being referred to is familiar, that is, already in the discourse model. Thus, to interpret the pronoun, there must be a male entity in the discourse model. Since a male entity was introduced into the model by the previous sentence, the pronoun is assumed to refer to that entity.

Overall, these developments in model-theoretic semantics indicate that the three components of semantics: meaning, truth and reference, can be formally specified. However, the formal specifications use either short fragments of text or they use artificial languages, such as logics. They also define truth with respect to a model and not with respect to the world. When we turn to psychological processing, it is not possible to confine ourselves to a fragment of natural language or to a model of the world. A psychological model must account for people's ability to grasp the sense of the sentences of a language, to recognize the situations in the world that make a sentence true, and to identify the specific situation in the world that the speaker intends to refer to. In other words, the three features of meaning identified by model theoretic semantics also have to be explained by a psychological theory of interpretation. However, they must do so by reference to entities and situations in the world and not in a simplified model of the world.

THE PSYCHOLOGY OF SEMANTIC INTERPRETATION

The process of understanding a sentence can be thought of as a process by which we come to know what situations are truthfully described by a sentence. One way in which this might be done is to take a sentence, or a representation of it, and construct a mental model of the situation described by the sentence, in the same way that we construct a model of a real situation during perception. Such a model can be thought of as the reference of the sentence, since it represents a specific situation described by the sentence. We must also have the ability to construct any number of models of the described situation, since the meaning of the sentence includes all the possible situations that fit the description. The potential to construct alternative models of the many different situations described by an expression is what enables us to grasp the meaning of a sentence, and to establish its truth value. The theory of mental models (Johnson-Laird, 1983) characterizes these abilities.

Mental Models

A mental model (Johnson-Laird, 1983) is an internal model of the situation described by the sentence. It is derived from a propositional representation of the sentence through the use of inferences based on general knowledge of the world.

Propositional representations contain both syntactic information and the meanings of individual words. They resemble surface structures and enable verbatim information to be retained for short periods of time. A mental model is constructed from the propositional representation together with inferences based on general knowledge. Consider, for example, sentence (4.6):

> The terrorists freed the hostages.   (4.6)

On hearing or reading a sentence like (4.6), the proposition expressed by the sentence is represented in memory. A proposition describes the elementary idea underlying the sentence. It consists of a predicate (or relation) and one or more arguments (e.g. Kintsch, 1974). Underlying the sentence above is the proposition:

> FREED(terrorists, hostages)   (4.7)

It consists of the predicate *freed*, and an ordered list of arguments, *terrorists* and *hostages*, where the first item in the list is the logical subject of the verb and the second item is the logical object. A propositional representation, therefore, consists of the concepts activated by the content words in the sentence, linked together in the ways specified by the syntax of the sentence. Notice that the proposition does not identify the reference of the expression, which must be inferred from background knowledge of typical situations involving terrorists and hostages. These inferences act on the propositional representation of the sentence to yield a mental model of the situation described by the sentence. The mental model can be regarded as a representative example of the set of situations described by the sentence. In the example above, the mental model will most probably encode the terrorists as members of a radical Arab organization, the hostages as nationals of a western country, and the act of freeing as taking place in South Lebanon. Of course, these inferences may be wrong, they are plausible rather than logical, based as they are on induction. But the main point here is that the inferences enable the listener to go beyond a propositional representation and construct a mental model of the situation described by the sentence; that is, they enable the listener to go beyond the meaning of the sentence to establish its reference.

Johnson-Laird regards the achievement of inferring the identity of an individual from a definite description as part of grasping the significance of an utterance. Barwise and Perry similarly regard inferring the identity of an individual as an important component of situation semantics. Its importance in comprehension can be judged by the study of Bransford and Johnson (1972).

Bransford and Johnson found that their subjects were unable to understand or comprehend a passage of prose unless they already knew what the passage was referring to. One of the passages they presented was the following:

> The procedure is actually quite simple. First you arrange things into different groups depending on their makeup. Of course, one pile may be sufficient depending on how much there is to do. If you have to go somewhere else due to lack of facilities that is the next step, otherwise you are pretty well set. It is important not to overdo any particular endeavour. That is, it is better to do too few things at once than too many. In the short run this may not seem important, but complications from doing too many can easily arise. A mistake can be expensive as well. The manipulation of the appropriate mechanisms should be self-explanatory, and we need not dwell on it here. At first the whole procedure will seem complicated. Soon, however, it will become just another

facet of life. It is difficult to see any end to the necessity for this task in the immediate future, but then one never can tell.

Subjects were either told the topic of the passage before hearing it, or immediately after hearing it, or not at all. All subjects were required to recall the passage and rate it for ease of comprehension. Only the first group of subjects – the one that was told the topic before hearing it – recalled the passage well and rated it as easily comprehended. Neither the group that was told the topic after hearing the passage but before the recall and rating tasks, nor the group that was not told the topic at all could recall or comprehend the passage. The topic of the passage above is washing clothes. Only knowledge of the topic allows the significance of the passage to be understood. For example, the referent of the procedure becomes known as well as the referents for the other noun phrases in the passage. Thus, a major feature of comprehension is a knowledge of the referents and this feature is captured by mental models.

According to Johnson-Laird (1983), the psychological procedures that construct, update, and evaluate mental models are as follows:

1. If a proposition makes no reference, either explicitly or implicitly, to an entity already in the current mental model, there is a procedure for constructing a new model.
2. If a proposition contains at least one entity that is in the current model, there is a procedure for adding the remaining information to the model. This information will consist of other entities, properties or relations.
3. If a proposition contains entities that are in two different models, there is a procedure that integrates these two separate models into a single model.
4. If all the referents in a proposition are in the current model, there is a procedure that verifies that the asserted properties or relations hold in the model.
5. If it is not possible to verify an assertion by the procedure above, there is a procedure that adds the property or relation to the model (see Johnson-Laird and Byrne, 1991).
6. If the verification procedure in (4) establishes that an assertion is true of the current model, there is a recursive procedure that checks whether the model can be changed to make the assertion false. It is this procedure that makes valid deductions possible.

7. If the verification procedure in (4) establishes that an assertion is false of the current model, there is a recursive procedure which checks whether the model can be changed to make the assertion true. It is this procedure that makes inductive inferences possible. For example, inferences based on stereotypes or default values, such as the inference that there are waiters or waitresses in a restaurant can be overruled if they turn out to be false according to later assertions in the discourse.

During comprehension, the propositional representation of an utterance elicits one of these seven general procedures as a function of its referring expressions, the current model, and background knowledge. This is how models are constructed (procedure 1), updated (procedures 2 and 5), integrated (procedure 3) and evaluated (procedures 4, 6 and 7). Some of these procedures can be illustrated with the sample discourse in (4.8).

Some men travelled to London.   (4.8)
They crashed the car at Bedford.

Once the first sentence has been interpreted to yield a proposition, procedure 1 constructs a model containing entities standing for *some men*, a location, *London*, and the relation of travelling. In order to construct a specific model, a default mode of travelling may be inferred, such as that the men travelled by train. The propositional representation of the second sentence contains the pronoun *they*, the definite noun phrase *the car*, the location, *Bedford* and the property of crashing. The semantics of definite noun phrases (including pronouns) assumes that they refer to familiar entities, that is, to entities that are already in the model (e.g. Heim, 1983; Kamp, 1981). Thus, on encountering *they*, the reader searches for entities in the model so that procedure 2 can be implemented. Since there are entities in the model that *they* can refer to, procedure 2 is implemented. The same procedure is adopted when *the car* is encountered: Since *the car* is a definite expression, the reader will search the current model for an entity standing for *car*. However, if the model of the first proposition has the men travelling by train, then there will be no such entity in the model. It is also not possible to infer the presence of a car from the contents of the current model, although this should be possible when a definite expression is used. Consequently, the verification procedure establishes that the second assertion is false of the current model. Procedure 7 checks whether the model can be changed to make the assertion true. Since the mode of travelling can be changed from going by train to going by car, this procedure is successful and the model is changed accordingly.

A mental model thus represents the reference of an assertion, that is, a representative example of the situation it describes. The two recursive procedures for revising the model (in conjunction with the propositional representation) characterize the meaning of the assertion, that is, the set of all possible situations that it describes. Any member of the set could in principle be generated from the propositional representation by these procedures. For example, the first sentence of the discourse above could be represented by an infinite set of possible models, depending in part on the number of men assigned to *some men*. The particular model that is constructed is simply a representative sample from that infinite set. The model can be revised, and the representative sample changed by the two recursive procedures. These procedures guarantee that, in principle, any one of the infinite number of possible models can be constructed. Since a mental model may have to be revised in the light of subsequent information, the semantic processes are non-deterministic.

Mental models are constructed from perception as well as language and it is this link with perception that ensures the link with reality and hence the link between language and the world. This grounding in perception also provides a way for the truth value of a discourse to be computed. A discourse is true if and only if there is at least one mental model of it that can be mapped into the real world, that is, the individuals represented in the model occur in the real world with the same properties and the same relations holding between them. Of course, there are very few discourses that we can evaluate directly, via perception, although we might be able to evaluate them indirectly, relative to an independent model of reality.

How plausible is the notion of a mental model? There is a considerable body of evidence to suggest that the representation of a sentence does indeed transcend its propositional interpretation. For example, Bransford and Franks (1971) presented subjects with sentences like the following:

> Three turtles rested on a floating log and a fish   (4.9)
> swam beneath them.

In a subsequent recognition test, they found that subjects were likely to assume that they had heard that the fish swam beneath the log. Thus the subjects made inferences from what they heard to construct a representation that contained more than was explicitly stated in the sentence. Similarly, Haviland and Clark (1974) proposed a 'given-new strategy' on the basis of their experimental results. They presented subjects with sentence pairs like the following:

Ed got some beer out of the trunk.   (4.10)
The beer was warm.

Ed got some picnic things out of the trunk.   (4.11)
The beer was warm.

They measured the time taken to read the second sentence and found that the times were longer in sentences like (4.11) than in sentences like (4.10). They argued that in (4.11) a bridging inference is required to identify the beer with one of the picnic things whereas a bridging inference is unnecessary in (4.10). This corresponds to the ways in which referents are identified or inferred in a model so that new information can be added to it.

A specific test of mental models was devised by Ehrlich and Johnson-Laird (1982). They presented subjects with materials like those shown in Table 4.1. In the continuous descriptions, each sentence begins by referring to the last mentioned entity, so a representation of the described spatial array could be constructed continuously. In the semi-continuous descriptions, each sentence begins by referring to an entity that is in the representation but is not the last mentioned entity. In the discontinuous descriptions, the second sentence refers to new entities, that is, they are neither recently mentioned nor already in the representation.

Thus, in continuous and semi-continuous descriptions it is possible to construct a mental model of the first sentence and progressively update it on reading sentences two and three. However, with the discontinuous descriptions, it is not possible to construct a single integrated model until the third sentence has been read, since the information in the second sentence is insufficient to enable the model of the first sentence to be updated.

Subjects were presented with the sentences of each description one at a time and the time taken to read and comprehend each sentence was measured. If the key feature for comprehension is the location of an

Table 4.1.   Examples of the materials used in Ehrlich and Johnson-Laird (1982)

Continuous description

The knife is in front of the pot
The pot is on the left of the glass
The glass is behind the dish

Semi-continuous description

The pot is on the left of the glass
The knife is in front of the pot
The glass is behind the dish

Discontinuous description

The knife is in front of the pot
The glass is behind the dish
The pot is on the left of the glass

---

entity in a model, then the time taken to read sentence three should be faster in the continuous and semi-continuous descriptions than in the discontinuous descriptions, since no model yet exists of the discontinuous description. The results supported this prediction. What seems to be important for comprehension is that each sentence can be integrated in a mental model as it is read. If this cannot be done, as with discontinuous descriptions, then comprehension is slowed.

The descriptions used by Ehrlich and Johnson-Laird were determinate: they were compatible with only one spatial layout. However, descriptions may also be indeterminate: they may be compatible with more than one layout, for example:

> The spoon is to the left of the knife.   (4.12)
> The plate is to the right of the spoon.
> The fork is in front of the spoon.
> The cup is in front of the knife.

Here, the plate could be either to the right or the left of the knife. Mani and Johnson-Laird (1982) found that if a description was indeterminate and more than one model could be constructed, then verbatim memory was better than memory for gist. By contrast, if the description was determinate and a single model could be constructed, then subjects remembered only the gist of the description. The description above would be a determinate one if the second line were changed to read:

The plate is to the right of the knife.

These findings suggest that wherever possible, people will construct a mental model of a description and forget the wording. When called upon later to recall the material, people describe the mental model, and this results in gist recall. However, if a mental model has not been formed, because there is no single model that fits the description, then a propositional representation is remembered, and this results in the words themselves being recalled.

This account of mental models shows how they can capture both the meaning and the reference of an expression. What remains to be considered, however, is the way in which other theories account for comprehension. In order to discuss mental models in this broader context, we will turn to word meanings and the ways in which words may be combined during comprehension to yield the meaning of the sentence as a whole. This involves a discussion of different views of comprehension.

THE MEANINGS OF WORDS AND THE MEANINGS OF SENTENCES

In general, theories of comprehension divide according to whether they regard the crucial component of semantics to be meaning (sense) or reference, and on whether they regard the end-point of comprehension to be a proposition or a representation that has been enriched by inferences. The theories that will be considered are those of Fodor, Fodor and Garrett (1975), Kintsch (1974) and Johnson-Laird (1983).

Fodor et al. and Kintsch regard meaning as the crucial ingredient of comprehension, rather than reference. Thus they focus on people's ability to recognize entailments, synonymy and ambiguity. They have, however, no mechanism for identifying the reference of an expression. They propose that the end-product of comprehension is a proposition and does not include any additional information. According to Fodor et al., the ability to recognize entailments, synonymy and ambiguity is due to an additional and optional inference mechanism, that is distinct from comprehension, and that is applied to a proposition. Johnson-Laird's theory contrasts with this view. First, Johnson-Laird disagrees with Fodor et al. by arguing that reference is a crucial ingredient of comprehension, not just meaning. According to Johnson-Laird, the procedures people use to establish the reference of a sentence also establish its meaning, thus ensuring that entailments, synonyms and ambiguities can be recognized. Johnson-Laird also disagrees with Fodor et al. and with Kintsch on what is regarded as the end-product of comprehension. For Fodor et al. and Kintsch, it is a proposition, unencumbered by inferences. For Johnson-Laird it is a mental model; that is, the propositional representation is enriched by inferences to yield a mental model.

It should also be noted that Kintsch (1988) has proposed a model of comprehension that involves three levels of representation: a syntactic representation, a propositional representation, and a situation model of the sentence. The propositional representation corresponds to his early view, described here, of the end-product of comprehension, but the situation model is comparable to Johnson-Laird's mental model. Consequently, Kintsch's (1974) distinction between comprehension and inferences has become blurred and he now seems to hold a view that is closer to Johnson-Laird's than to the view of Fodor et al.

Word Meaning

In truth-conditional semantics, sentence meaning is taken as basic and words are characterized in terms of the systematic contribution they make to sentence meaning. However, a complete psychological theory of comprehension will need to account for the way in which word meanings are represented.

We have seen that the interpretation of a sentence involves the specification of the conditions that make the sentence true. Thus, our account of word meaning should be in terms of the systematic contribution a word makes to the truth conditions of sentences in which it occurs. Consider the sentences in (4.13) to (4.16):

The cat chased the dog.   (4.13)

Bill chased his sister.   (4.14)

The little boy chased the ball.   (4.15)

The cat caught the dog.   (4.16)

These sentences have certain aspects of meaning in common. In each case, the entity referred to in the subject position has followed the entity referred to in the object position with the intention of catching it. In addition, the conditions necessary for the truth of (4.13) differ from those necessary for the truth of (4.16) solely in respect of the meaning difference between chase and catch. Thus the interpretations assigned to words contribute in a systematic way to the truth conditions of the sentences in which they occur. Fodor et al.'s theory of meaning postulates and Johnson-Laird's theory of mental models represent two distinct attempts to explain how this systematic relationship is exploited in comprehension.

Meaning Postulates

Fodor et al. (1975) propose that the end-product of comprehension should be as close to the original sentence as possible because comprehension is very fast; too fast, they argue for any inferencing to take place. They propose, therefore, that the end-product of comprehension is similar to its deep structure representation. A sentence such as *John killed Mary* is represented by a proposition of the form *KILL*(John, Mary), where *kill* is a relation and *John* and *Mary* are arguments. This proposition is the end-product of comprehension.

In order to account for the entailment from *John killed Mary* to *Mary died*, Fodor et al. propose that people may choose to apply inference rules or meaning postulates to the proposition. Meaning postulates were introduced into logic by Carnap (1952). They have been used by him and others, to capture entailments that depend on the meanings of content words, such as *kill*, or *bachelor*, rather than on the meaning of the logical words, like *if*, *and*, *not*, and so on.

For example, meaning postulates for the verb *to kill* are:

For any X and Y, if X killed Y, then X caused Y to die.   (4.17)
If X caused Y to die, then Y died.

A meaning postulate for the word *bachelor* is:

If X is a bachelor, then X is unmarried.   (4.18)

According to Fodor et al., meaning postulates are stored in long-term memory. They are retrieved if they are needed to recognize entailments, synonymy, or ambiguity. If the meaning postulate in (4.18) is activated on encountering the word *bachelor*, then the entailment from *bachelor* to *unmarried* will be recognized. Two words have the same meaning if they have the same meaning postulates, and a word is ambiguous if more than one set of meaning postulates is associated with it.

For Fodor et al., then, the end-product of comprehension is a proposition, where each word is represented as a unit. It is not decomposed into underlying elements. Whether or not meaning postulates will be applied depends on how the sentence is used. Thus, the theory accounts for comprehension by explaining the ability to recognize relations between sentences, but it ignores the ability to recognize the relations between language and the world.

Mental Models

We have already seen that Johnson-Laird (1983) assumes that a propositional representation is necessary for the construction of a mental model. However, unlike Fodor et al. and Kintsch, Johnson-Laird does not assume that a proposition is the end-product of comprehension. He argues instead that the construction of a mental model is crucial for adequate comprehension. The reason for this is that it is only through the construction of a mental model that the significance of a sentence is grasped. The significance of an utterance goes beyond a proposition because it depends on knowing the referent of an expression. The study by Bransford and Johnson (1972) that was cited earlier highlights the importance of understanding what the words of a text refer to. Meaning postulates, however, have nothing to say about this aspect of comprehension, since they do not consider the way in which the reference of a word or sentence is understood. Indeed, as Johnson-Laird points out, the theory cannot fulfil the requirements of model-theoretic semantics. This is because propositions do not refer to model-theoretic entities, or entities in the world, and so they do not provide an interpretation of a sentence. They can account for the way that the conceptual content of a sentence is grasped, but not for the understanding of reference.

One argument that Johnson-Laird uses to support his claim that reference is the key to comprehension is illustrated by sentence (4.19):

They are very rich. (4.19)

In this sentence, the word *they* is ambiguous. But its ambiguity concerns its reference not its meaning. To understand the sentence, therefore, it is necessary to identify the referent of *they*. If rich means wealthy, you will infer that *they* refers to a set of people. If rich means fruity you may infer that *they* refers to cakes. Theories that account only for meaning cannot explain how sentences like (4.19) are understood. This observation, together with the results of studies like those of Bransford and Johnson (1972), Bransford and Franks (1971), and Haviland and Clark (1974) suggest that comprehension does involve a grasp of the reference of an expression as well as its meaning and that theories that consider only meaning are therefore problematic.

According to Johnson-Laird's theory, one sentence entails another if a mental model of the entailed proposition is contained in the mental model of the sentence. Two sentences are synonymous if they are consistent with the same mental models, and a sentence is ambiguous if it is compatible with two or more mental models. The theory therefore accounts for meaning as well as reference, although the degree to which different mental models can be distinguished becomes an important issue in this context. We will now examine the way in which the theory of mental models accounts for the meaning and reference of a word and how words are combined to yield the meaning and reference of a sentence.

Johnson-Laird defines word meanings as concepts having both intensions and extensions (Miller and Johnson-Laird, 1976). The intension of a concept – what brings out its relationship with other concepts – has two components: a schema that characterizes the causal relations underlying the concept, and a taxonomy in which each schema is located. The extension of a concept – the set of things that are instances of the concept – is determined by the second component: the particular taxonomy in which the schema occurs. Thus, whether or not something is judged to be a cat depends on its similarity to typical cats as well as its similarity to other mammals, such as typical dogs, typical tigers, and so on.

How do the truth conditions of words in the lexicon combine to yield a mental model of a sentence? Johnson-Laird's theory makes use of procedural semantics; that is, the semantic or conceptual components of a word are used in the procedures that construct and manipulate mental models. Consider the example in (4.20) which is taken from Johnson-Laird (1977).

A boy pushed the bicycle.   (4.20)

When the indefinite determiner is identified during comprehension, its semantic function is executed. The semantics of the indefinite article indicate that something new is being introduced and so a new memory location is set up to accept the incoming new information in the noun. When the word *boy* is encountered, an entity representing a boy is stored in that location. The meaning of a word is an infinite set of individuals, but we do not represent the complete set, only a representative example (a referent) that satisfies the conditions of being a boy. Thus, as in Kamp's (1981) discourse representation theory, an indefinite determiner introduces an entity into the model.

Next the verb *pushed* is encountered. Its meaning is characterized by a schema consisting of a set of conditions that say what kind of action would make it true that somebody X pushed something Y. Miller and Johnson-Laird specify these conditions as follows:

Do $(x, e1)$
& cause $(e1, e2)$
& $e2 = $ move (y)

(This can be roughly translated as: somebody, x, does something, $e1$, and this event ($e1$) causes a second event, $e2$, which causes y to move.) When this meaning is retrieved from long-term memory, the representation of an action corresponding to these conditions is constructed in the model. The model now consists of an entity representing *boy*, and a representation of the action, *pushed*. Since boys typically can push things, the entity for *boy* is assigned to the x argument of the action.

In the second noun phrase the determiner is definite, which means that something familiar is being referred to. Thus, the definite article triggers an instruction to expect a known object, that is, to look in the mental model for an entity that was previously introduced that stands for a bicycle. However, the noun *bicycle* has not been encountered before and so there is no entity standing for it in the model. A new memory location is therefore created for the entity that represents a bicycle, through the use of bridging inferences (Haviland and Clark, 1974). As before, the entity depicting a bicycle is a representative example of the set of entities referred to by bicycle. Since bicycles can move, the entity can be assigned to the y argument of the verb meaning. The result is a mental model that represents the situation described by the sentence. Of course, we may only grasp the meaning of the sentence and so we may end up with a superficial propositional representation of the kind proposed by Fodor et al. But in order to grasp the significance of sentences we need to go beyond their meanings to their referents and construct mental models.

SUMMARY

Semantics requires a specification of the meaning of a sentence, its truth value and its reference. Model theoretic semantics describes these components of semantics through the use of a model. The meaning of an expression is thus defined as all the situations in the model that made the expression true. An expression is true if there is at least one situation in the model that makes it true, and false otherwise. Traditionally, model-theoretic semantics have not specified the reference of an expression, that is, the unique entity in the model referred to by a sentence, unless there is only a single entity that makes the expression true. However, more recent semantic theories have proposed ways in which the referent of an expression might be computed, either through the use of contextual constraints, as advocated by Barwise and Perry (1983) or through the use of entities in a discourse model as advocated by Kamp (1981) and Heim (1983).

Psychological accounts of comprehension cannot maintain the simplicity of formal semantic theories, since people judge the truth of a sentence by reference to the world, not by reference to a model. Nevertheless, psychological theories that propose that people construct mental models, or situation models, can account for the way that people grasp the meaning and reference of a sentence as well as its truth value (e.g. Johnson-Laird, 1983). Johnson-Laird suggests that people initially compute a propositional representation of a sentence, and then use inferences based on general knowledge in conjunction with the propositional representation to construct a mental model of the situation described by the sentence. The mental model serves as the referent of the sentence, while the recursive procedures that enable people to revise mental models, together with the propositional representation, show how people are able to compute the range of situations that make a sentence true; that is, they show how people grasp the meaning of a sentence. Finally, the presence of individuals in the world, or in an independent mental model of the world, who are identical to those in a mental model, guarantees the truth of an assertion.

The theory of mental models differs from other theories of comprehension by taking reference as a crucial ingredient of semantics that needs to be explained. The procedures that are proposed to explain reference include recursive procedures that enable meaning or sense to be explained as well. Other theories (e.g. Fodor, Fodor and Garrett, 1975) take meaning as the crucial ingredient and leave reference unexplained. The results of studies by Bransford and his colleagues (e.g. Bransford and Johnson, 1972; Bransford and Franks, 1971) and by Haviland and Clark (1974) indicate that an understanding of reference is crucial for comprehension, thus supporting the theory of mental models. Johnson-Laird also makes use of a procedural semantics, whereby the meaning components of words are used as procedures to construct a mental model. In this way he explains how the meanings of words are combined to construct a mental model of the meaning of the sentence. In such a manner are sentences comprehended.

CHAPTER 5 The comprehension of texts

This chapter considers the comprehension of continuous prose. It concerns the way that information from different sentences is integrated into a single representation. Like the discussion in Chapter 4, the discussion deals with semantics rather than pragmatics. That is, it deals with the truth-conditional aspects of meaning.

The chapter begins with an overview of theories of text comprehension that propose that different types of representation are constructed during comprehension. The evidence for propositions and mental models is then reviewed, and this is followed by a discussion of inferences. People do not make all possible inferences during comprehension. Consequently, constraints on inferencing are also discussed and pronoun comprehension is used as a case study to show how different kinds of knowledge constrain the number of inferences that are made. Lastly, two different views of the way in which knowledge is organized in long-term memory are discussed. These are Schank's (Schank and Abelson, 1977; Schank, 1982) notion of scripts and, more recently, memory organization packets, and Kintsch's (1988) notion of an unstructured connectionist network. Both views attempt to explain how the organization of knowledge constrains inferences to allow the rapid retrieval of relevant general knowledge during comprehension.

THE MENTAL REPRESENTATION OF INFORMATION IN TEXTS

People have proposed that two distinct types of representation are constructed during reading and these have often been portrayed as competing theories. One view suggests that texts are represented as propositions that, together with some minimal inferences, form what has been called the text-based representation (e.g. Kintsch and van Dijk, 1978; McKoon and Ratcliff, 1980). An alternative view proposes that comprehension relies on representational elements that reflect aspects of the real-world situations that are described by the text (e.g. Bransford, Barclay and Franks, 1972; Schank and Abelson, 1977; Sanford and Garrod, 1981). More recently, however, theorists have suggested a combined approach to representational issues, such that both kinds of representation contribute to comprehension (e.g. Glenberg, Meyer and Lindem, 1987; van Dijk and Kintsch, 1983; Johnson-Laird, 1983; Speelman and Kirsner, 1990).

Johnson-Laird (1983) argues that text comprehension involves both a linguistic (propositional) representation and a mental model. A propositional representation is very similar to the wording of the text, except that the units are concepts rather than words and that the syntactic relations are specified. A mental model represents the state of affairs described by the text. It is structurally similar to part of the world rather than to any linguistic structure. Information that is not explicitly mentioned in a text can be included in a mental model, by means of inferences from general knowledge acting in conjunction with the propositional representation.

Van Dijk and Kintsch (1983) have made similar suggestions. They propose three levels of representation: a surface, or syntactic level, a propositional text base, and a situation model. At the surface level, the text is represented by the exact words and phrases used. At the text-based level, the semantic content of the text is represented, not the original wording. This level is comparable to Johnson-Laird's propositional representation. At the situational level, the situation described by the text is represented, detached from the text structure proper and embedded in pre-established fields of knowledge. This level is comparable to Johnson-Laird's mental model.

These representations form the episodic memory for the text. They can be thought of as being held in a distinct episodic store that therefore contains all the information stated in the text together with additional (inferred) schema-based information (see, for example, Bower, Black and Turner, 1979). Alternatively, only the new information may be held in a distinct episodic memory for the text, with the old and inferred information being simply tagged in long-term memory as part of the text (e.g. McKoon, Ratcliff and Seifert, 1989). The evidence presented in this chapter seems to favour the latter view. However, regardless of the precise relationship between episodic and long-term semantic memory, it is evident that these different representations are constructed during comprehension. In the next section, the evidence for them is reviewed.

Propositions are considered first, then mental models, then evidence for their co-existence is considered, as is evidence showing the conditions that favour one kind of representation over another.

EVIDENCE FOR PROPOSITIONS AND MENTAL MODELS

Propositions

Numerous experiments have investigated the 'psychological reality' of propositions. Studies of memory reveal that, in general, people recall complete propositions, not isolated elements (e.g. Kintsch, 1974), thus supporting the view that propositions are semantic units. This is the case even when the propositions are not very plausible units. For example, Goetz, Anderson and Schallert (1981) used sentences like:

The comedian supplied glassware to the convicts. (5.1)

The bedraggled intelligent model sang. (5.2)

Preformed associations or familiarity play little or no role with these sentences; nevertheless, people were just as likely to recall them as whole propositions as they were more plausible sentences. Thus, what is processed as a propositional unit gets recalled together, irrespective of plausibility and familiarity. Reading-time studies also support the idea that propositions are processing units. Thus, Kintsch and Keenan (1973) showed that the time taken to read a sentence depends on the number of propositions that the sentence expresses and not the number of words in the sentence.

Mental Models

Evidence for mental models has already been presented in Chapters 1 and 4 (Barclay, 1973; Bransford and Franks, 1971; Bransford and Johnson, 1972; Haviland and Clark, 1974; Ehrlich and Johnson-Laird, 1982). Morrow and his colleagues have also investigated mental models (e.g. Morrow, Greenspan and Bower, 1987; Morrow, Bower and Greenspan, 1989). In their studies, mental models were specifically contrasted with propositions.

Morrow, Bower and Greenspan (1989) argue that readers build a situation model organized around protagonists, and that the spatial location of a protagonist is an important determinant of accessibility. In one experiment, they asked subjects to memorize a diagram of a building depicting the layout of rooms and describing the objects within the rooms. Subjects then read narratives that described someone moving through the building from one room to another. At specific points in the narratives, subjects were presented with probe words that were the names of two objects and they had to say as quickly as possible whether the objects were in the same room or different rooms. The results showed that subjects responded quickly to the two probe words for objects in the same room when the room was close to the protagonist. For example, when probed after the sentence *Wilbur walked from the storage area into the wash room,* subjects were faster to respond to the probe words when the two objects came from the room that the protagonist had moved to (the wash room in the example above) than when they came from the room that he or she had left (the storage area in the example above). There was also a tendency for the response times to increase as the distance between the objects and the protagonist increased, thus supporting the view that the accessibility of information depends on the location of the protagonist in the model, not on the accessibility of propositions.

Subsequent experiments extended these results and showed that the room toward which the protagonist was moving was also highly accessible, that the same findings emerged when the location of the protagonist was not explicitly mentioned and had to be inferred, and that a location that the protagonist was thinking about was more accessible than his or her actual location. Thus, the accessibility of objects depended on their relevance to the actions of the protagonist in the situation and not on their presence in a propositional representation. Overall, therefore, these studies provide clear support for the view that people construct mental models of the text during comprehension.

Propositions and Mental Models

Evidence is accumulating to support the view that both types of representation are constructed when people read texts (e.g. Glenberg, Meyer and Lindem, 1978; Schmalhofer and Glavanov, 1986). In addition, there are studies that show that people remember texts as either propositions or mental models depending on features such as the task (e.g. Garnham, 1981, 1987), the text (e.g. Mani and Johnson-Laird, 1982), and the reader's level of expertise (e.g. Kintsch, Welsh, Schmalhofer and Zimny, 1990).

Schmalhofer and Glavanov (1986) tested van Dijk and Kintsch's (1983) proposal that people construct three types of representation: syntactic, propositional and situational. They asked subjects to read brief computer-programming manuals and then attempt to recognize original and related statements. Subjects were presented with four kinds of recognition sentence: (1) the original sentence, (2) a paraphrase of the original, which substituted a synonym for one of the words in the original, (3) an inference statement which described something inferred by the original but not explicitly stated, and (4) a contextually related sentence, which was not inferrable but which followed from the general context.

The original sentence is compatible with all three types of representation – syntactic, propositional and situational. The paraphrase is consistent with the propositional and situational representations but not with the syntactic, which represents the actual words that were used. The inference statement is compatible only with a situational representation, not with a syntactic or propositional one. The contextually related sentence is not compatible with any of the representations. Schmalhofer and Glavanov argued that if people do construct these representations, then recognition should depend on the type of recognition sentence. Recognition should be best for original statements, next best for paraphrases, next best for inference statements and worst for contextually related. The results bore out these expectations, thus supporting the idea that people construct all three kinds of representation. Furthermore, it seems that these representations have different decay rates. Syntactic representations decay the most rapidly and situational representations are the most resistant to forgetting (Kintsch, Welsh, Schmalhofer and Zimmy, 1990).

Van Dijk and Kintsch (1983) suggest that comprehension is strategic. That is, people use heuristic strategies in the construction of representations. We saw in Chapter 3 how strategies might be used to construct syntactic representations (e.g. Frazier, 1987). Van Dijk and Kintsch propose that strategies are also used to construct propositions (e.g. if the subject noun phrase describes a person, assume that the person is an agent in the proposition) and situation models (e.g. assume that the first noun phrase is the topic of the text; assume that subject pronouns refer to the topic). If performance is strategic, then we should find that people will favour one kind of representation over another if one is easier to construct than another. Johnson-Laird also stresses the voluntary nature of mental models suggesting that they may not always be constructed. The evidence favours these proposals. Whether or not a situational (or mental) model will be constructed depends on the text, the task, and the knowledge of the reader.

Mani and Johnson-Laird (1982) showed that the nature of the text determines whether or not a mental model will be constructed. They found that a determinate spatial description was remembered as gist, while a non-determinate spatial description was remembered verbatim. These findings suggest that wherever possible, people will construct a mental model of a description and forget the wording. At recall, subjects describe the mental model, and this results in gist recall. However, if there is no single model that fits the description, then a mental model is much less likely to be constructed and a propositional representation must be used instead, which results in the words themselves being recalled.

Garnham (1987) showed that the goals of comprehension may determine whether or not a mental model is constructed (see also Johnson-Laird and Stevenson, 1970). Garnham exploited the fact that the representation of the text by means of propositions and the representation of the situation by means of mental models do not always coincide. He pointed out that two statements such as:

The man standing by the window shouted to the host.   (5.3)

The man with the martini shouted to the host.   (5.4)

have different meanings, hence they are represented by different propositions. However, in the appropriate context they may have the same significance, that is, they may refer to the same individual, and hence they may be represented by a single individual in a mental model.

Garnham presented subjects with short texts that contained two sentences about a man standing by the window. One group of subjects was given instructions that encouraged comprehension. They were asked to check that the passage sounded natural. A second group of subjects was given memory instructions. They were told that they would have a memory test after the passage had been presented. The passage included two critical sentences. One, shown in (5.5), was the third sentence in the passage:

By the window was a man with a martini.   (5.5)

The other, shown in (5.6), was the sixth sentence:

The man standing by the window shouted to the host.   (5.6)

On a subsequent recognition test, Garnham found that subjects who were given comprehension instructions tended to say (wrongly) that the following sentence had occurred in the passage:

The man with the martini shouted to the host.   (5.7)

However, subjects who knew that their memories would be tested, correctly recognized the original sentence. These results suggest that when people are trying to understand a passage, they construct a model of it, but when they are trying to remember the passage, they are more likely to construct propositions.

The importance of knowledge for the construction of a mental model has been reported by Kintsch, Welsch, Schmalhofer and Zimmy, 1990. They report an experiment in which novices and experts were asked to read short passages from a highly technical text introducing the programming language LISP. The novices had no programming experience while the experts were proficient in PASCAL (but had no experience of LISP). The experts, therefore, should have a schema for programming concepts that they could use to understand the text. The novices, on the other hand, have no such schema available, although they could understand the words and phrases of the text.

After reading the texts, subjects verified whether or not a test sentence was true. Test sentences contained either old (verbatim) information, paraphrased information, inferred information, or incorrect information. The major difference in the results for the two groups lay in their performance with the inferred test sentences. Six seconds or more after reading the test sentence, experts were more likely to accept the inference statements as true than were the novices. These results suggest that the experts, but not the novices, have constructed a mental model of the text.

Overall, therefore, the evidence supports the view that distinct types of representation are required for text comprehension. These representations have different decay rates and different situations favour their construction. If a text is compatible with more than one mental model, if subjects are deliberately trying to memorize the text, or if the subjects have little or no specific knowledge of the concepts being described, then people will tend to rely on a propositional representation and not construct a mental model. However, if the text is compatible with a single mental model, if subjects are trying to comprehend rather than memorize the text, or if the subjects have specific knowledge of the relevant concepts so that inferences can be made, then people will construct a mental model. The ability to make inferences is obviously crucial for the construction of mental models. The next section, therefore, presents a discussion of different types of inferences and of their possible role in comprehension.

THE USE OF INFERENCES

Inferences flesh out a text with additional information retrieved from long-term memory so that what is stored is the information in the input plus information that was not stated but inferred. However, one of the biggest problems in research into text comprehension is to determine what (and when) inferences are made. In the 1960s, the end-product of comprehension was commonly thought to be a linguistic, propositional representation that, by definition, does not include non-linguistic information. Thus, the possibility that inferences were a part of comprehension seemed most unlikely. Many people, therefore, argued that inferences were not part of comprehension proper but part of a separate optional inference process (e.g. Fodor, Fodor and Garrett, 1975; Kintsch, 1974; Kintsch and van Dijk, 1978).

However, beginning with the work of Bransford and his colleagues in the early 1970s (e.g. Barclay, 1973; Bransford and Franks, 1971; Bransford and Johnson, 1972), it became increasingly clear that full comprehension went beyond a linguistic representation to a conceptual representation in which the original linguistic information was no longer available. These ideas were crystallized in the work of Johnson-Laird (1983) on mental models, which specified what the conceptual representation might be like – a mental model of the situation described by the sentence. With this distinction between a propositional representation of linguistic meaning and a mental model of the situation, it became possible to see how inferences might contribute to comprehension: they are used to construct a mental model from a propositional representation (van Dijk and Kintsch, 1983; Johnson-Laird, 1983).

People normally distinguish between bridging inferences and elaborative inferences. If the inference is drawn in order to establish coherence between the present piece of text and the preceding text, then it is a bridging inference (Haviland and Clark, 1974). If an inference is not needed for coherence, but is simply drawn to embellish the textual information, then it is an elaborative inference. Take the following example:

> John drove to London. (5.8.a)
>
> The car broke down at Bedford. (5.8.b)

In (5.8.b) there is no antecedent for the definite noun phrase *the car*. In order to construct a mental model of the situation, therefore, it is necessary to infer that it was a car that John drove. This is a bridging inference (Haviland and Clark, 1974). It bridges two sentences so that a single integrated mental model can be constructed. A bridging inference is made only when it is required to make the text cohere, as in the above example, where the presence of a definite noun phrase implies that the car in question is already known to the reader. However, the same inference could have been constructed when the first sentence (5.8.a) was read. Then the inference would have been an elaborative one. It would add sensible information to the textual information but it is not essential to the coherence of the text.

When are Inferences Made?

The extent to which inferences are made varies quite considerably, from the knowledge-rich inferences of experts to the failure to infer by novices (Schmalhofer et al., 1990). This means that inferences are not necessarily made during comprehension. Indeed, there are indefinitely many inferences that could be made from a text. If all of them were made, comprehension would be prohibitively slow. It is necessary to discover, therefore, which of these many inferences are drawn.

Bridging inferences

Bridging inferences appear to be necessary for comprehension. They integrate the information from different sentences into a single representation. A number of experiments have indicated that such inferences are made while the sentence is being read. For example, Haviland and Clark (1974) showed that where sentences required a bridging inference they had longer reading times than sentences that did not and they suggested that the increased reading time was used to make the bridging inference. More recently, however, there has been some doubt about results such as these on methodological grounds (Keenan, Potts, Golding and Jennings, 1990; McKoon and Ratcliff, 1990). The slow reading times, for example, may reflect reduced comprehensibility rather than the construction of bridging inferences (McKoon and Ratcliff, 1980). However, the results of a study by Singer (1980) suggest that bridging inferences but not elaborative inferences are made during comprehension.

Singer (1980) presented subjects with sentence pairs: a context sentence and a target sentence. Subjects were asked to say whether the target sentence was true or false given the context sentence. The context sentence contained either an explicit antecedent, an antecedent that could be inferred by means of a bridging inference, or an antecedent that could be inferred only by means of an elaborative inference. The time taken to verify the target sentence, which referred to the antecedent, was measured. An example of the sentences is given below:

Context sentences:

(a) The pitcher threw the ball to first base.
    The runner was half way to the second. (explicit
        antecedent)

(b) The pitcher threw to first base.
    The ball sailed into the field. (bridging inference required)

(c) The pitcher threw to first base.
    The runner was half way to the second. (elaborative
        inference possible)

Target:

The pitcher threw a ball.

Context (a) explicitly states that the pitcher threw a ball, hence the target can be verified directly. In context (b), a bridging inference, that the pitcher threw a ball, is needed to link the word *ball* in the second sentence with the information in the first sentence. In context (c), the first sentence permits the elaborative inference that the pitcher threw a ball, but the inference is not necessary for comprehension of either the first or the second sentence. If the inferences are made in (b) and (c), then the time taken to verify the target should be as fast as in context (a). But if the inferences are not made, then the time to verify the target should be slow. The results showed that verification times for the target were fast in the (a) and the (b) contexts, but slow in the (c) context, and therefore suggest that the bridging inference had been made in context (b) but that the elaborative inference had not been made in context (c). In general, therefore, it seems that bridging inferences are made during comprehension.

Elaborative inferences

The results of Singer's (1980) experiment suggest that elaborative inferences are not made during comprehension. In fact, elaborative inferences pose the greatest problems for accounts of comprehension since they are not strictly needed at all. It is important to establish, therefore, whether they are made, and if so, what constrains their use.

Investigations of elaborative inferences pose problems, however. The task used to detect inferences and the time at which tests of inference are made both determine whether or not inferences will be detected (Keenan et al., 1990; McKoon and Ratcliff, 1990). For example, if a memory task is used and inferences are observed, as was the case with the original Bransford and Franks (1971) experiment, then it is impossible to tell whether the inferences were made during comprehension or retrieval. This problem applies to many of the studies of inference, and there are several good sources that discuss both theoretical and methodological issues (Garnham, 1985; Keenan et al., 1990; McKoon and Ratcliff, 1990).

A number of different kinds of elaborative inference have been studied experimentally. Three common examples are: instrument inferences (e.g. inferring *broom* from *sweep the floor* – Singer, 1979); instantiation of general terms (e.g. inferring *bottle* from *the container contained cola* – Anderson and Ortony, 1975); and likely consequences of events (e.g. inferring *dead* from *the actress fell from the 14th floor* – McKoon and Ratcliff, 1986). The results from experiments have been mixed, some finding support for elaborative inferences and others failing to find support. However, McKoon and Ratcliff (1986) suggest that elaborative inferences take time to develop. Hence they will only be detected in tasks in which there is a delay between the sentence licensing the inference and the test for the inference. They also suggest that elaborative inferences may be only minimally encoded into memory. For example, McKoon and Ratcliff (1986) presented subjects with short texts containing the following predicting sentence:

> The director and the cameraman were ready to shoot   (5.9)
> closeups when suddenly the actress fell from the 14th storey.

A control condition replaced the predicting sentence with the following control sentence:

> Suddenly the director fell upon the cameraman,   (5.10)
> demanding close-ups of the actress on the 14th storey.

Subsequently, subjects were presented with a test word (*dead*) and asked to decide as quickly as possible whether or not it had appeared in the text. The test word was preceded by either a neutral priming word (*ready*) or a priming word from the sentence (*actress*). If subjects had made the elaborative inference that the actress was dead then they should wrongly decide that the test word had appeared in the text, regardless of which priming word preceded it.

The results showed that when the test word was preceded by *actress* subjects said, incorrectly, that *dead* had occurred in the text. On the basis of this finding, McKoon and Ratcliff argued that the inference was made while reading the text: reactivation of the original proposition by *actress* seems to reactivate the inference as well. However, when the test word was preceded by a neutral word, *ready*, subjects said, correctly, that the critical word had not appeared in the text. On the basis of this result, McKoon and Ratcliff argued that the inference was only minimally encoded in memory while reading: it was not sufficiently encoded to reactivate the inference in the absence of the *actress* priming word. They speculate that the minimal encoding of the inference might be in terms of a few semantic features, such as *something bad happened*, or that it might be encoded as *dead*. The latter encoding is then suppressed by information that *dead* was not explicitly stated. Sanford (1990) also argues that inferences are often very sketchy and may not be fully fleshed out during comprehension. Indeed, in a discussion of instrument inferences, Garnham (1985) suggests that neither inferred nor explicitly stated instruments that are highly probable are explicitly encoded in a mental model. Instead, they are reconstructed from general knowledge when needed. Such a view could be regarded as similar to the idea that only new information is held in a distinct episodic memory for the text, while old and inferred information is simply tagged in long-term memory as having occurred in the text (McKoon, Ratcliff and Seifert, 1989). Overall, then, it seems that elaborative inferences can be made during comprehension, but only very slowly and without being fully represented (if at all) in a mental model. The next section examines how different sources of knowledge place constraints on the number of inferences that are made.

CONSTRAINTS ON INFERENCES

When presented with a sentence like:

The actress fell from the 14th floor.   (5.11)

why do we draw the inference that the actress died or that something bad happened, rather than that she was by an open window or a myriad of other irrelevancies? The number of possible inferences is exceedingly large and without firm guidance, a processing system could not function properly for very long. What is it then, that constrains the inferences that we make? The answer seems to be knowledge; knowledge about syntax, about semantics, about texts, about concepts, and about the world. In short, knowledge about anything constrains the construction of mental models, and so restricts the inferences that are made.

Constraints on the Interpretation of Pronouns

To illustrate how inferences can be constrained by different kinds of information, we will focus on the interpretation of pronouns. It is not possible to discuss the large volume of work that has been conducted on pronoun comprehension. However, this section is intended to show how knowledge about syntax, semantics and texts reduces the range of inferences that are needed, and how general knowledge acts as a context that filters out unnecessary inferences and not just as a store from which inferences are derived.

Pronouns provide an ideal test bed for the view that inferencing is constrained by different kinds of information. In particular, syntactic, semantic and textual constraints each may establish a link between an antecedent and a pronoun so that inferences need only be used to check that the hypothesized link is plausible.

Syntactic constraints

Consider the following sentence:

John said that Bill liked him.   (5.12)

In this sentence, syntactic knowledge tells us that the pronoun *him* cannot refer to Bill (Chomsky, 1981). If a speaker had intended the pronoun to refer to Bill, then a reflexive would probably have been used instead.

There is evidence to support the view that such syntactic constraints are used to limit the search for an antecedent. For example, Nicol (1988) presented subjects with sentences like the following:

The boxer told the skier that the doctor for the team   (5.13)
would blame himself for the recent injury.

The boxer told the skier that the doctor for the team   (5.14)
would blame him for the recent injury.

In the first sentence, the reflexive pronoun *himself* must refer to *the doctor*, while in the second sentence, the personal pronoun *him*, cannot refer to *the doctor*, but can refer to either *the boxer* or *the skier*. Sentences like these were presented auditorily, and subjects were asked to make a lexical decision to visually presented word or non-word targets. The visual target was presented immediately after the pronoun and in the critical cases was either an associate of a previously mentioned noun phrase or a control word matched in length and frequency. The results showed that with sentences like (5.13) subjects were faster at making a lexical decision about the associate of *doctor* than about the control word, but that there was no difference between lexical decision times for associates to *boxer* or *skier* and their respective control words. These results suggest that the syntactically permissible antecedent *doctor* is reactivated when the reflexive pronoun is encountered and that the syntactically impermissible noun phrases are not.

Conversely, with sentence (5.14) the opposite pattern of results was obtained. Decision times were fast for associates to *boxer* and *skier* but not for the associate to *doctor*. Once again, the results suggest that the syntactically permissible antecedents are activated while the syntactically impermissible antecedent is not. Thus, the results support the view that syntactic information constrains the search for a pronoun's antecedent. Furthermore, these constraints act very quickly since their results are apparent immediately after the pronoun has been encountered.

Semantic constraints

Consider the following sentence:

A man came in. He was very late. (5.15)

The pronoun *he* in this example, is normally taken to refer to the man. However, there is nothing in the syntax of the sentence that could contribute to this interpretation. Instead, semantic knowledge, through consideration of a discourse model (Kamp, 1981), assigns the pronoun *he* to the antecedent *a man*. Thus, on encountering the noun phrase *a man*, an entity that stands for a man is introduced into the discourse model. The subsequent pronoun acts as an instruction to look for an antecedent in the discourse model that agrees with the pronoun in number and gender. In the example, there is only one such entity in the model and so the pronoun can be assigned to that entity. Thus, the search is limited to the contents of the discourse model.

The evidence supports this view. Numerous studies have shown that people take longer to identify the antecedent of a pronoun when more than one entity is compatible with it than when only one entity is compatible. Thus assignment times are faster with sentences like (5.16) than with sentences like (5.17) (Erhlich, 1980):

Jane blamed Bill because he spilled the coffee. (5.16)

John blamed Bill because he spilled the coffee. (5.17)

Furthermore, it seems that these constraints, like syntactic constraints, apply very rapidly. Stevenson (1986) found that, shortly after a pronoun was encountered, both potential antecedents were activated when both were compatible with the pronoun in number and gender.

However, only one antecedent was activated when the other was incompatible with the pronoun.

Textual constraints

Numerous studies have shown that certain entities have a privileged status in a text and that pronouns are understood through accessing this privileged entity (e.g. van Dijk and Kintsch, 1983; Chafe, 1972; Gernsbacher and Hargreaves, 1989; Sanford and Garrod, 1981). This privileged entity has been variously called the focus (e.g. Garrod and Sanford, 1985), the hero (e.g. Clancy, 1980), the actor focus (Sidner, 1983) and the topic (e.g. Kieras, 1981). Here, the term 'topic' refers to the privileged entity.

A study that illustrates the importance of the topic is one by Anderson, Garrod and Sanford (1983). They asked subjects to read short texts like the following:

At the cinema   (5.18)

Jenny found the film rather boring.
The projectionist had to keep changing the reels.
It was supposed to be a silent class.

Ten minutes/Seven hours later the film was forgotten.

She/He had fallen asleep and was dreaming.

In the text, *Jenny* is the topic character, while *the projectionist* is the non-topic character and is tied to the *cinema* scenario. The fourth sentence either maintains the scenario by referring to a short time interval or changes the scenario by referring to a long time interval so that it is clear Jenny is no longer at the cinema. The last sentence uses a pronoun to refer to either the topic or the non-topic character. The results showed that regardless of the length of the time interval, reading times for the last sentence were uniformly fast when the pronoun referred to the topic character. However, when the pronoun referred to the non-topic character, reading times were faster after a short time interval but not after a long time interval. This suggests that the topic character is always accessible as an antecedent for a pronoun, but a non-topic character is only accessible when the relevant scenario is activated.

One way to explain the notion of topic and its role in pronoun comprehension is to say that pronouns can only refer to entities that are present in the current short-term memory store (van Dijk and Kintsch, 1983; Sanford and Garrod, 1981). Sanford and Garrod distinguish between aspects of text memory that are either in explicit or implicit focus. Explicit focus has a limited capacity, is based on entities explicitly mentioned in the text, and constitutes short-term episodic memory for the text. Implicit focus is based on information from the current scenario or script and constitutes the currently accessible part of long-term memory. The two components together capture the same information as a mental model, but explicitly mentioned entities are distinguished from inferred entities.

Sanford and Garrod (1981) suggest that the antecedent for a pronoun must be in explicit focus, while the antecedent for a definite noun phrase may be in either explicit or implicit focus. In other words, the topic of a passage is to be found in explicit focus. Consider the following (modified) examples from Sanford (1989):

> Erica unlocked the door with difficulty.   (5.19)
> It tended to stick.

The pronoun *it* is assigned to the antecedent *the door*, which is in explicit focus. By contrast, in the following sentence:

> Erica unlocked the door with difficulty.   (5.20)
> The key tended to stick.

The definite noun phrase, *the key*, is only in implicit focus, since it was not explicitly mentioned in the first sentence. It is brought into explicit focus through the use of bridging inferences. These inferences, however, could not be used to interpret the pronoun in (5.19) as referring to *the key*. Only definite noun phrases can have antecedents in implicit focus. It seems likely, therefore, that the topicalized entity in a text has privileged status because it is held in explicit focus. This idea is supported by a study by Garrod and Sanford (1985). They found that a definite noun phrase was interpreted rapidly regardless of whether the antecedent was the topic or the non-topic, but that pronouns were interpreted rapidly only if the antecedent was the topic. Overall, assignment to the topic can be seen as a way of constraining inferences, since the inferences need only be used to confirm the hypothesized link between a pronoun and an antecedent.

General knowledge

The context in which a pronoun occurs, what situation the sentence describes, seems to be used very rapidly to constrain the interpretation of a pronoun. Consider the following example, from Haugeland (1985):

> We bought the boys apples because they were so hungry.   (5.21)

> We bought the boys apples because they were so cheap.   (5.22)

These two sentences are identical until the last word, which radically affects the interpretation of each sentence. In the first case, general knowledge associates hunger with people and so we infer that the pronoun, *they*, refers to *the boys*. In the second case, general knowledge associates cheapness with products that are bought and so we infer that *they* refers to *apples*. The last word in each sentence, triggers a series of inferences based on general knowledge of probable events that enable the ambiguous pronoun to be interpreted almost instantaneously.

Another example comes from Sanford and Garrod (1981) and it also illustrates the speed with which knowledge about probable events is used in comprehension:

> John was on his way to school.   (5.23.a)

> He was terribly worried about the maths lesson.   (5.23.b)

> Last week, he had been unable to control the class.   (5.23.c)

> It was unfair of the teacher to leave him in charge.   (5.23.d)

> After all, it's not usually part of a janitor's duties.   (5.23.e)

In this passage, the (c) sentence deliberately violates the assumption made while reading the first sentence, that John was a schoolboy, and the (e) sentence violates the revised assumption that John was a teacher. The text illustrates the ease and speed with which different components of general knowledge can be retrieved: as the events change, so the inferred identity of John changes.

These examples suggest that contextually relevant inferences based on general knowledge are retrieved very rapidly in comprehension.

The way in which knowledge is organized in long-term memory has been used to explain this facility and to show how knowledge itself constrains inferencing by providing a context in with the sentences are understood. These ideas about knowledge organization are discussed in the next section.

THE ORGANIZATION OF KNOWLEDGE

One of the real puzzles of language comprehension is how we are able to retrieve rapidly and efficiently the relevant general knowledge from our vast store in long-term memory. One attempt to address this problem is script theory (e.g. Schank and Abelson, 1977). Scripts encode stereotypical situations in independent semantic networks. However, the use of scripts was soon found to be insufficient to account for the pervasive use of general knowledge, so Schank (1982) revised his view of scripts to include what he called memory organization packets (or MOPs). A more radical solution to the problem of how relevant general knowledge is retrieved so rapidly has more recently been proposed by Kintsch (1988), who argues that general knowledge is represented in an unstructured connectionist network.

Scripts

Scripts contain information about stereotypical roles and events in everyday activities, such as visiting a restaurant. Their virtue lies in their ability to store all the information about a particular activity together. So, for example, on encountering the word *restaurant* in a text, the complete script is activated as a unit. This allows inferences to be made about the presence of a waiter, reading the menu and so on, even though the information is not explicitly stated in the text.

Despite their usefulness, there are a number of inadequacies in scripts as a complete explanation of the role of inferences in language understanding. For one thing, inferences are nowhere near as widespread as script theory would predict. For another, there would have to be an enormous proliferation of scripts for all possible sequences of events: travelling by plane, going to work, watching the television, visiting the theatre, and so on. This suggests that there needs to be a level of abstraction beyond scripts that characterizes activities that are common to a number of scripts. Sitting in a waiting room, for example, is an activity that is common to scripts for *visiting the bank manager, going to the dentist, going to the doctor,* and so on.

Thus, people may have specific scripts for visiting doctors or dentists. But they may also have more general superordinate scripts that contain the events that are common to all visits to professionals. Such observations led Schank to suggest that people's knowledge is not stored in the form of preset sequences of actions. Instead our knowledge of likely script events can be brought together to create a script-like representation whenever that is required. Schank (1982) proposes that memory organization packets underlie this ability.

Memory Organization Packets (MOPs)

MOPs represent collections (or packets) of knowledge around a central theme. They 'abstract' away from the specific situations and represent knowledge that is derived from a number of situations that have things in common. In order to interpret a particular visit to a restaurant, the relevant MOPs are recalled in order to construct a superscript for that particular occasion. Thus, the only part of the old restaurant script that would still be stored as a sequence of routine actions are actions that are specific to restaurants, for example, summoning waitresses and reading menus. All the other events would be part of the more general memory representations about entering buildings, tipping, paying bills and eating.

The results of studies by McKoon, Ratcliff and Seifert (1989) support the use of MOPs. They presented subjects with a set of stories in which pairs of stories shared the same MOP. For example, there were two stories about *going to the beach.* At the end of the set of stories, the subjects were presented with a series of test phrases one at a time and they had to decide as quickly as possible whether each test phrase was OLD or NEW. The test phrases were either related to the MOPs or unrelated to them.

The results showed that MOP-related test phrases from the stories were recognized very rapidly if they were preceded by a MOP-related phrase from *either* story. However, if they were preceded by phrases that were unrelated to the MOP (but still in the story), recognition was facilitated only for the test phrase that was from the same story. McKoon et al. argue that these results support a view that says that on reading a story, MOP-related events are tagged in the generalized MOP representation. This representation is assumed to contain all the

MOP-related events used in the stories. Hence facilitation occurs with MOP-related phrases from either story. Information in a story that is not related to a MOP is encoded separately with pointers to the MOP-related information of the story. Hence a phrase facilitates recognition of the unrelated target only if it is from the same story.

The notion of MOPs gives some much needed flexibility and generalizability to Schank's original work on scripts. Nevertheless, there are still things that are hard to account for. There is still an enormous number of MOPs, for example – one for each kind of action that we are familiar with. A computer simulation of language comprehension that uses MOPs (Schank, Lebowitz and Birnbaum, 1978) illustrates the difficulties. The simulation is very good at selecting only the appropriate senses of words; for example, that *sprayed* refers to bullets in *The gunman sprayed the street,* but only because the simulation is limited to a single domain, that of terrorism. The program has a great deal of in-depth knowledge about this limited domain. People, however, have vast amounts of knowledge about a very wide range of everyday domains; and it is the explanation of our human ability to encode and retrieve massive amounts of everyday knowledge that remains so elusive.

A Connectionist Account of Knowledge Retrieval

Kintsch (1988) proposes a different solution to the difficulties that were addressed by MOPs. He presents a computer model that uses a connectionist representational system. In fact it is a hybrid connectionist model since the processing is distributed and parallel but the units are concepts and propositions. Another feature that makes it a hybrid model is that it uses production rules to construct propositional representations when interpreting a text. To explain Kintsch's model, we will first outline its main features and then show how it exploits a connectionist knowledge base to overcome the problems of how the rapid retrieval of relevant general knowledge occurs in comprehension.

The general features of Kintsch's model draw on his earlier views of text processing that were described by Kintsch and van Dijk (1978) and van Dijk and Kintsch (1983). Processing begins with the abstraction of a propositional representation from a parsed linguistic string. The parser itself is not part of the model so the input to the system is the syntactic information that enables propositions to be constructed. The output of the parser, therefore, is the input to the model of text processing and corresponds to a surface representation of the text. The propositional representation consists of propositions that represent the linguistic meaning of the text, propositions that are the results of bridging inferences made to make the text cohere, and propositions (called macropropositions) that represent the gist of the text. These propositions form the text base, and they all deal with representations of the text proper. In addition, however, text comprehension results in the construction of a situation model, which is not a representation of the text itself but of the situation described by the text. Kintsch's model, however, concentrates on the processes involved in constructing the propositional representation.

As the text is read and propositions are constructed, they are stored in a memory buffer of limited capacity. New propositions entering the buffer become connected, via bridging inferences, to those still residing in the buffer after the previous sample was taken. Comprehension takes place in cycles, and at each cycle propositions are constructed and enter the buffer. A number of propositions, such as those that represent the topic of the text, are held in the buffer until the next cycle. The result of this process is that the propositions of the discourse become linked in a coherent connected structure. A macrostructure is constructed from these propositions to represent the inferred topic.

One of the most important changes in Kintsch's recent model compared to his earlier ones is that general knowledge (called the knowledge base) is represented in a connectionist network in which related concepts and propositions have excitatory connections and contradictory or mutually exclusive concepts and propositions have inhibitory connections. For example, the concept representing the meaning of the word *bank*, in the sense of money, has excitatory connections to concepts concerning money and financial institutions and inhibitory connections to concepts concerning an alternative (river) meaning of *bank*. The model has two components, a construction component and an integration component.

Construction

The text base is constructed in four phases. First, the concepts referred to in the sentence are activated in the knowledge base and linked together to form a proposition according to the syntactic information.

Propositions are constructed one phrase at a time, and new phrases are added to the current proposition wherever possible. When this is not possible, as in garden path sentences (see Chapter 3) then more than one proposition is constructed for the same sentence. The resulting propositions are stored in the memory buffer. Second, elaborative inferences are made. Propositions that are close associates of the concepts in initial propositions are activated and these are also read into the buffer. This process is context-free. For example, associates of both meanings of the word *bank* would be activated if that word occurred in the sentence. Third, additional propositions are constructed as a result of bridging inferences and inferences about the topic of the text. Fourth, the interconnections between all these propositions are specified according to their strengths in the knowledge base, and their relations in the sentence.

Integration

After all the propositions have been constructed, the integration process takes place. Activation is spread around the system so that some propositions drop out of the buffer and only the highly activated ones remain (see, e.g. Waltz and Pollack, 1985). The highly activated propositions constitute the text representation formed on each processing cycle. It may include not only text propositions but also knowledge-based inferences and macropropositions. Construction and integration take place in short cycles, roughly corresponding to short sentences or phrases. Thus, integration may occur at any time in the construction phase to eliminate some of the constructed propositions. For example, integration may eliminate inappropriate associates generated at stage two before the inferences of stage three are made.

An illustration

Kintsch describes these processes by referring to the sentence, *Lucy persuaded Mary to bake a cake*. Stage one of the construction process leads to a single proposition:

PERSUADE (LUCY, MARY (BAKE (MARY, CAKE)))   (5.24)

Stage two activates propositions that are closely associated with the concepts in the proposition. For example, the propositions that are close associates of BAKE in the knowledge base include the following (in the knowledge base, propositions contain general terms, such as *agent* = *person;* during comprehension, individuals referred to in the sentence are substituted for these general terms):

LIKE (MARY, EAT (MARY, CAKE))   (5.25)

PUT (MARY, CAKE-IN-OVEN)

RESULT (BAKE (MARY, CAKE), HOT (CAKE))

PREPARE (MARY, DINNER)

Not all of these inferences will be relevant in the context of the complete text, but context is not taken into account at this stage.

After the undirected elaboration of stage two, more specific, bridging inferences yield additional propositions in stage three. For example, other propositions in the buffer will be examined to see if the representation for *Lucy* can be linked to the same person mentioned in the other propositions. The same will occur for *Mary*. Macropropositions are also inferred at this stage. Both directed and undirected associative inferences are used for this, since the strategies for selecting the topic take account of information from various sources. In a simple case like the sentence above, where no context is provided, the inference process has to fall back on some default strategies and, using the syntax as a guide, selects the main verb as the topic. Thus, propositions that are closely associated with PERSUADE in the knowledge base are activated. In stage four, the activation weights are specified. To take the example of the word *bank* again, the assigned activation weights will be the same as those in the knowledge base, where close associates of the *money* concept will have strong excitatory links as will the close associates of the *river* concept. But all the *money* associates will have strong inhibitory links with all the *river* associates. Going back to the *persuade* example, the closeness of the concepts in the propositions representing the original sentence will also contribute to the strength of the excitatory links.

In the integration process, elaborative inferences are likely to be eliminated in the simple *persuade* example above, since they are not connected to other propositions in the text base. However, in the presence of a preceding context, such as, *Lucy made tomato soup and sautéed some pork chops with herbs. She set the table and persuaded Mary to bake a cake,* the integration process has very different results. PREPARE (LUCY, DINNER) emerges as the dominant macroproposition because most of the other propositions in the text base contribute to its activation level. That the cake was hot, or that she put it into the oven, disappear from the representation with activation levels close to zero.

The model accounts well for the time course of the activation of words in a discourse context. Kintsch (1988) cites a study by Till, Mross and Kintsch (1988) in which subjects were asked to read sentences like *The townspeople were amazed to find that all the buildings had collapsed except the mint*. After the last word (*mint*) the subjects were presented with test words or non-words at different time intervals after the word *mint* had been read. The subjects had to decide as quickly as possible whether the letter string was a word or not. The time taken to complete these lexical decisions indicated the activation level of the concepts underlying the test words. The results showed that a context-appropriate associate of *mint* (e.g. *money*) was activated by 200 milliseconds after mint had been presented. *Mint* would have been only partially processed in this time. Context-inappropriate associates (e.g. *candy*) were also activated by 200 milliseconds. However, by 400 milliseconds, activation of the inappropriate associate had disappeared. Finally, an inference word concerning a possible topic (e.g. *earthquake*) was activated only some 1,000 milliseconds after the word *mint* had appeared.

Kintsch's model simulates these results. Stage two of the construction process initially activates both meanings of *mint*, together with their associates, so that both appropriate and inappropriate associates are immediately activated. The integration process produces high activation levels for propositions related to the building meaning of *mint* and so the inappropriate candy associate is no longer activated. Inference strategies also try to find out what the text is about. One such strategy is to look for causal explanations, which is the strategy that people seem to use when faced with the sentence above. Thus, the model also searches for causal explanations and eventually adds propositions to the text base to indicate that an earthquake caused the building to collapse. However, considerable time is needed for these elaborative inferences to be made, hence they are only activated some 1,000 milliseconds after the word *mint* has been seen.

Thus, the model explains the rapid access to general knowledge by means of a context-free process of activation of the nearest neighbours of the original proposition in the general knowledge net. This activates a lot of irrelevant material. However, Kintsch argues that the price to be paid for such promiscuity is low. The connectionist network rapidly removes inconsistencies and irrelevancies. What is gained is flexibility and context-sensitivity. This use of a hybrid model that combines symbolic representations with connectionist parallel processes in a network may prove to be a powerful combination for explaining people's facility for combining information from a number of different knowledge sources very rapidly.

SUMMARY

The comprehension of text results in the construction of different types of representation – surface, propositional and situational. A surface representation encodes verbatim information, a propositional representation encodes the meaning of the text and a situation (or mental) model encodes the situation described by the text. A body of evidence testifies to the existence of these representations and to the fact that the nature of the text, the goals of the reader, and the reader's knowledge all affect the ease with which a mental model may be constructed.

A mental model provides a single, integrated representation of the text and bridging inferences are frequently needed for this. Elaborative inferences, such as assuming that a specific instrument has been used or that certain consequences follow, may also be used to construct a mental model. The evidence suggests that these inferences, and highly probable stated information as well, are only weakly encoded, perhaps by being tagged in long-term memory as having occurred in the text rather than being copied into a separate episodic store.

The fact that people do not make all possible inferences during comprehension seems to be due to constraints imposed by different sorts of knowledge, syntactic, semantic, textual, conceptual and probabilistic. The interpretation of pronouns, for example, is constrained by all these kinds of knowledge. The first three limit the use of inferences by proposing interpretations that are then checked for plausibility. The latter two, which concern general knowledge, constrain inferences because of the way that knowledge is organized in long-term memory. Scripts constrain inferences to those that are relevant to the script, while a connectionist system constrains inferences through its interconnected network of excitatory and inhibitory links. These ensure that only relevant inferences receive sufficient activation to form part of the final interpretation of the text.

The distinction between propositions and mental models shows how inferences contribute to comprehension: they are used to construct a mental model from propositions. The distinction also allows specific proposals to be made concerning the contents of episodic memory for a text. The evidence seems to suggest that only new information is explicitly stored in episodic memory, while old and inferred information is tagged in long-term memory.

CHAPTER 6   Conversation and discourse

This chapter focuses on pragmatics. In doing so it concentrates on conversations rather than written texts since much of the work on pragmatics has focused on conversations. The chapter emphasizes communication: how do we come to understand the meaning that a speaker intends to convey?

As we saw in Chapter four, semantics means different things to different people. The same is true of pragmatics and of the distinction between semantics and pragmatics. To clarify the issues involved, consider a simple distinction, one that says that semantics concerns linguistic knowledge while pragmatics concerns non-linguistic world knowledge. Such a distinction might lead us to say that pragmatics is concerned with contextual influences on meaning, since the use of context requires inferences based on non-linguistic general knowledge. This view would be consistent with Montague's (1968) definition of formal pragmatics as the study of indexical expressions, that is, expressions that require context for their interpretation. However, it runs counter to current work on formal semantics, which holds that an account of context is part of a truth conditional semantic theory (e.g. Barwise and Perry, 1983).

Alternatively, the above distinction between linguistic and non-linguistic knowledge might lead us to equate linguistic knowledge with the subject matter of semantic theory and non-linguistic knowledge with the subject matter of a cognitive theory. On this view, semantics would be concerned with truth conditions while pragmatics would be concerned with the assumptions people make when speaking and the inferences listeners make to recover those assumptions. Such a view is similar to a proposal by Gazdar (1979), which has achieved a degree of support from both linguists and psychologists. Gazdar suggested that pragmatics is the study of meaning minus the study of truth conditions. That is, pragmatics is concerned with the non-truth conditional aspects of meaning, such as whether a speaker intends to make a request, ask a question or make an assertion, for example. This notion of pragmatics relies heavily on the ideas of Grice (1975) who held that a listener needs to discern the speaker's intentions in order to work out what is meant (or implicated) by an utterance.

Gazdar's view has been strongly contested by Wilson and Sperber (1981). They argue that pragmatic principles, such as those underlying speaker intentions, are needed to determine linguistic sense and reference and cannot be confined to non-truth conditional aspects of meaning. A similar argument arises in the psychological literature on metaphor, where Glucksberg and Keysar (1990) propose that literal category statements, such as *a dog is an animal*, are interpreted in accordance with Gricean (Grice, 1975) principles. These differing views indicate that the distinction between semantics and pragmatics is very hard to pin down. This is not surprising given the intimate relation between semantics and general knowledge, and given the different views of semantics that were outlined in Chapter 4.

One way to think about the relationship between semantics and pragmatics is to make a threefold distinction between sense, reference and pragmatics. The sense of a sentence, the proposition it expresses, can be thought of as the linguistic meaning or intension of a sentence. The reference of a sentence can be thought of as the link between language and the world, the particular situation that is described by the sentence, that is, its extension. Pragmatics can be thought of as the non-linguistic component: what the speaker and listener contribute to communication over and above the linguistic meaning. In this tripartite distinction, sense can be regarded as purely linguistic, dependent only on syntax and semantics, while pragmatics can be regarded as purely non-linguistic, dependent on general non-linguistic knowledge. By contrast, reference does not seem to fall neatly into either of these categories since it depends on both linguistic and non-linguistic knowledge for its resolution, a dependence that was highlighted in the discussion of mental models in Chapter 4, and in the section on pronouns in Chapter 5. That is, determination of the reference of a sentence requires knowledge of the set of situations that makes the sentence true. This yields the truth conditions of the sentence and can be regarded as linguistic knowledge. However, determination of reference also requires the ability to infer the specific situation that the speaker intends to refer to. This involves inferences based on non-linguistic knowledge and so is an aspect of pragmatics. Thus it can be argued that both linguistic knowledge and non-linguistic knowledge are required to establish reference, and therefore that the truth conditions of a sentence are determined by the outcome of pragmatic processes and not just by linguistic processes. This view is consistent with the views of Sperber and Wilson (1986) and of Glucksberg and Keysar (1990). The evidence to be discussed in this chapter supports such a view.

So far in this book, in Chapters 4 and 5, discussions of non-linguistic knowledge have been confined to discussions of knowledge of concepts and of the probability of events in the world. However, Grice (1975) emphasized aspects of general knowledge that were more social in their orientation, since they were concerned with the nature of social interactions and with the importance of the intentions of the participants in a conversation. These aspects of general knowledge form the traditional subject matter of pragmatics.

Grice tried to account for what people meant as opposed to what they said. For Grice (as for Gazdar), what people mean is governed by pragmatic principles while what they say conforms to truth conditional semantics. He outlined four conversational maxims that participants in a conversation adhere to and that enable the speaker to make *conversational implicatures*, that is to implicate something over and above the explicit proposition being expressed. Grice tried to explain how listeners discern these implicatures.

Grice's account was vague in many respects and left a number of unanswered questions that have since been addressed by others. Thus, Sperber and Wilson (e.g. 1986) replaced Grice's four conversational maxims by a single principle of relevance. They also extended Grice's notion of pragmatics to apply to truth conditional aspects of meaning, that is, to sense and reference, as well as to implicatures. Clark and his colleagues (e.g. Clark and Marshall, 1981) also focus on the way in which participants in a conversation can discern each others' intentions. He spells out the ways in which participants can infer (by induction) that certain assumptions, or beliefs, are held in common. These mutual beliefs are said to be crucial for successful communication. All these ideas are discussed in this chapter. They show how conversational principles, as well as the more cognitive aspects of general knowledge that have been discussed in previous chapters, constrain the range of inferences that are needed to yield a unique interpretation of an utterance.

Grice's work emphasized a distinction between literal and intended meanings (or direct and indirect speech acts). This distinction highlights the importance of non-literal figurative language such as the language of metaphor, simile and irony. Psychological studies of metaphor have also extended and developed the ideas of Grice to show how metaphors are understood. These studies, too, are discussed in this chapter.

LITERAL AND INTENDED MEANINGS

Austin (1962) distinguished between locutionary and illocutionary acts. The locutionary act is roughly equivalent to uttering a sentence with a certain sense and reference. It corresponds to the literal or linguistic meaning of the sentence. The illocutionary act is what is done when the sentence is uttered. That is, a sentence may fulfil the illocutionary act of promising or threatening or requesting and so on. Searle (1969) made a similar distinction but he also pointed out that on many occasions people use indirect rather than direct speech acts, that is, the intended meaning differs from the literal meaning of the sentence. For example, a direct request is made in (6.1):

Please open a window. (6.1)

But in an appropriate context, the same request can be made indirectly as in (6.2):

It's hot in here. (6.2)

In an indirect speech act the literal and intended meanings may diverge. The literal meaning of (6.2) concerns the temperature and lies in the domain of semantics, but the intended meaning of (6.2) is a request to open a window and lies in the domain of pragmatics. How do listeners figure out what meaning was intended by the speaker? The first attempt to answer this question is due to Grice (e.g. 1975).

The Co-operative Principle and Conversational Implicatures

Grice distinguished between what is said: the intended sense and reference of the utterance, and what is tacitly implicated. He argued that what is said, the literal meaning, is largely determined by linguistic rule, while what is implicated, the intended meaning, is largely determined by conversational maxims.

According to Grice, conversation works because the two (or more) parties mutually agree to co-operate in accordance with particular maxims. This mutual agreement enables the listener to work out the intentions of the speaker. Thus participants in a conversation adhere to a co-operative principle. Furthermore, each participant assumes that the other participant is adhering to it. Adherence to the principle means adherence to four conversational maxims. These are:

1. The maxim of quantity: say as much as is needed to be informative but no more than is needed.
2. The maxim of quality: only say what you know to be true.
3. The maxim of relation: make your contribution relevant to what has gone before.
4. The maxim of manner: be clear, brief and to the point.

Each participant agrees to conform to these maxims and, to the co-operative principle, assumes that the other participant is conforming to them. A conversational implicature is invited when one participant appears to flout a maxim deliberately, or when the participant does deliberately flout a maxim. (A maxim may also be violated if it conflicts with another, as when quality – being truthful – conflicts with quantity – being informative. But violations of this kind do not lead to implicatures.) On encountering an apparent violation, the listener does not assume that the speaker is abdicating from the co-operative principle. Instead, the listener tries to make sense of the seeming violation by assuming that the speaker intends to convey a meaning that is different from the literal one. Grice (1975) gives the following example:

A. Smith doesn't seem to have a girlfriend these days.   (6.3)
B. He's been paying a lot of visits to New York lately.

B's response appears to violate the maxim of relation: it seems irrelevant to A's concerns. However, according to Grice, the response implicates that Smith has, or may have, a girlfriend in New York. B must be taken to believe this implicature in order to preserve the assumption that he or she is observing the maxim of relation. In this example, a conversational implicature is a proposition that the hearer must take the speaker to believe in order to preserve the assumption that the co-operative principle and maxim of relation have been obeyed. Grice proposes that these are only apparent violations because the connection between A's remark and B's remark is very obvious.

Blatant or deliberate violations occur when the relevance of the remarks is less obvious. In such cases, the listener assumes that the co-operative principle is still being observed and so assumes that the speaker is trying to convey an implicature. Grice gives examples of a flouting of the maxim of quantity, such as *war is war*. Such patent tautologies are totally uninformative at the level of linguistic meaning and so infringe the maxim of quantity: say as much as is needed to be informative. They are, however, informative at the level of what is implicated, and so the listener recognizes the implicature. Conversational implicatures are not logical inferences; they are inductive rather than deductive. Thus, they cannot be explained by a semantic theory that is primarily concerned with entailment and truth conditions.

THE THEORY OF RELEVANCE

Sperber and Wilson (1986) have modified Grice's theory in two main ways. First, they argue that pragmatic principles are used to interpret literal as well as non-literal meanings, and so are not confined to the interpretation of non-literal meanings. They therefore dispute Grice's alignment of linguistic meaning (semantics) with truth conditions and the speaker's intended meaning (pragmatics) with implicatures. Second, they replace the co-operative principle and its four associated maxims with a single principle of relevance. Sperber and Wilson also adhere to Fodor's (1983) modularity assumption, that is, they assume a central cognitive system served by specialized input modules, such as those of vision and language.

Pragmatics and Truth Conditions

Sperber and Wilson point out that there are two aspects to literal or asserted meaning. One is the truth conditions of a sentence that specify the circumstances in which it would be true. That is, the truth conditions determine the set of situations of which the sentence could be a correct description. This yields a range of possible situations that could be described by the sentence. In Chapter 4 this aspect of semantics was identified with the sense of a sentence. However, knowing the set of situations that could be described by a sentence does not guarantee successful communication. For that, the second aspect of the asserted meaning is required. This is the determination of the particular situation that the speaker intended to refer to. In Chapter 4 this aspect of semantics was identified with the reference of the sentence. Sperber and Wilson argue that reference is grasped through the use of implicatures, that is, it is pragmatically, not just semantically, determined. Sperber and Wilson's initial point of departure from Grice, therefore, is in their adoption of the use of implicatures for determining aspects of the asserted meaning as well as the intended meaning. This allows them to consider all cases of intended meaning, whether asserted or implicated, and not just those situations where the intended meaning is different from the literal meaning.

Sperber and Wilson distinguish between the linguistic code and inferential processes. The linguistic code is the basic meaning of a sentence without any inferences. It often consists of incomplete propositions. The inferential processes (entailments, implicatures and presuppositions) use the linguistic meaning as evidence for deriving a set of implied propositions that are intended by the speaker. The real work of understanding an utterance is carried out by these inferential processes. The truth conditions of an assertion are assigned to the outcome of this inferential process and not to the linguistic meaning of the sentence.

Relevance

Sperber and Wilson's principle of relevance, which replaces Grice's co-operative principle, states that: *The speaker tries to express the proposition which is the most relevant one possible to the hearer.* According to Sperber and Wilson, the search for relevance is a fundamental cognitive activity. On hearing an utterance, therefore, inferences are made to yield a unique interpretation that is consistent with the requirements of relevance. The principle of relevance operates in conjunction with a principle of minimal effort that asserts that people make as little effort as possible that is consistent with maintaining relevance. If the utterance is not sufficiently relevant in the initial context, it is unlikely that its relevance will be increased by further extensions of the context. Thus, the search for context will cease and the communication will fail. Taken together, the principles of relevance and of minimal effort act as constraints on possible inferences. Only those that are consistent with relevance and so are easily accessible will be derived.

There are two types of inferences (or implicatures) in Sperber and Wilson's theory, contextual assumptions and contextual implications. Contextual assumptions are made by the speaker when making an utterance and by the listener when interpreting it. These contextual assumptions, together with the utterance itself, serve as premises to which rules of deduction then apply. The conclusion drawn from these premises is a contextual implication. Thus, contextual implications are deduced from the assertion itself and from the context, not from either in isolation. Consider the following example (from Carston, 1988):

A.Have you read Susan's book?   (6.4)
B.I don't read autobiographies.

implicated premise: Susan's book is an autobiography.
implicated conclusion: B hasn't read Susan's book.

What ensures that the listener makes the intended implicatures and not some others? Sperber and Wilson use the notion of mutual manifestness. A fact is manifest to a person if he or she is capable of representing it mentally. If two or more individuals have a mental representation of the same fact, then it is mutually manifest. According to Sperber and Wilson, both the principle of relevance and the principle of minimal processing are mutually manifest facts. Thus, implicated premises are identified because they lead to an interpretation consistent with the principle of relevance and because they are manifestly the most easily accessible premises to do so. The implications are selected because the speaker must have intended the listener to derive them, or some of them, given that the utterance was intended to be manifestly relevant to the hearer. Thus, implicated premises and implicated conclusions are both identifiable as parts of the first inferable interpretation consistent with the principle of relevance.

What are the sources from which the context can be derived? That is, what is the context that is assumed by the listener? According to

Sperber and Wilson, an initial context consists of the interpretation of the immediately preceding utterance in the conversation or text. The hearer first attempts an interpretation in this context by looking at what contextual implications or implicatures can be drawn from it. This situation would be the normal state of affairs when the utterance has no additional covert meaning. If this is insufficient to satisfy the principle of relevance, then the context can be expanded in three different ways. First, the hearer can add to the context what is remembered from earlier portions of the conversation, or previous conversations with the same speaker. Second, the hearer can retrieve general world knowledge that is activated by the concepts which underlie the utterance or the context. Finally, the hearer can add contextual information about whatever he or she is attending to at the time the conversation is taking place. In brief, the context is culled from previous discourse, general knowledge of the world, and the situation in which the discourse occurs.

The Modularity Assumption and the Nature of the Central Processor

Sperber and Wilson argue that the construction of the initial linguistic code is a function of the language module. By contrast, the inferential processes form the central cognitive system. However, Sperber and Wilson's account differs from Fodor's account of modularity because they assume that the central processor is deductive (hence it is responsible for contextual implications). Fodor, however, assumes that the central cognitive system is inductive. Of course, the contextual assumptions are inductive, but Sperber and Wilson have little to say about these. Instead they devote their attention to specifying the logical rules of the central processor that enable the contextual implications to be deduced.

A Critique of Relevance Theory

There have been a number of criticisms of Sperber and Wilson's theory. Many of them can be found in the commentary on Sperber and Wilson's (1987) article in the journal *Behavioural and Brain Sciences*. I will just mention two here. First, a number of their claims are either psychologically implausible or untested. The view that the cognitive system consists of deductive rules, for example, runs counter to much of the work on deduction that suggests that many seemingly logical inferences are in fact arrived at through inductive processes (see Stevenson, in press, and Chapter 7). The view that people conform to a principle of minimal effort begs the question of what counts as 'effort' in psychological terms and is not based on any clear psychological principles. Indeed, Garnham (1987) found evidence to suggest that highly probable elaborative instrument inferences, like highly probable explicit instruments, are not encoded at all beyond a surface level. Such evidence runs counter to the view that the most easily accessible inferences are the ones that will be derived.

Second, Sperber and Wilson claim that their principle of relevance together with the principle of minimal effort is sufficient to yield a unique interpretation of any utterance. This is a very strong claim and a number of people have taken issue with it. In particular, Clark and his colleagues have consistently argued that the concept of mutual belief is crucial for successful communication (e.g. Clark and Carlson, 1982; Clark, 1987; Gerrig, 1987).

MUTUAL BELIEF

Like Sperber and Wilson, Clark assumes that pragmatic inferences are used to determine a unique interpretation of the linguistic meaning of an utterance. Like Sperber and Wilson, therefore, he does not confine pragmatic inferences to the determination of conveyed rather than literal meaning. For example, Clark (1979) argues, on the basis of answers to a range of indirect requests, that both the literal and intended meanings of a message are available to the listener and that the one that is finally selected depends upon such things as the conventionality of the linguistic form of the request, the transparency of the request, the plausibility of the literal meaning, and the speaker's imputed goals and plans. In short, the linguistic information and the contextual information combine to constrain the interpretation.

Clark differs from Sperber and Wilson in the mechanism that is used to constrain the inferences. While Sperber and Wilson use relevance and minimal effort to constrain inferences, Clark uses mutual belief. Clark's overall programme began with his given-new strategy

(Haviland and Clark, 1974). All of the work described below can be regarded as successive attempts to spell out in more detail the processes that enable the intended bridging inferences to be made.

Mutual Belief

Grice defined speaker meaning as follows:

> 'S (the speaker) meant something by x' is (roughly) equivalent to 'S intended the utterance of x to produce some effect in an audience by means of the recognition of his [sic] intention'.

However, this definition will not work unless the speaker and the audience mutually know the effects particular utterances are intended to produce (Schiffer, 1972). A speaker who intends an utterance to be interpreted in a particular way must also expect the hearer to be able to supply a context that allows that interpretation to be recovered. A mismatch between the context envisaged by the speaker and the one actually used by the hearer may result in a misunderstanding. In other words, there needs to be a stronger constraint on possible inferences than knowledge of the intention of the speaker. Unfortunately, Schiffer's notion of mutual knowledge runs into severe difficulties on other grounds, namely that it requires an infinite number of steps, a requirement that runs counter to the finite nature of psychological processing. Sperber and Wilson use the notion of mutual manifestness to solve this problem. Mutual manifestness is a weaker notion than mutual knowledge since it does not involve knowledge of what the speaker believes and of what the speaker believes the listener believes and so on. However, Clark argues that this weaker notion is insufficient to guarantee successful communication and that the stronger notion of mutual knowledge or mutual belief is needed. Clark solves the problem of an infinity of conditions by proposing that people use a number of heuristics to infer by induction the existence of mutual belief. Clark goes on to show how mutual beliefs are negotiated by the participants in a conversation.

Clark and Marshall (1981) construct a series of scenarios to demonstrate the necessity for mutual belief. Consider the following example (modified from Clark and Marshall, 1981, p.13):

On Wednesday morning Ann and Bob read the early edition of the newspaper, and they discuss the fact that it says that *A Day at the Races* is showing that night at the Roxy. When the late edition arrives, Bob reads the movie section, notes that the film has been corrected to *Monkey Business*, and circles it with his red pen. Later Ann picks up the late edition, notes the correction, and recognizes Bob's circle round it. She also realizes that Bob has no way of knowing that she has seen the late edition. Later that day Ann sees Bob and asks, 'Have you ever seen the movie showing at the Roxy tonight?'

The question is, which film should Bob take Ann to be referring to? Although Bob and Ann both know that the film showing at the Roxy is *Monkey Business*, and Ann knows that Bob knows that it is, this degree of shared belief is not enough to guarantee successful communication. What is needed in addition is that Ann knows that Bob knows that Ann knows that the film is *Monkey Business*. Otherwise, there is no guarantee that Bob will realize that *the movie at the Roxy tonight* uniquely describes *Monkey Business*.

But even that degree of mutual belief is not enough. Imagine a slightly different version of the above scenario. One in which Ann, not Bob, sees the change of film in the paper and marks it with a blue pen. Later that day, without Bob noticing, she sees Bob pick up the paper and read the section that Ann has marked. Now Bob knows that Ann knows that the film is *Monkey Business*. And Ann knows that Bob knows this. But Bob does not know that Ann knows that Bob knows. So once again the reference will fail to refer uniquely to *Monkey Business*. What is at stake here is the need for Ann not only to know what the film is but to know that Bob knows what it is too, and to know that Bob knows that she knows what it is, and to know that Bob knows that she knows that he knows, and so on indefinitely. Similarly, Bob must not only know what film is showing, but must also know that Ann knows what it is, and that she knows that he knows that she knows what it is, and so on indefinitely. This is mutual knowledge (Schiffer, 1972) or common knowledge (Lewis, 1969).

The idea that people need to use knowledge of this infinitely regressive sort is very implausible. Psychologically it would result in a processing and capacity explosion that would render communication impossible. Clark and Marshall propose that mutual belief can be achieved without having to check that an infinite series of mutual belief statements are true. They suggest that people use a mutual belief induction schema together with evidence (or grounds) for mutual belief.

Mutual Belief Induction Schema

Clark and Marshall propose (after Lewis, 1969) that the existence of mutual belief can be inferred through the use of a mutual belief induction schema that enables participants in a conversation to use appropriate evidence or grounds (G) to infer mutual belief. This schema is as follows:

1. A and B have reason to believe that G holds.
2. G indicates to A and B that each has reason to believe that G holds.
3. G indicates to A and B that p (where p stands for the proposition that is mutually believed).

With this induction schema, all that is needed for mutual belief is to find grounds (G) that satisfy the three conditions above, apply the schema (together with certain assumptions about the other person, such as that the other person is rational), and infer the mutual belief. The infinite character of mutual belief is no longer a problem. However, what is required is a means of determining the evidence, or grounds, from which mutual belief can be inferred. According to Clark and Marshall, this evidence is evidence of triple co-presence, that is the co-presence of the speaker, the listener, and a target object. The task for the listener therefore is to determine when triple co-presence occurs. Clark and Marshall propose that co-presence heuristics enable co-presence to be determined and hence used to infer mutual knowledge.

Co-presence Heuristics

Co-presence is of three kinds: physical co-presence, linguistic co-presence and community membership.

Physical co-presence

Evidence of physical co-presence is the simultaneous presence of A, B and the object of mutual belief. For example, if two people are sitting at a table that has a candle on it, and each can see the other attending to the candle as well as to the other person, then all A and B have to do is to assume that the other is attending to both the candle and their partner, and, roughly, that the other is rational and so making similar assumptions. Then they can inductively infer mutual belief of the candle.

Linguistic co-presence

Evidence of linguistic co-presence is the simultaneous co-presence of A, B and the linguistic identification of the object of mutual belief. If A tells B, *I bought a candle today*, each is aware that A has identified a candle and each is aware that the other is attending to the speech act. A and B can both use this evidence to inductively infer mutual belief in the existence of the candle.

Community membership

At the most general level, once A and B have evidence that they mutually believe that they are adult humans, they can assume as mutual beliefs everything that adult humans are assumed to know or believe. This includes general beliefs about the world as well as specific knowledge associated with both being members of a particular culture (such as a Western culture), of a particular country (such as England), or a particular city (such as Durham), or a particular profession (such as psychology) and so on.

Each of these three kinds of evidence enables mutual beliefs to be readily available when a speaker assumes that the listener already knows something (such as the film showing at the Roxy). During conversation the participants make use of these mutual beliefs to ensure successful communication. The speaker presupposes some prior belief when he or she has reason to believe that it is a mutual belief and can readily be inferred. The listener interprets what is said on the understanding that the speaker will presuppose only what is mutually believed. For this to be possible, Clark and Marshall suggest that both the speaker and the listener have two distinct discourse models in memory. One is a model of the speaker and the other is a model of the listener. For example, Ann, as speaker, will have a model of the things that she wishes to talk about, and she will also have a model of what she believes Bob's state of knowledge of these things to be. Knowledge of the contents of both these models will guide her conversation. (See also Johnson-Laird and Garnham, 1980.) This then is how Clark constrains the range of inferences that are needed to identify a unique interpretation.

Establishing Mutual Beliefs

How are mutual beliefs established in new encounters, such as those involved in chatting to a stranger at a party? Clark and Wilkes-Gibbs (1986) suggest that they are the result of a collaborative process between the speaker and the hearer. According to Clark and Wilkes-Gibbs both participants in a conversation adhere to the principle of mutual responsibility. This states that:

> The participants in a conversation try to establish, roughly by the initiation of each new contribution, the mutual belief that the listeners have understood what the speaker meant in the last utterance to a criterion sufficient for current purposes.

This principle also embodies the view that the participants try to minimize their joint effort. They do not aim for perfect understanding of each utterance, only understanding that is sufficient for the purposes of the discourse.

Clark and Wilkes-Gibbs conducted an experiment to test their view that mutual beliefs are collaboratively established. They gave sets of 12 abstract shapes to a speaker and a hearer. The speaker had to get the listener to arrange his or her shapes in the same order as the speaker's. Thus the speaker had to find a way of referring to each shape that the listener would understand. The subjects repeated this task six times, each with a different order. The results showed that fewer words were used to describe each figure as the trials progressed, that the number of speaking turns decreased as the trials progressed, and that more words were used to describe figures early in the order than late. Taken as a whole, these results suggest that both the speaker and the listener contributed to the establishment of a satisfactory reference.

The quantitative results were supplemented by a qualitative analysis of the exchanges to investigate how collaboration occurred. This qualitative analysis suggested that participants engage in what Clark and Wilkes-Gibbs call the acceptance process, which consists of the speaker presenting a noun phrase to the listener who responds to it. This cycle is repeated until a noun phrase is accepted. The example below shows how the speaker presents a noun phrase on each of the six trials:

> Trial 1. All right, the next one looks like a person who's   (6.5)
> ice-skating, except they're sticking two arms out in front.
> Trial 2. Um, the next one's the person who's ice-skating that
> has two arms?
> Trial 3. The fourth one is the person ice-skating with two arms.
> Trial 4. The next one's the ice-skater.
> Trial 5. The fourth one's the ice-skater.
> Trial 6. The ice skater.

On the first trial, the speaker describes the figure using an indefinite reference (*a person who's ice-skating*), thus creating linguistic co-presence. After that, the speaker refers to the figure with a definite reference (e.g. *the person who's ice-skating*). The listener responds by accepting, rejecting, or postponing judgement on the noun phrase. Below is an example of a speaker's reference being rejected by the listener who offers an alternative reference. The speaker accepts this alternative and then the listener signals acceptance by saying *okay*.

> A. Okay, and the next one is the person that looks like   (6.6)
> they're carrying something and it's sticking out to the left.
> It looks like a hat that's upside down.
> B. The guy that's pointing to the left again?
> A. Yeah, pointing to the left, that's it! (laughs)
> B. Okay.

These examples illustrate how the participants mutually assume responsibility for establishing a successful reference. According to Clark, such collaborative negotiation suggests that the need to draw on large bodies of general knowledge may be unnecessary during the normal course of conversations, since much of the conversational groundwork goes into establishing a referential language that is unique to that conversation and that guarantees the correct choice of referent (see also Garrod and Anderson, 1987).

Critique of Mutual Belief and General Summary

Sperber and Wilson (1986) argue against Clark by saying that there can never be any certainty of mutual belief and so an individual may be wrong in assuming it. However, communication is frequently very uncertain and we can never really be sure that we have been understood or have successfully understood others. Thus the possibility that an individual may be wrong in assuming mutual knowledge seems consonant with the nature of conversations.

Like Sperber and Wilson, Clark denies the sharp distinction made by Grice between a literal linguistic meaning and a non-literal meaning. Also like Sperber and Wilson, he tries to spell out the processes that constrain inferencing. The fact that we can never be certain that we have adequately understood another person is captured by the inclusion of inductive inferences, inferences that are plausibly but not necessarily true.

Both relevance and mutual knowledge are presented as a sufficient solution to the problem of constraining inferences. However, given the indefinitely large number of inferences that it is possible to derive from an utterance, it may be more reasonable to assume that both notions have a role to play. One possibility, for example, is that mutual belief, rather than mutual manifestness, acts in conjunction with the principle of relevance to constrain inferences. In addition, it would seem sensible to modify some of the other claims of relevance theory to render them compatible with psychological observations. Thus, the central processor might be thought of as manipulating mental models (Johnson-Laird, 1983; Johnson-Laird and Byrne, 1991) rather than as a deductive system. And the notion of minimal effort needs to be reconciled with the evidence concerning the kinds of inferences that people make. Overall, though, both theories make serious efforts to specify the processes that enable relevant inferences to be made quickly and efficiently during comprehension.

A large part of the discussion so far has emphasized the role of pragmatic principles in the interpretation of linguistic meaning, particularly reference. It is time, therefore, to turn our attention to situations where the intended and the literal (linguistic) meanings diverge. Thus, the next section is devoted to a discussion of the comprehension of metaphors, which are characterized by such divergence.

THE COMPREHENSION OF METAPHOR

Psychological investigations of the comprehension of metaphor highlight two related issues. One mirrors the discussion so far, and concerns whether or not literal and figurative meaning are constructed by the same or by different processes; that is, whether or not truth conditional aspects of meaning are affected by pragmatic as well as linguistic processes. The other mirrors the literature on concepts and concerns the extent to which general knowledge is involved in metaphor comprehension. Understanding metaphors, such as, *My job is a jail*, seems rather like deciding whether or not an instance (*my job*) is a member of a conceptual category (*jails*). General knowledge, as opposed to similarity of features, figures heavily in work on concepts (see Chapter 8), so it is not surprising to find this same debate occurring in work on the comprehension of metaphors.

In this discussion of metaphors, the terminology introduced by the literary theorist I.A. Richards (1936) will be used. The main subject will be referred to as the topic of the metaphor, the secondary subject, which is used to characterize the topic, will be referred to as the vehicle of the metaphor, and the features that are central to the metaphor's interpretationwill be referred to as the ground of the metaphor. Thus, in *My job is a jail*, *my job* is the topic, *jail* is the vehicle, and unpleasant, confining, involuntary situations make up the ground.

Stages in the Comprehension of Figurative Language

The three-stage view

Early views of the comprehension of metaphor reflected the views of Grice (1975): that the literal meaning of an utterance is computed first, this is then checked against context and if it is found to be inappropriate, an alternative figurative meaning is constructed instead. Only if the literal meaning is discarded are pragmatic inferences brought into play. This has been characterized as the three-stage view of metaphorical comprehension (Clark and Lucy, 1975) and can be described as follows:

1. Derive a literal interpretation of an utterance.
2. Assess the interpretability of that utterance against the context of the utterance.
3. If that literal meaning cannot be interpreted, then and only then derive an alternative non-literal interpretation.

This sharp distinction between literal meaning, governed by linguistic principles, and figurative or intended meaning, governed by pragmatic principles, is evident in a number of views of metaphorical comprehension, such as Gentner's structure mapping model (e.g. Gentner and Clement, 1989), and Ortony's salience imbalance model (Ortony, 1979). For example, according to Ortony's salience imbalance model, the literal meaning of a metaphor is a category statement. In the example above, *my job* is a member of the category *jail*. This literal meaning is obviously false since a job is not literally a jail. The literal meaning, therefore, violates Grice's maxim of quality: do not say anything that you believe to be false. So it cannot be the intended meaning. Ortony proposes that the intended meaning is a comparison statement, that is, a simile. This is much weaker than a category statement, since it is something that can be true. Thus, the speaker really intends to say that *my job is* like *a jail*.

This fits into the three-stage view as follows:

1. Compute the literal meaning. This is a (false) category statement.
2. Assess the interpretability of the utterance against an assessment of the context: uttering a false statement violates Grice's maxim of quality. On the assumption that the speaker is still adhering to the co-operative principle, he or she must mean something else.
3. Since the literal meaning cannot be interpreted, derive an alternative non-literal meaning: the something else must be a comparison statement.

The single-stage view

An alternative to the three-stage view is held by Glucksberg (e.g. Glucksberg and Keysar, 1990) and also by Gibbs (e.g. 1984). Glucksberg argues that metaphors, like the one above, are intended as category statements and that is how they are comprehended. He suggests that both literal and metaphorical statements (e.g. *A bird is an animal*, a literally true category statement, and *My job is a jail*, a literally false category statement) are interpreted in the same way. They are understood as class inclusion statements in which the first element in the sentence is assigned to the class specified by the second element. Thus, the same processes are used to comprehend literal and metaphorical category statements. The evidence for these two views is presented below.

Models of the Comprehension of Metaphors

The salience imbalance model

Once the intended meaning of a metaphor has been computed at stage three, Ortony proposes that metaphors, like literal comparison statements, are understood by finding features that are shared by the topic and the vehicle. With literal statements of similarity, the two elements share features that are salient for both; with metaphors, on the other hand, salient features of the vehicle are not in fact salient for the topic. According to Ortony, these shared features that are salient for the vehicle but not for the topic are crucial for interpreting metaphors and they form the ground of the metaphor.

This view is compatible with the Gricean distinction between linguistic (literal) and conversational (intended) meaning. However, Glucksberg and Keysar (1990) point out that each of the stages has been disconfirmed at one time or another. First, Ortony, Schallert, Reynolds and Antos (1978) have shown that when metaphors are comprehended in context, they do not take longer to understand than comparable literal statements. This contradicts stage one of the three-stage view that claims that the literal meaning must be understood before the intended meaning can be derived. Similar results have been obtained with other types of non-literal speech such as idioms (e.g. *kick the bucket)* and indirect requests (e.g. *Can you tell me the time?*) (Gibbs, 1984).

Second, Glucksberg, Gildea and Bookin (1982) found that people cannot help interpreting the figurative meaning of a metaphor. When asked to decide whether class inclusion statements were literally true or false, subjects took longer to respond 'false' when the statement had a metaphorical interpretation (e.g. *Some desks are junkyards*) than when it had not (e.g. *Some desks are roads*). Thus, the view that metaphorical meanings are computed only if the outcome of stage two is negative is also disconfirmed: subjects seem unable to avoid the metaphorical interpretation.

Third, Gildea and Glucksberg (1983) showed that the comprehension of ambiguous metaphors is facilitated by context. For example, the metaphor *some marriages are iceboxes*, could mean that some marriages are seen as lacking in interpersonal warmth. Gildea and Glucksberg found that the metaphorical meaning was computed more rapidly when it was preceded by a context sentence, regardless of whether the context sentence specified the literal interpretation of temperature (e.g. *winters are cold*) or the metaphorical interpretation (e.g. *people are cold*). Gildea and Glucksberg argue, therefore, that the comprehension of metaphorical statements requires the same kind of contextual support as the comprehension of literal statements. This contradicts stage three of the three-stage view, which assumes that metaphorical meanings require both more and different contextual supports than do literal meanings. Thus, the evidence for the three-stage view is not compelling. Without clear evidence for the three-stages, there can obviously be no support for the more specific proposal of Ortony's that metaphorical comprehension depends crucially on shared features that are salient for the vehicle but not for the topic. (However, Tourangeau and Rips (1991) have shown that this salience imbalance does not typify the shared features in a metaphor.)

The attractive feature of the three-stage view is that it postulates a straightforward view of comprehension, one in which the component processes can be clearly specified since linguistic processes can be described independently of pragmatic processes. Rejecting the model means that this simplicity must be abandoned. It also means that the major task for people who advocate a single-stage view in opposition to the three-stage view is to specify the processes involved and to show how they account for the comprehension of both literal and non-literal meaning. This is what Glucksberg and Keysar (1990) have tried to do in their class-inclusion model.

The class-inclusion model

The basic argument is that pragmatic inferences are needed to interpret literal statements as well as metaphorical ones. So all the processes of comprehension, syntactic, semantic and pragmatic are common to the two types of meaning. Which particular interpretation is computed depends upon the particular set of inferences that are triggered for the utterance's comprehension.

One argument that Glucksberg and Keysar use to support the view that pragmatic inferences are needed to interpret literal category statements is that these statements often have alternative non-literal meanings. For example, the statement:

Dogs are animals   (6.7)

is literally true. However, if the listener assumes that the speaker is being informative, in line with Grice's maxim of quantity, then the interpretation will depend on what the listener knows (and what the listener assumes the speaker believes the listener knows and so on). If the listener does not know that dogs are animals, then the literal meaning is informative. But if the listener already knows this, then the statement might be interpreted instead as saying that dogs do not have human-like features and so should not be treated like people. In other words, the literal interpretation, and not just the non-literal interpretation, uses Grice's maxim of quantity. Pragmatic inferences are used for literal meanings, too.

According to Glucksberg and Keysar, therefore, the processes involved in interpreting both literal and non-literal category statements require the use of context. Context determines whether or not a statement is an identity statement and if not, whether it is a literal or a non-literal category statement. For example, in the metaphor *cigarettes are time bombs*, the vehicle refers to both a well-known category (actual bombs) and an unfamiliar category (the class of deadly and temporally unpredictable things, etc.). Contextual inferences are needed to decide which category is intended. The metaphor vehicle is treated as an unfamiliar category that must be constructed on the spot. That people can construct unfamiliar categories easily, and that such concepts are context dependent has been shown by Barsalou (1983) in his work on goal-directed concepts. Barselou's work suggests that most class-inclusion statements are context dependent, the precise meaning of the category term depending on the instance. Thus, in *cigarettes are time bombs*, the relevant category includes both general features, such as the unpredictability of a negative future event, and specific features, such as death by lung disease. In *people are time bombs*, the specific features include emotional explosions but not lung disease. The set of relevant features that characterize both the topic and the vehicle is determined during comprehension.

This view of metaphorical comprehension comes down firmly on the side of having the same set of processes determine both literal and figurative meanings. It therefore coincides with the view that pragmatic processes are not separable from the truth conditional aspects of meaning. In particular, they are not separable from those processes that fix a unique reference for a sentence. In order to decide whether or not a sentence is true it is necessary to construct a unique interpretation. And this depends on context.

The Role of Knowledge in the Comprehension of Figurative Meaning

Much conceptual behaviour requires the use of general knowledge (see Chapter 8). This is particularly the case with the formation of new concepts, such as *apartment dog* (e.g. Murphy, 1988, 1990). Indeed, such novel concepts might be seen as posing a comprehension problem that is similar to that posed by novel metaphors, such as *my accountant is a spreadsheet* (from Glucksberg and Keysar, 1990).

Theories of metaphorical comprehension are divided on whether they opt for a model that proposes that formal rules are used (such as might describe a judgement of similarity among features) or a model that proposes that general knowledge is used. Both the theories of metaphorical comprehension discussed so far subscribe to the view that a system of formal rules will suffice. Both Ortony and Glucksberg assume that the topic and the vehicle of the metaphor can be represented as sets of features. In Ortony's model, the features of the vehicle are compared to the features of the topic. In Glucksberg and Keysar's model the features that represent the metaphor are determined by the combination of the topic and the vehicle, and the similarity of the two sets of features depends on this combination. Thus, although the similarity metric is different in the two cases, the recourse to a ruled-based system that uses similarity of features is the same. This contrasts with the proposals of Lakoff and Johnson (1980) who argue that the comprehension of a metaphor is dependent on the use of large-scale conceptual structures. The contrast between the two classes of theory parallels the contrast between feature-based theories and knowledge-based theories that are used to explain the comprehension of concepts (e.g. the similarity-based theory of Smith and Osherson (1984) and Smith, Osherson, Rips and Keane (1988) versus the knowledge-based theory of Murphy (1988, 1990)).

Since the feature similarity theory is the simpler theory, we need to ask whether the evidence on metaphorical comprehension forces us to assume the involvement of general knowledge over and above the use of feature similarity. It seems that it does. In particular, a study by Tourangeau and Rips (1991) asked subjects (among other things) to list features that characterized either the topic or the vehicle of a metaphor and to say what the metaphor meant. They found that many of the features in the interpretation of the metaphor were emergent, that is, present in the interpretation but not in the lists of features of either the topic or the vehicle alone. In addition, when subjects were asked which of two interpretations best captured the meaning of a metaphor, they overwhelmingly selected the interpretation that contained emergent features. Thus, the features associated with the meaning of the metaphor cannot be a function of the similarity between the features shared by the topic and the vehicle, since many of the features associated with a good interpretation of a metaphor are not shared by either the topic or the vehicle. The interpretation, therefore, must have made use of additional background knowledge over and above the shared features. In line with such observations, Glucksberg (1991) has suggested that people may use conceptual knowledge of the domains specified by the topic and the vehicle to understand novel metaphors, such as those encountered in both scientific and literary contexts. However, he suggests that in everyday discourse use of such knowledge is rarely necessary, because, consistent with the co-operative principle, speakers do not (or try not to) use metaphors that listeners cannot readily interpret.

Summary

It seems, therefore, that when literal and non-literal meanings diverge, as in metaphors, it is still unnecessary to assume that different processes are used to interpret the two meanings. Literal category statements as well as metaphorical ones need pragmatic inferences for their interpretation. Such a view is consistent with the notion that general knowledge, and not just linguistic knowledge (in the form of features) is required to interpret category statements. It is possible that such general knowledge may be needed only to comprehend novel metaphors.

SUMMARY

There has been much debate over whether or not linguistic meaning is distinct from non-linguistic meaning. It seems that, as far as psychology is concerned, the distinction is hard to maintain. Pragmatic inferences are needed to interpret the sense and reference of an utterance as well as the utterance's implicatures. The way that such inferences are constrained has been studied extensively, and Grice's original ideas on the subject have been considerably modified. One modification replaces Grice's co-operative principle with a principle of relevance, although the psychological evidence for this proposal is lacking. Another spells out how mutual knowledge can be inferred, and it seems that people are quite skilled at establishing mutual belief.

Much of the work on relevance and mutual knowledge concentrates on cases where pragmatic inferences are needed to interpret linguistic meaning, particularly reference. The study of metaphor, however, focuses on utterances where the literal and non-literal meanings diverge. Here, too, it seems that a common set of principles, syntactic, semantic and pragmatic, are needed to interpret both of these meanings. Metaphors, therefore, seem to be interpreted in the same way as literal category statements, and general knowledge is required for their interpretation, at least when they are first encountered.

CHAPTER 7   Deductive reasoning

Deductive reasoning is concerned with logical reasoning, that is, with rationality: the ability to reason according to the rules of logic. There has long been a debate over whether or not people are logical, and this debate is reflected in theories of deduction, which can broadly be divided into those that assume rationality and those that do not.

Non-Logical theories assume that people are not rational and so use *ad hoc* heuristics and rules of thumb to make a best guess at a solution (e.g. Woodworth and Sells, 1935). Logical theories assume that people are rational and they fall into two main groups: general-purpose theories and domain-specific theories. General-purpose theories (or syntactic theories) propose that people possess a mental logic: a set of domain-free, general-purpose logical rules that are used in every situation (e.g. Braine, 1978). Domain-specific theories account for the fact that the content of a problem frequently affects how easily it is solved. Two major variants within this general group are semantic theories and rule-based theories; that is, the use of mental models (e.g. Johnson-Laird, 1983; Johnson-Laird and Byrne, 1991) and the use of domain-specific rules (e.g. Cheng and Holyoak, 1985; Cosmides, 1989) respectively. Those who favour mental models propose that people use inferences based on general knowledge to construct a mental model of the situation described by the premises. On this view, logical behaviour is due to the manipulation of mental models: the search for alternative models that are consistent with the situation. People are logical, therefore, but do not possess a 'mental logic'. Instead, logical inferences result when alternative models are successfully considered. Those who favour domain-specific rules argue that people can reason logically only if they are familiar with the domain and if the relevant domain-specific rules are triggered by the situation.

This chapter focuses on two of the logical theories: the general-purpose, or syntactic, view and the domain-specific, semantic (mental models) view. Some non-logical theories will be reviewed in the discussion of syllogistic inference. Discussion of domain-specific rules will be postponed until Chapter 11 on hypothesis testing. Before the theories are discussed, however, a review of some logical issues is necessary.

LOGICAL ISSUES

Deduction

One way to define a deductively correct argument is to say that its conclusion is true in any state of affairs in which its premises are true. Thus, the deduction in (7.1) is logically impeccable:

If John finishes his book,   (7.1)
John will go to the cinema.
John finishes his book.

Therefore, John will go to the cinema.

In a state of affairs in which John finishes his book and in which if he finishes his book he will go to the cinema, it will certainly be true that he will go to the cinema. The inference is deductively valid. The validity of an argument depends, therefore, on the relation between the truth of the premises and the truth of the conclusion. This means that a conclusion can be valid even though its premises or its conclusion happen to be false in the actual state of affairs. For example, in (7.2), both the second premise and the conclusion are false in the current state of affairs.

If the moon is made of green cheese,   (7.2)
the moon will soon be eaten.
The moon is made of green cheese.

Therefore, The moon will soon be eaten.

Nevertheless, in those states of affairs in which the moon is made of green cheese and in which if the moon is made of green cheese it will soon be eaten, it will be true that the moon will soon be eaten. As in (7.1), the inference is logically impeccable (although slightly bizarre to an inhabitant of earth who does not read children's stories).

Proof and Validity: Syntax and Semantics

Validity is a semantic notion: it is based on the ideas of model-theoretic semantics that were discussed in Chapter 4. However, modern logic also specifies a proof-theoretic system that contrasts with a model-theoretic system. A proof-theoretic system defines formal derivations of proofs. It consists of rules for deriving just those inferences that are valid. These rules are formal and depend on the form of the premises, not their meanings. Proof, therefore, is a syntactic notion.

There are several ways of formalizing proof procedures for deductive arguments. One procedure starts with a set of rules that tell us when sentences of one form follow immediately from sentences of another form. To determine whether a particular argument (which consists of premises and a conclusion) is deductively correct, we apply one of these rules to the premises of the argument and see what sentence follows from them. If the conclusion of the argument is identical to this newly derived sentence, we have succeeded in proving the argument correct. If not, we continue by again applying a rule to both the original premises and the newly derived sentence. This procedure continues until a sequence of rules is found that will produce the conclusion and so indicate that the argument is correct. The entire set of sentences that we have derived is the proof of the argument, and the argument itself is said to be provable. Of course, if the argument is deductively incorrect, we will never succeed in deriving the conclusion.

One example of a rule in the system might be the following:

> From a sentence of the form if p then q and another   (7.3)
> of the form p, the sentence q follows.

Here p and q stand for arbitrary sentences. This rule is sufficient to show that the arguments in (7.1) and (7.2) are correct, since each conclusion can be derived in one application of (7.3) to the premises. The premise, *If John finishes his book, John will go to the cinema* in (7.1) exactly matches the *if p then q* form in the rule, with p equal to *John finishes his book* and q equal to *John will go to the cinema*. Similarly, the second premise is *John finishes his book*, which we have just set equal to p. *John will go to the cinema* therefore follows from (7.3). Since this is the conclusion of (7.1), the argument is provable. (7.3) corresponds to a logically valid argument known as *modus ponens* and it will be encountered again when propositional inferences are discussed.

The distinction between a syntactic system that proves that an argument is correct and a semantic system that defines valid inferences is reflected in the major classes of theories that have been proposed to account for people's ability to make deductive inferences. On the one hand, there are syntactic theories, which claim that people are able to make valid deductions because they have a formal (syntactic) logic in their heads (e.g. Inhelder and Piaget, 1958). These theories attempt to specify the rules of inference that people use (e.g. Braine, Reiser and Rumain, 1984; Rips, 1983). On the other hand, there are semantic theories which claim that people are able to make valid deductions because they construct a model of the situation described by the premises, try to derive a conclusion from that model, and then search for alternative models of the premises that refute the conclusion (e.g. Erickson, 1974, 1978; Guyote and Sternberg, 1981; Johnson-Laird, 1983; Johnson-Laird and Byrne, 1991).

Theoretical Issues

A theory of reasoning needs to show how reasoning occurs: what processes facilitate correct performance and what processes lead people into error. Syntactic theories propose that people use mental rules of logic to derive conclusions, a process that is error free. Errors arise in the processes of comprehension, not logic, so that premises other than those intended are constructed. But given the constructed premises, the reasoning is logical. Logical competence, therefore, is distinct from performance, which is contaminated by comprehension processes. Semantic theories propose that people construct a mental model of the situation described by the premises, from which a tentative conclusion can be derived. Alternative models of the premises are then constructed and if the initial conclusion is true in all of them, the conclusion is deductively valid. If the conclusion is not true in all of the models, then the conclusion is not valid. Semantic theories, therefore, do not distinguish between comprehension and inference: both are implicated in a theory of performance.

PSYCHOLOGICAL STUDIES OF REASONING

Traditionally, three types of logical problem have been studied and these are discussed in turn below. The discussion starts with studies of transitive inference because the traditional accounts of these problems can be regarded as precursors to the current syntactic and semantic views of reasoning. They provide, therefore, a good basis for introducing some of the key features of the current alternatives. This is followed by a description and evaluation of syntactic and semantic views in relation to propositional and syllogistic reasoning. In general, the results seem to favour the semantic, mental models, account, but it needs to be borne in mind, that different people may use different procedures (syntactic or semantic) and that people may change with practice from a semantic to a syntactic strategy.

Transitive Inferences

Transitive inferences are inferences that depend on relational terms, such as *taller than, bigger than, to the right of* and so on. The inference specifies the relation between the items that are not explicitly linked in a premise. Two examples of transitive inferences are shown below:

A is better than B	(7.4)	A is worse than B	(7.5)
A is worse than C		C is better than B	
C is best		C is best	

Problems like these (often called three-term series problems, or linear syllogisms) are very easy to solve. Hence research has concentrated on the time taken to evaluate or derive the conclusions. People invariably take longer to evaluate the conclusion in (7.4) than in (7.5). Thus, theoretical accounts of transitive inferences have concentrated on trying to explain the differences in difficulty of different kinds of problems.

Traditional accounts, the precursors to current views, emphasized the distinction between the use of a propositional representation and the use of a spatial representation to solve these problems.

Clark (1969) proposed a linguistic model of transitive inference that assumed that each premise was represented as a separate proposition and that no attempt was made to integrate the two propositions, and hence derive an inference, until a question was asked about the conclusion (e.g. *who is best?*). Clark accounted for the differences in difficulty of different problems in terms of the propositional (linguistic) complexity of the premises and whether or not the propositional form of the question was congruent with the propositional form of the premises.

For example, the propositional representations of the two premises in (7.4) can be described as follows:

B is least good   (7.6)
A is middle
C is least bad

The difficulty of the inference in (7.4) is because the conclusion C *is best* (or C *is most good*) is not congruent with the propositional form of the premise information about C, which is C *is least bad*.

By contrast, the propositional representations of the two premises in (7.5) can be described as follows:

A is most bad   (7.7)
B is middle
C is most good

The ease with which the inference in (7.5) can be derived is because the linguistic form of the conclusion C *is best* (or C *is most good*) is consistent with the propositional form of the premise information, C *is most good*.

De Soto, London and Handel (1965) and Huttenlocher (1968) proposed an alternative spatial model, which supposes that people construct an integrated spatial array of the information in the premises and read off the conclusion from this array. De Soto, London and Handel also proposed that an array is easier to construct from top to bottom (or left to right) than from bottom to top (or right to left). In addition, the construction of a spatial representation is facilitated if the first item is an end anchor. An end anchor is an item that occurs at one of the two ends of the spatial array. Thus, according to this theory, (7.4) is harder than (7.5) because in (7.4) the first item in each premise is the middle term whereas in (7.5) the first item in each premise is an end anchor.

A decision as to which of these two theories was the most plausible was never fully resolved, since they could both account for the range of experimental results. However, the theories highlight a distinction between propositional representations, on the one hand, and spatial representations, on the other. This distinction marks a distinction between a purely linguistic representation (propositions) and an integrated semantic representation that encodes the content, and not just the form, of the premises.

Current syntactic theories assume that people construct propositional representations of each of the premises, while current semantic theory assumes that people construct a single semantic representation of the two premises. Specifically, people construct mental models of the situation described by the premises. However, the current theories go further than the original linguistic and spatial theories described above by specifying the nature of the operations that enable deductions to be made. Syntactic theories assume that a set of rules, sensitive to the form of the premises, are applied to propositions to derive a new proposition that is a logical conclusion of the premises. Semantic theories assume that people construct alternative models of the premises to determine whether or not a potential conclusion is true in all the possible models. Byrne and Johnson-Laird (1990) have attempted to adjudicate between these two views and have concluded that the evidence favours the use of mental models rather than the application of rules to propositions. They therefore conclude that people construct an integrated representation of the content of the problem (a mental model) that includes a potential conclusion. Finding a conclusion, therefore, depends upon the ability to construct mental models.

There is, though, evidence to suggest that there are individual differences in the extent to which people rely on one of these two forms of representation (e.g. Shaver, Pierson and Lang, 1975). Furthermore, a study by Wood (1969) produced results to suggest that, with practice, subjects switch from using mental models to using rules applied to propositions. Results such as these suggest that people can use rules if they are highly practised. The same may therefore be true of performance with propositional or syllogistic reasoning.

Propositional Inference

Propositional reasoning involves reasoning about an assertion that states a relationship between two propositions. An example is shown in (7.8).

> If it's a Friday, then we go to the pub.   (7.8)
> (or: If p then q.)

The first proposition (*It's a Friday*) is called the antecedent. The second proposition (*we go to the pub*) is called the consequent. The relation between the propositions is conveyed by the words from the logical vocabulary, such as *if, then, and, or* and *but*. The assertion is followed by another assertion that describes a state of affairs indicating the truth value of either p or q (for example, *it's a Friday* indicates that p is true). A valid conclusion is one that is true in the same states of affairs in which the premises are true.

Evidence suggests that certain propositional inferences are more difficult to make than others, and some errors, known as fallacies, are very common (e.g. Rips and Marcus, 1977; Wason and Johnson-Laird, 1972). In general, the valid inference known as *modus tollens* is more difficult than the valid inference known as *modus ponens*; common fallacies are affirming the consequent and denying the antecedent.

Modus ponens was described in (7.3) above. *Modus tollens* is a rule that says:

> From a sentence of the form *If p then q* and another of the form *not q*, the sentence *not p* follows.

Thus, in the pub example, if you are now told *We do not go to the pub*, the conclusion *It is not a Friday* follows from *modus tollens*. Equivalently, a semantic account of validity would say that in a state of affairs in which it is true that we do not go to the pub and in which if it is Friday, we go to the pub, then it is also true that it is not a Friday. In general, people have much greater difficulty in making *modus tollens* inferences than in making *modus ponens* inferences.

However, if we are told the following:

> If it's a Friday then we go to the pub.   (7.9)
> It isn't Friday.

it does not follow that *We do not go to the pub*. There is no syntactic rule of inference that sanctions this conclusion, and it should be clear that the conclusion is not true in the same states of affair in which the premises are true. For example, the premises, but not the conclusion, include states of affair in which it is also true that we go to the pub on Wednesdays as well as Fridays. This inference is due to the fallacy of denying the antecedent. Similarly, if we are told the following:

> If it's a Friday then we go to the pub.   (7.10)
> We go to the pub.

it does not follow that *It is Friday*. Again, there is no syntactic rule of inference that sanctions this conclusion, and the conclusion is not true in the same states of affair in which the premises are true: our going to the pub on Wednesday, for example. This is the fallacy of affirming the consequent. The valid inferences and fallacies are listed in Table 7.1.

Table 7.1.   Valid inferences and common fallacies made in propositional inference

Valid inferences		
	modus ponens	*modus tollens*
	if *p* then *q*	if *p* then *q*
	p	not *q*
	q	not *p*
Fallacies		
	Affirming	*Denying*
	the consequent	*the antecedent*
	if *p* then *q*	if *p* then *q*
	q	not *p*
	p	not *q*

Theories of deduction try to account for the ease with which people can recognize *modus ponens*, their difficulty with *modus tollens*, and the frequency of the fallacies of denying the antecedent and affirming the consequent.

Syntactic theories

Syntactic theories conform to the view that people have a mental logic, or set of inference rules in the mind (e.g. Braine, 1978; Braine, Reiser and Rumain, 1984; Rips, 1983). Errors are said to be due to processes that are independent of logical reasoning. Specifically, contextual and pragmatic aspects of comprehension convert the original premises into different ones. The conclusions that are accepted are logical consequences of these changed premises. According to syntactic theories, the first step in reasoning is to construct the logical form of the premises by representing them in an internal language that matches the structure of the inference rules. Formal rules of inference are then used to derive a conclusion.

The work of Braine and his colleagues (Braine, 1978; Braine, Reiser and Rumain, 1984) is representative of the syntactic view. Braine describes a number of mental inference rules (or schemas) for the logical connectives *and, or, if,* and *not.* Braine et al. found that people who have not been tutored in logic can indeed solve purely arbitrary problems with great accuracy. For example, subjects can solve problems of the following form:

> If there is a B, then there is a T.   (7.11)
> It is false that there is not a B.
>
> There is a T?

Braine and his colleagues have proposed a total of 16 inference schemas, which people use to reason logically. For example, problems like (7.11) are solved by the sequential application of two inference schemas, P5 and P12:

> P5   It is false that it is false that *p*.   (7.12)
>
>   *p*
>
>   *p*
>
> P12   if p then *q*   (7.13)
>
>   *p*
>
>   *q*

P12 corresponds to *modus ponens,* which is therefore a straightforward application of an inference schema and so is very easy. Braine also accounts for people's poor performance on *modus tollens* as well as for the ease with which people commit the fallacies of affirming the consequent and denying the antecedent. Braine argues that there is not a natural rule of inference that corresponds to *modus tollens.* He takes up a suggestion that was made by Wason and Johnson-Laird (1972) and proposes that a *modus tollens* inference is made by deriving a *reductio ad absurdam.* Suppose subjects are presented with the following premises:

> If there is a G, then there is a P.   (7.14)
> There is not a P.
>
> There is not a G?

According to Braine, Reiser and Rumain (1984), subjects correctly accept this conclusion as valid by means of the inference schemas, P15, P12 and P16:

	if p then q	(premise)	(7.15)
	not q	(premise)	
P15	suppose p		
P12	if p then q	(from premise 1)	
	p	(from P15)	
	q	(incompatible with premise 1)	
P16	p has been supposed		
	q is incompatible with not q		
	Therefore, not p		

It is as if the subject said to him or herself: Suppose p were present. Then q would have to be. But q isn't present, so p must be absent.

Braine argues that the greater the number of inference rules that have to be used, the more difficult will be the inference. Since the derivation of *modus tollens* requires the application of three inference rules it should prove difficult relative to *modus ponens*, which is, of course, the case. In fact Braine, Reiser and Rumain 1984; (see also Rips 1983), have observed a good correlation between the number of steps involved in a derivation and the difficulty of evaluating the inference.

But what about the fallacies? How do syntactic theories account for them? These systematic errors cannot be attributed to corresponding inference rules, because the rules are designed to characterize logically correct inferences, not incorrect ones. Proponents of syntactic theories attribute the errors to the comprehension process. In particular, they suggest that the fallacies are due to conversational implicatures (Grice, 1975). That is, they are due to principles of conversation, not to the logical properties of *if*. Thus, the fallacies are invited by our understanding of language and by our general knowledge. For example, if someone says to you: *If you lean out of the window you'll fall* then your knowledge of the situation will lead you to make the invited inference: *If you don't lean out of the window you won't fall*. This is the obverse of the original rule and is, of course, the fallacy of denying the antecedent. But it is very hard to resist this invited inference if the warning is to be taken seriously (Geis and Zwicky, 1971). The speaker would be violating Grice's maxim of quantity (be informative) if she knew that you would fall whether you leaned out of the window or not. Hence the syntactic theorists argue that the fallacy of denying the antecedent is made because the *modus ponens* inference schema is applied to the obverse of the original rule. Similarly, affirming the consequent is made through the application of the *reductio* argument to the invited obverse rule. Thus, the fallacies are a result of the correct application of the inference schemas to a new interpretation of the rule.

Semantic theories

The theory of mental models (Johnson-Laird, 1983) is a psychological theory of the mental representation of meaning. It assumes that once there is an adequate explanation of language comprehension, there is no need for the mobilization of an elaborate machinery for reasoning, such as the inference schemas of the syntactic theorists. Instead, reasoning depends on the search for counter-examples to conclusions. Difficulties in reasoning arise because memory limitations constrain the search for counter-examples.

Although semantic theories do not suppose that people possess the formal rules of logic, these theories do need to show how logical inferences can be made. After all, logic itself is a product of human intellectual endeavours. But the theories must also show how people more readily accept certain inferences rather than others. This means that they must show how *modus ponens* is easier than *modus tollens*. The theories must also show why people are prone to the logical fallacies.

How might a propositional inference be derived from a mental model? In model theory, a conditional statement such as:

$$\text{if } p \text{ then } q \tag{7.16}$$

is true if, and only if, q is true in every state of affairs in which p is true. Thus, Johnson-Laird and Byrne (1989) suggest that it requires a mental model that indicates the relationship between the ps and the qs:

$$
\begin{aligned}
p &= q \\
p &= q \\
  & q \\
  &\cdots
\end{aligned}
\tag{7.17}
$$

Each line in (7.17) represents an alternative possible contingency. The = sign indicates that the propositions denoted by p and q are both true.

Thus, whenever p is true, q is true, but there may also be states of affairs in which q is true in the absence of p, hence the q on its own in line three. The three dots indicate uncertainty about *not p* and *not q*.

Some information is therefore explicit in the model (the information stated in the premise), but other information may be represented only implicitly (information about *not p* and *not q*). If p is asserted, the explicit information makes it easy to read off from the model that q must also be the case: Whichever instance of p is selected, it is always associated with a q in the model. This simulates *modus ponens* without the need for a formal rule. Now consider *modus tollens*, the inference *not p* from the assertion *not q*. Information about *not q* is only represented implicitly in the model, so it is necessary to add representations of the states of affairs corresponding to *not p* and *not q*. This results in a model of the following form:

$$
\begin{aligned}
p &= q \\
p &= q \\
\text{not } p &= q \\
\text{not } p &= \text{not } q \\
\text{not } p &= \text{not } q
\end{aligned}
\tag{7.18}
$$

Now when the premise *not q* is presented, the lines corresponding to q can be eliminated, producing the following model:

$$
\begin{aligned}
\text{not } p &= \text{not } q \\
\text{not } p &= \text{not } q
\end{aligned}
\tag{7.19}
$$

This model can be scanned to yield the conclusion *not p*. Whichever instance of *not q* is selected, it is always associated with *not p*. Thus, according to this theory, *modus tollens* is harder than *modus ponens* because it calls for implicit information about the complements of p and q to be made explicit.

Johnson-Laird and Byrne go on to suggest that the fallacies of denying the antecedent and affirming the consequent arise because the following item in the model:

$$
\text{not } p = q
\tag{7.20}
$$

is either omitted or forgotten. Of course, if the context of the assertion seduces the reasoner into accepting the invited obverse inference:

$$
\text{if not } p \text{ then not } q
\tag{7.21}
$$

then the item:

   not $p = q$

will not be represented at all. This account is comparable to the account given by the syntactic theorists, but the explanation is different. There is no application of inference rules to the obverse premise; instead, conclusions are read off from mental models.

Thus, mental models provide a semantic account of propositional reasoning that renders the use of inference schemas unnecessary.

Syllogistic Inference

A syllogism consists of two premises and a conclusion, each of which can occur in one of four moods. An example of each mood is shown below, along with its usual mnemonic:

All A are B	(a universal affirmative premise)
Some A are B	(a particular affirmative premise)
No A are B	(a universal negative premise)
Some A are not B	(a particular negative premise)

The arrangements of the terms in the premises can occur in one of four figures:

A–B	All A are B	B–A	All B are A
B–C	All B are C	C–B	All C are B
A–C	All A are C	B–A	All B are A
C–B	All C are B	B–C	All B are C

There are a number of features of syllogistic inference that theoretical accounts need to consider. One feature is the effect of content on performance. It appears to be very difficult to accept valid conclusions that contradict strong beliefs about the world. For example, nearly everyone accepts the valid conclusion in (7.23):

   Philosophers are all human.   (7.23)
   All human beings are fallible.

   Therefore, Philosophers are fallible.

By contrast, hardly anyone accepts the equally valid conclusion in the syllogism of the same form in (7.24) (Lefford, 1946):

War times are prosperous times.   (7.24)
Prosperity is highly desirable.

Therefore, Wars are much to be desired.

In (7.24) the conclusion runs counter to most people's beliefs.

A second feature of syllogistic reasoning is that some syllogisms are very easy and nearly everyone gets them right, but others are very difficult and nearly everyone gets them wrong. For example, nearly everyone draws the valid conclusion from the syllogism in (7.25):

Some of the artists are beekeepers.   (7.25)
All of the beekeepers are chemists.

Therefore, Some of the artists are chemists.

However, hardly anyone draws the valid conclusion from the syllogism in (7.26) (Johnson-Laird and Bara, 1984):

None of the artists are beekeepers.   (7.26)
All of the beekeepers are chemists.

Therefore, Some of the chemists are not artists.

Some theories of syllogistic reasoning have emphasized the errors which people make. These are non-logical theories and they propose *ad hoc* heuristics to explain the errors.

Non-logical theories

Woodworth and Sells (1935) proposed the atmosphere hypothesis that states that people may be seduced by the atmosphere of the syllogism (Woodworth and Sells, 1935). This atmosphere effect has been expressed most clearly by Begg and Denny (1969):

> If one of the premises contains *some*, then subjects will prefer a conclusion containing *some*. Similarly, if one of the premises contains a negative, then they will prefer a conclusion containing a negative.

However, the atmosphere effect does not always occur. If it did, then subjects would never say that there was no valid conclusion when asked to produce their own conclusions to syllogisms (Johnson-Laird and Steedman, 1978). Furthermore, the atmosphere effect is more likely to occur with valid than with invalid syllogisms, which suggests that people may use some logical ability to distinguish between valid and invalid inferences. In addition, the effects of atmosphere may be overruled by a figural effect, which is where the form of a conclusion is influenced by the figure of the syllogism. Premises in the figure:

A–B
B–C

tend to elicit conclusions of the form: A–C, while premises in the figure:

B–A
C–B

tend to elicit conclusions of the form: C–A. In the former case, the order of terms in the conclusion mirrors the order of the terms in the premises. In the latter case, where an end term is subject in only one of the premises, that term tends to occur as the subject of the conclusion. If the valid conclusions are inconsistent with these biases, then errors are likely to arise. However, these errors do not necessarily coincide with the atmosphere effect.

Another non-logical theory, the conversion hypothesis, was proposed by Chapman and Chapman (1959). They suggested that people illicitly convert *All A are B* into *All B are A*, and *Some As are not Bs* into *Some Bs are not As*. However, it appears that people rarely make these conversion errors when presented with a single premise and asked to select Euler circles that represent the relationship between the two terms. This suggests that the errors occur during the reasoning process rather than during initial interpretation (Newstead, 1990). Revlis (1975) and Revlin and Leirer (1978) have attempted to embed the conversion hypothesis in a specific performance model that assumes that the converted premise is the most dominant interpretation. However, subsequent studies have not supported this proposal (e.g. Dickstein, 1981; Newstead, 1989).

The non-logical theories concerning atmosphere and conversion assume that when solving logical problems, people are swayed by incidental aspects of the task, such as its wording. As such, they emphasize the factors that affect inferential performance but do not address the issue of how logical reasoning occurs. For this, we need a theory that explains not only why people make the kinds of errors described above but how logical reasoning is possible at all. As with propositional reasoning, two classes of theory attempt this kind of explanation: syntactic theories (e.g. Henle, 1962; Braine and Rumain, 1983) and semantic theories (e.g. Erickson, 1974; Guyote and Sternberg, 1981; Johnson-Laird, 1983; Newell, 1981). We will begin with semantic theories, since they give the most explicit accounts of syllogisms.

Semantic theories

Semantic theories all assume that an inference is derived from a mental representation of the states of affairs described by the premises. The mental representations that have been proposed include Euler circles (Erickson, 1974, 1978), and mental models (Johnson-Laird, 1983; Johnson-Laird and Steedman, 1978; Johnson-Laird and Bara, 1984).

Euler circles Erickson (1974, 1978) has proposed a three-stage model of syllogistic inference in which reasoners construct representations that

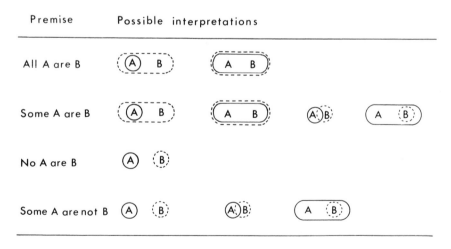

Figure 7.1 Euler circles representing the possible interpretations of the premises used in syllogisms (adapted from Gilhooly (1982); reproduced by permission of Academic Press)

are analogous to Euler circles. During stage one, people interpret the premises; during stage two, they combine the information in the two premises; and during stage three, they make a response.

Erickson's theory acknowledges the fact that there are a number of possible interpretations for each premise in a syllogism. These interpretations can be characterized by Euler circles and are shown in Figure 7.1.

Erickson proposed that people construct only one interpretation of each premise during stage one. He based this proposal on the results of studies in which subjects were asked to draw Euler circles corresponding to the statement *All A are B*. Approximately 40% of responses were set identity interpretations (the second interpretation in Figure 7.1), while 60% were set inclusion interpretations (the first interpretation in Figure 7.1).

In stage two, the interpretations of the two premises must be combined to produce a conclusion. However, there may be several possible combinations of the two premises. For example, the premises:

All C are B   (7.27)
All A are B

can be combined in five different ways. Consequently, Erickson proposed that people typically construct some but not all combinations of the premises, and that some combinations are more likely than others. To examine how subjects combine premises, Erickson gave two Euler circles to subjects and then asked them to draw the conclusion. He found a consistent pattern of combinations for each interpretation of the premises.

For example, when subjects were presented with the Euler circles of premises in (7.27), the five combinations were not equally likely. When the two Euler circles corresponded to the set identity interpretations, all subjects drew a combination that also represented set identity. However, when the Euler circles corresponded to the set inclusion interpretations, only 20% of the subjects chose a set identity combination. Another 20% chose an overlapping relation between A and C, while 10% chose disjoint sets for A and C, and 50% produced no combination at all.

Erickson (1978) used these percentages, together with the probabilities of constructing each interpretation to predict the probabilities of the actual responses given to syllogisms in a number of studies. The theory proved to be a good predictor of people's performance on both valid and invalid syllogisms. However, in order to predict performance on tasks requiring a verbal response, Erickson was forced to fall back on the atmosphere effect. This was because some combinations of premises can be described in more than one way: two overlapping sets, for example, can be described as *Some A are C* or as *Some A are not C*.

Johnson-Laird and Bara (1984) point out a number of difficulties with this theory. They claim that it denies the possibility of human rationality, since it proposes that people do not consider all the combinations of premises. However, given that people do make logical errors, it also fails to give an adequate explanation of people's performance. For example, as mentioned above, the syllogism in (7.25) is very easy and nearly everyone gets it right. But it requires 16 different Euler combinations. This contrasts with the syllogism in (7.26) that hardly anyone ever gets right. But it requires only six different combinations (Johnson-Laird and Bara, 1984). We would expect a theory of performance to predict a correlation between the number of combinations and difficulty, but this seems not to be the case. In addition, Erickson's theory provides no account of the figural effect, or of the error of responding 'no valid conclusion' when there is a valid conclusion. Thus, Erickson's theory based on Euler circles does not seem very successful.

Mental models The theory of mental models assumes that mental models have the same structure as the situations that they represent. Thus, a finite set of individuals is represented not by a circle, but by a finite set of mental tokens. Further tokens represent properties and relations between individuals (Johnson-Laird, 1983). The theory assumes that reasoning depends on three main stages. First, the premises are understood, that is, a mental model of the state of affairs they describe is constructed that incorporates any relevant general knowledge. Second, if possible, a novel conclusion is read off from the model; and third, a search is made for alternative models of the premises that refute the conclusion. The problem that is addressed by Johnson-Laird is how to explain both the errors people make and correct performance. The theory claims that mental models represent all the possible interpretations of the premises, thus making logical performance possible. However, errors arise because people find it difficult to construct alternative models. According to Johnson-Laird, the reason why some syllogisms (like the one in 7.25) are very easy and some (like the one in 7.26) are very difficult is because the very easy problems only require one model while the very difficult ones require multiple models.

The way that mental models enable deductions to be made can be illustrated with a one-model and a two-model problem. A one-model problem is shown in (7.28), where the valid conclusions have been capitalized.

Some A are B   (7.28)
All B are C

SOME A ARE C
SOME C ARE A

A model of the first premise, *Some A are B* is constructed by positing an arbitrary number of As and indicating that some of those As are Bs:

$a = b$ (7.29)
$a = b$
$Oa \quad Ob$

The items preceded by O are optional. They indicate that there may be some As that are not B and some Bs that are not A. We can now add the information in the second premise (*All B are C*) to the model by indicating that all of the Bs are Cs. Again, there may be some Cs that are not Bs:

$a = b = c$ (7.30)
$a = b = c$
$Oa \quad Ob = c$
$\qquad \quad Oc$

This results in an integrated representation of the two premises that links the two end terms, A and C. The conclusion *Some A are C* is consistent with this representation and so is regarded as a tentative conclusion. A search for alternative models now takes place. The search is carried out by a deductive process that tries to construct alternative models that are also true of the premises but in which the tentative conclusion is false. Since it is not possible to construct an alternative model in the example above, the original conclusion *Some A are C* is a valid conclusion.

The example in (7.31) is a two-model problem and so is not evaluated quite so easily; (again, the valid conclusion is capitalized):

> Some A are B $\qquad$ (7.31)
> All C are B
>
> NO VALID CONCLUSION
> Some A are C
> Some C are A

The first premise (*Some A are B*) is constructed in the same way as the first example. When the second premise (*All C are B*) is encountered, an integrated model is constructed:

$$
\begin{array}{rcl}
a & = & b & = & c \\
a & = & b & = & c \\
Oa & & Ob & = & Oc \\
& & Ob &
\end{array}
\qquad (7.32)
$$

Two conclusions are consistent with this model, *some A are C*, and *some C are A*. The deductive component now attempts to construct alternative models that are consistent with the premises. In this case, there is an alternative model that refutes the initial conclusions:

$$
\begin{array}{rcl}
a & = & b \\
a & = & b \\
Oa & & Ob & = & c \\
& & Ob & = & c
\end{array}
\qquad (7.33)
$$

The initial conclusions, therefore, cannot be valid conclusions. Furthermore, there is no conclusion that is compatible with both the alternative models, so there is no valid conclusion. People frequently make errors with syllogisms of this kind and erroneously conclude that *Some A are C*, or *Some C are A*, because they fail to evaluate alternative models.

Not all multiple model problems result in 'no valid conclusion'. A conclusion will be valid if it is true in all the alternative models. For example, the syllogism in (7.34) is a three-model problem that has a valid conclusion:

> All B are A $\qquad$ (7.34)
> No B is C
>
> No C are A
> Some C are not A
> SOME A ARE NOT C

The first invalid conclusion results when people fail to consider the first alternative model. The second invalid conclusion arises from a failure to consider the second alternative model. The three models are shown below:

$$
\begin{array}{llll}
a = b & a = b & a = b & (7.35) \\
a = b & a = b & a = b \\
Oa \\
\\
\quad c & Oa = c & Oa = c \\
\quad c & \quad c & Oa = c
\end{array}
$$

In this example, the first invalid conclusion (*No C are A*) conforms to the atmosphere effect. Johnson-Laird and Bara (1984) claim that atmosphere errors are a consequence of the failure to consider alternative models.

Processing difficulties may also arise when the premises are integrated to form an initial model. The ease of interpretation depends on the figure of the syllogism. For example, with the figure A–B, B–C it is relatively straightforward to integrate the two premises: the two instances of the middle term (B) occur one after the other. With the figure A–B, C–B (e.g. *All A are B, All C are B*), the integration of the premises requires the model of the second premise to be switched round. With the figure B–A, C–B, the initial model is based on the second premise and the interpretation of the first premise is recovered in order to integrate it into the model. In this latter example, the procedure results in a preference for conclusions of the form C–A. This is because the order in which information is added to the model is retrieved on a 'first in, first out' basis and ordered in the same way in the conclusion. The need to rearrange the premises to maintain a consistent order of the terms is therefore said to underlie the figural effect.

The use of optional elements in the models allows one model to capture the content of the assertion. It contrasts with the use of two separate Euler diagrams, one representing set inclusion and one representing set identity. However, the optional elements seem the most vulnerable to memory loss when processing demands are high (Johnson-Laird and Bara, 1984; Newstead, 1990).

Overall, then, mental model theory proposes that the number of models that are described by the premises explains which syllogisms will be easy and which will be difficult (e.g. Johnson-Laird and Bara, 1984; Johnson-Laird and Byrne, 1989), and the process of integrating the premises in working memory explains the figural effect (e.g. Johnson-Laird and Bara, 1984). Erroneous conclusions that conform to the atmosphere effect are explained by the failure to consider alternative models in multiple-model problems. Finally, the loss of optional elements when processing demands are high explains those errors that suggest that the subject has illicitly converted the terms in the premises (Newstead, 1990). The question remains, however, of how well syntactic theories account for these phenomena.

Syntactic theories

There have been no detailed suggestions of formal rules of inference for quantified assertions, but in an attempt to distinguish between semantic and syntactic accounts, Johnson-Laird and his colleagues (e.g. Byrne and Johnson-Laird, 1990; Johnson-Laird, Byrne and Tabossi, 1989) have examined inferences based on multiply quantified premises, such as:

> All of the authors are in the same place as all of the   (7.36)
> barristers.
>
> All of the barristers are in the same place as all of the cyclists.
>
> Therefore, All of the authors are in the same place as all of the
> cyclists.

Since current syntactic theories do not specify the inference schemas needed for such syllogisms, Johnson-Laird et al. constructed a possible syntactic theory based on the logic of multiply quantified assertions and the inference schemas of Braine (1978).

They argued that a syntactic account of quantified assertions should reveal a close relationship between the number of steps in the derivation and inferential performance. They presented subjects with problems for which they had calculated the number of steps required to solve the problem syntactically, and the number of mental models required to solve the problem semantically. The following example is a one-model problem that has 19 steps in its derivation:

> None of the authors is in the same place as any of the   (7.37)
> barristers.
>
> All of the barristers are in the same place as all of the cyclists.
>
> Therefore, None of the authors is in the same place as any of the
> cyclists.

The following is a three-model problem that also has 19 steps:

None of the authors is in the same place as any of the (7.38)
barristers.

All of the barristers are in the same place as some of the cyclists.

Therefore, None of the authors is in the same place as some of the cyclists.

or, equivalently:

Some of the cyclists are not in the same place as any of the authors.

They had other problems where the number of models was constant but where the number of steps in the syntactic proofs diverged. The predictions were that if people use mental models to derive valid inferences, then the one-model problems should be easier than the multiple-model problems. By contrast, if people use mental rules of logic, then problems with short derivations should be easier than problems with long derivations. The results supported the semantic view: subjects found one-model problems easier to solve than multiple-model problems, regardless of the number of steps in the syntactic derivation. These results, therefore, support the view that people use semantic procedures to derive valid conclusions rather than formal rules of inference.

The effects of belief on syllogistic reasoning

According to syntactic theories, belief effects must occur during comprehension, not when logical inferences are deduced. By contrast, semantic theories argue that beliefs can affect the reasoning process itself and not just comprehension. However, in most studies that reveal a belief bias effect, processes of comprehension cannot be disentangled from processes of deduction. Consequently it is difficult to determine where the effect occurs. In fact, the effect may also occur at a stage after the reasoning process: subjects may choose to accept a conclusion when it seems true and to reject it when it seems false.

A study by Oakhill, Johnson-Laird and Garnham (1989) attempted to tease out these different possibilities to determine the locus of the believability effects. The basic proposition that they tested was that beliefs influence the reasoning process, not just comprehension or choosing a conclusion. They proposed that if the initial model leads to a tentative conclusion that is believable, then it is likely to be accepted without any further attempt to find alternative models. Conversely, if the initial model leads to a tentative conclusion that is unbelievable, then it is likely to be scrutinized more closely and lead to attempts to formulate alternative models that disprove it. That is, the believability of the initial tentative conclusion will affect the likelihood of continuing the reasoning process.

They tested this proposal by asking subjects to solve syllogisms like those in (7.39):

> All of the communists are golfers.   (7.39)
> Some of the golfers are Marxists.
>
> Some of the communists are Marxists. (believable)
> Some of the Marxists are communists. (believable)
>
> All of the communists are golfers
> Some of the golfers are capitalists
>
> Some of the communists are capitalists. (unbelievable)
> Some of the capitalists are communists. (unbelievable)

The conclusions in the examples above are all invalid, but are likely to be accepted if people fail to search for alternative models. In the first example, the initial model that people construct will be:

$$
\begin{aligned}
c &= g = m \\
c &= g = m \\
Og &= m
\end{aligned}
\tag{7.40}
$$

which supports the tentative conclusion, *Some of the communists are Marxists*, or equivalently, *Some of the Marxists are communists*. By a similar process, the initial model that is constructed for the second example supports the tentative conclusion, *Some of the communists are capitalists*, or equivalently, *Some of the capitalists are communists*. In both examples, however, the correct conclusion is that there is 'no valid conclusion', which is discovered when an alternative model is constructed:

$$
\begin{aligned}
c &= g \\
c &= g \\
Og &= m \\
Og &= m
\end{aligned}
\tag{7.41}
$$

Oakhill, Johnson-Laird and Garnham (1989) found that people were more likely to draw one of the invalid conclusions with problems like the first example, where the initial tentative conclusions are believable, than with problems like the second example, where the initial tentative conclusions are unbelievable. Oakhill et al. argued, therefore, that the results supported the semantic, mental model, theory rather than the syntactic theory. Initial tentative conclusions do not figure in syntactic theories and so these theories cannot explain the results. However, in mental model theory, the initial tentative conclusion appears as a consequence of the initial model. Overall, therefore, mental model theory seems to provide the most comprehensive account of syllogisms.

SUMMARY

In this chapter, two alternative theories of deductive reasoning have been discussed: proof-theoretic syntactic theories and model-theoretic semantic theories. In all three kinds of reasoning that have been considered – relational, propositional, and syllogistic – evidence was cited to support the view that people make valid deductions by manipulating mental models. Nevertheless, the possibility that inference rules are used cannot be ruled out, since it may be that the appropriate set of rules has yet to be formulated. In addition, there is evidence from transitive inferences to suggest that people may switch from a semantic to a syntactic mode as they become practised in the task.

However, the bulk of evidence seems to favour mental models. They also have the merit of explaining both errors and correct performance by recourse to a single principle, in contrast to syntactic theories that assume that errors are due to a separate comprehension mechanism. Mental models, therefore, seem to give the best account of the delicate interplay between form and content, between deduction and induction, that invariably arises in human reasoning.

CHAPTER 8   Concepts: features, similarity and theories

Objects and events in the environment can be seen from many different points of view. To borrow an example from Gelman (1990), children may treat the objects used in a counting lesson in a counting relevant way. On the other hand, they may not. They may prefer to treat the objects as things to bite or things to bang on the table or things to throw on the floor. As the activities vary, so too do the properties of the objects that are seen as important. If something is used to bang on the table it must be rigid and a reasonable size. But if the same object is used for counting, then its rigidity and size can be ignored. What is it then that causes children, and adults, to categorize objects and events in the ways that they do? Proposed answers to that question form the subject matter of this chapter.

Concept learning, induction, pervades all of our cognitive life. By grouping things together into a single category we are able to make sense of the world and carve it into manageable chunks. Imagine living in a world where each object is in a category of its own and not grouped with other objects. The resulting cognitive overload would defeat our memory systems and, equally drastically, we would be unable to make inferences and predictions about the world. In short, we would be unable to learn. Not only do concepts themselves have to be learned, but having concepts enables further learning to occur. For example, children must learn that there is a category to which all birds belong. But having learned such a concept, they can then use it to make inferences about new instances they encounter. Once they are in possession of the concept, then merely by knowing that an animal is a bird, they are able to infer a number of other things about the animal, such as that it probably has feathers and wings, probably flies and probably sings.

OVERVIEW OF THE CHAPTER

For many years, the classical view of concepts held sway in psychology. This view held that the mental representation of a concept consists of a list of features that are each necessary for category membership. For example, to check if something is a triangle it is only necessary to check that it has each of the three properties of being a closed geometrical form, having three sides, and having interior angles that add up to 180 degrees. Concept learning involved the gradual realization that certain things, such as triangles, were members of the same category because they had the same features in common.

In the 1970s doubts about this classical position began to emerge, resulting in the anti-classical view that concepts are represented probabilistically; that is, the representation of a concept consists of a set of correlated attributes that are characteristic or typical of a concept. The probabilistic view rejects the notion that there are necessary and sufficient features that define a concept, and sees learning as the detection of feature clusters that determine category membership. However, despite their surface differences, both the classical view and the probabilistic view shared the same set of assumptions about the nature of concepts: that the meaning of a concept can be fully described by lists of features and that concept learning involves the detection of features.

Eventually, a number of lines of evidence began to make it increasingly clear that something was missing from these accounts. This something was an underlying principle, or theory, that would bind concepts together more firmly than do sets of features and that would make the concepts cohere; a theory that would give a reason for grouping diverse entities together into a single category. In other words, part of the meaning of a concept may be the apprehension of the theoretical relations that explain why a set of correlated features occur together. According to the theory-based view, the fact that instances of a category share a set of features is a consequence of the causal relationships that underlie a person's knowledge of a concept. On this view, concept learning is constrained by people's causal theories about the world. Indeed, constraints are often seen as innate principles that limit the kinds of things that can be learned.

The emphasis in the chapter, therefore, is on two major (related) shifts in thinking about concepts. One shift is from the view that concepts are represented as features, to the view that they are represented as theories. The second is from the view that people learn concepts by noticing which features go together and grouping objects according to those features, to a view that people learn the concepts that they do because they are biologically constrained to learn certain concepts and not others. Finally, the precise relationship between theories and features and the possible role that each might play in the learning of concepts will be discussed.

THE CLASSICAL VIEW

A concept has an intension, what the concept means, and an extension, what the concept refers to. The classical view holds that a concept's intension consists of the set of attributes that define the concept, while the extension is the set of entities that are members of the concept. For example, the intension of the concept *bachelor* includes the attributes male, adult, and unmarried, while the extension of *bachelor* is all the individuals in the world who possess this set of attributes.

This view of concepts carries with it two notions that could be said to characterize the classical view. These are that concepts are arbitrary and that concepts form discrete, all-or-none categories. The arbitrary assumption means that features are associated with objects in a random and arbitrary way, and the task of the concept learner is to attend to the features that are relevant to the concept and to ignore all the irrelevant features. For example, a concept such as *red squares* has two defining features – the colour red and the shape square. All other features of red squares, such as their size, weight, type of material and so on are irrelevant to the concept. The all-or-none assumption says that instances either are or are not members of a category. An instance either has the defining features, in which case it is a member of the concept, or it has not, in which case it is not a member of the concept. There is no room for fuzziness or blurring at the edges. A modern version of this classical view of concepts can be seen in Collins and Quillian's (1969) model of semantic memory.

TROUBLES WITH THE CLASSICAL VIEW

In a comprehensive review of the literature, Smith and Medin (1981) concluded that the classical view was in grave trouble. The arguments against the view are many and varied, but the most serious problems can be summed up very easily: concepts do not all have defining features, they are not arbitrary, and they are not all-or-none.

Concepts do not have Defining Features

There have been many arguments against the view that concepts consist of necessary and sufficient features. Wittgenstein (1953) used the example of games and challenged people to discover their necessary and sufficient features. He coined the term 'family resemblance' to describe the way that instances of a concept are similar to each other. Rosch and her colleagues (e.g. Rosch, 1973; Rosch and Mervis, 1975) conducted numerous studies supporting the view that categories are organized around family resemblances among the members rather than around necessary and sufficient features. For example, Rosch and Mervis asked subjects to list the features associated with 20 instances of concepts such as *furniture, fruit, clothing* and *vehicles*. The results showed that for a given concept, subjects never listed the same set of features for all 20 instances. In fact, only very rarely was there a unique feature that was shared by every instance. Where this did happen, the feature was so general that it described a number of other concepts too, for example the feature *you eat it* for instances of the concept *fruit*. On the other hand, a person may list *juicy* as a feature of oranges, but not all fruits are juicy. Thus Rosch and Mervis found no evidence for defining features. Instead, instances of a concept seemed to be organized according to a set of overlapping features since they are shared by some but not all instances. Work of this kind led to the probabilistic view of concepts: that they consist of characteristic rather than defining features.

Concepts are not Arbitrary

Rosch's work on overlapping features led her to the view that concepts have internal structure. That is, instances of a concept are either good, poor, or medium examples of the concept. For instance, Rosch (1975) asked subjects to rate instances of different categories according to how well each instance fitted the subject's view of the concept. The results showed that subjects ranked the instances in a consistent manner. For example, robin and wren are good examples of the concept *bird*, bat and penguin are poor examples, while chicken and parrot are medium examples. Rosch and Mervis (1975) went on to show that good examples (or prototypes) share a large number of common features, poor examples share few, if any, common features, while medium examples fall between these two extremes. As a consequence

According to the classical view, all examples of a concept are equally good because they all possess the requisite defining features. Experience and a large body of evidence undermine this claim, beginning with Rosch's (1975) rating study that was mentioned above. It has also been shown that people can answer category membership questions more rapidly for good examples than for poor examples (Smith, Shoben and Rips, 1974). Such typicality effects seem to be ubiquitous: they hold for artistic style (Hartley and Homa, 1981), chess (Goldin, 1978), emotion terms (Fehr, 1988; Fehr and Russell, 1984), medical diagnosis (Arkes and Harkness, 1980), and person perception (Cantor and Mischel, 1977).

The presence of typicality effects undermines another aspect of the classical view: that there is an effective procedure for determining concept membership, which is to check for defining features. If features are only characteristic and not defining, then there may well be difficulties in determining concept membership. The idea that some instances are only poor examples of a concept renders this possibility even more likely. Indeed there are numerous cases where it is not clear whether or not an instance belongs to a category. Should a picture be considered furniture? What about a clock? Or a rug? People not only disagree with each other about concept membership but also contradict themselves when asked about membership on separate occasions (e.g. Barsalou, 1989).

All in all, the classical view of concepts has not stood the test of time. These and other problems have led to a disenchantment with it and it has since given ground to the alternative anti-classical, probabilistic view.

THE PROBABILISTIC VIEW

The probabilistic view holds that there are no defining features of a concept, only characteristic ones, and it comes in two main versions.

One is the prototype version (e.g. Rosch, 1975; Rosch and Mervis, 1975), which holds that a concept is represented as a summary set of the features that are typical of the concept. This summary representation is an example or ideal that possesses all the characteristic features of a concept. An object is considered to be a member of a concept if it has sufficient similarity to the prototype. The general notion is that, based on experience with examples of a concept, people abstract out the central tendency or prototype that becomes the summary mental representation for the concept.

The second, more radical, version is the exemplar view of Smith and Medin (1981). The exemplar view denies that there is a single, summary representation of a concept and claims instead that concepts are represented by means of examples. On this view an object is considered to be a member of a concept not because it is similar to some prototype but because it reminds the person of a previous similar example.

A considerable amount of research has contrasted prototype and exemplar representations (see, for example, Medin, 1986; Medin and Smith, 1984; Oden, 1987). However, for the purposes of this chapter, I will ignore their differences and consider the merits and drawbacks of both alternatives as examples of the probabilistic view of concepts.

The probabilistic view holds that membership of a concept is determined by whether an object is sufficiently similar either to the prototype or to a set of encoded examples, where similarity is based on matches and mismatches of independent features. The critical assumption of the view is that the typicality of an instance reflects its similarity to the prototype or example. Specifically, the more frequently the properties of an instance occur among concept members in general (the greater its family resemblance) the more typical is the instance. Thus typical instances are categorized more rapidly than atypical ones because the more similar an instance is to the representation of the concept the faster one can tell that it exceeds some threshold level of similarity.

It seems, therefore, that the probabilistic view provides a better fit to the data than the classical view. The evidence mentioned above, which posed problems for the classical view, all supports the probabilistic view. There is also evidence to suggest that the learning of concepts is influenced by their internal structure. For example, children learn concepts best if they are presented with good rather than poor examples of the concept, and they learn the good examples of a concept more rapidly than the poor examples (Mervis and Pani, 1980).

PROBLEMS WITH THE PROBABILISTIC VIEW

Despite its seeming fit with the data, problems have also arisen with the probabilistic view of concepts. These problems seem to hinge on three main issues: the view that family resemblance predicts typicality, the way that concepts are combined to form new concepts, and the use of feature similarity to explain conceptual coherence. The last two issues are not specific to the probabilistic view, since they also apply to the classical view, but the discussion will mainly apply to the probabilistic view.

Does Family Resemblance Predict Typicality?

According to the probabilistic view, family resemblance predicts typicality: the more features an instance shares with other instances of the concept, the more typical it is. There are a number of studies in the literature that contradict this claim. People have found typicality effects that cannot be explained by family resemblance, either because the concepts involved are classical concepts (e.g. Armstrong, Gleitman and Gleitman, 1983), or because typicality arises for some other reason, such as relevance to a goal (e.g. Barsalou, 1985).

Armstrong et al. focused on two measures commonly used by Rosch and her colleagues to show typicality effects: ratings of typicality of concept examples, and reaction times to identify legitimate examples. They asked whether data that showed a strong correlation between degree of typicality and reaction times should necessarily imply that the meaning of the term involved was a probabilistic concept. To assess this possibility, they used classically defined concepts like *odd number* and showed that subjects did indeed rate some instances as more typical of the concept than others. For example, 7 and 13 were rated as more typical odd numbers than 15 and 23. Moreover, as with object concepts, people were faster to judge that a typical instance is a member of the concept than that an atypical instance is. Thus well-defined concepts can yield empirical results very much like those that purportedly were evidence for a family resemblance view of concepts. This makes it difficult to interpret the typicality effects that have been used to support the probabilistic view, since concepts that cannot possibly be probabilistic show the same kinds of effects.

Barsalou's work (e.g. 1985) also queries the notion that family resemblance predicts typicality. He found that goal-derived concepts give rise to typicality effects. Goal-derived concepts are those that are created during our efforts to achieve certain goals. For instance, a goal to lose weight can lead to a concept of *foods not to eat on a diet*; a goal to go camping can lead to a concept of *things to take on a camping trip*. Typicality effects in these goal-derived concepts cannot be due to family resemblance, since the instances are defined by their relevance to the current goal and not by feature similarity. Thus, typicality effects cannot conclusively support a family resemblance structure for concepts, since they arise in situations where family resemblance is not applicable.

Conceptual Combination

Most of the time we combine concepts with other concepts, as for example, when we combine words into phrases and sentences during language comprehension. So a theory of concepts needs to be able to explain how concepts are combined. According to the classical view, a combined concept, such as a *pet fish*, is formed by taking the intersection of the set of all things that are pets and the set of all things that are fish. This view has a great deal of trouble with many complex concepts. Murphy and Medin (1985) give examples like *ocean drive, expert repair* and *horse race*. These concepts are not intersective at all. Ocean drives are not both oceans and drives. Horse races are not both horses and races. It appears, therefore, that no single relation, like set intersection, can describe all or even most complex concepts. Furthermore, even when set intersection can apply, concepts do not combine in a straightforward way. For instance, *fake* may mean something different when applied to *gun* and when applied to *tan*. *Good* means something different when applied to *person* and when applied to *knife*. Thus, although the classical view gives a simple account of how concepts might combine to form new concepts, this simple account cannot explain the facts.

The same facts must also be accounted for by the probabilistic view. But this view has an added level of complexity when considering combined concepts. This is that the family resemblance structure of concepts needs to be taken into account in conceptual combination. The natural way to do this would be to say that the typicality of an instance in the individual concepts predicts its typicality in the combined concept. There is evidence though that this is not the case. Medin and Shoben (1988) found that people rate metal spoons as more typical of spoons than wooden spoons. In a straightforward account of conceptual combination, therefore, metal spoons should also be judged more typical than wooden spoons in the combined category of *large spoons*. But they are not. People find wooden spoons to be the most typical. The problem, then, for the probabilistic view is to explain how concepts combine in a way that predicts the typicality of instances of the combined concept.

Fuzzy set theory, which is a brand of set theory, would seem to be an obvious tool to use since it was specifically designed to manipulate concepts that have degrees of category membership. However, fuzzy set theory is unable to make the right predictions (Osherson and Smith, 1981). For example, according to fuzzy set theory, a goldfish should be less typical of the combined concept *pet fish*, than it is of the concept *fish*, because *pet fish*, unlike *fish*, includes features that are typical of pets in general and these are not likely to be features of goldfish. Yet intuitions suggest that a goldfish is more representative of pet fish than it is of either constituent: pet or fish. In general, the formula based on fuzzy set theory will always yield a typicality value of an instance in the combined concept that is less than the instance's typicality in the individual concepts, and this is often counter to actual typicality ratings.

Some more recent feature-based attempts at explaining conceptual combinations that produce the expected typicality effects have met with more success (e.g. Hampton, 1987, 1988; Smith, Osherson, Rips and Keane, 1988). Smith et al. have proposed a model that accounts for adjective–noun combinations, like *red fruit*, and for adverb–adjective–noun combinations, like *very red fruit*. They do this by using representations of concepts that contain attribute-value pairs. Thus the representation of the concept *fruit* includes the attribute colour, and this attribute can take one of three values: red, green or brown. In addition, each attribute has a weighting that indicates its importance in identifying instances, and each value has a weighting that reflects its subjective likelihood of appearing in an instance. The representations of instances of fruit will include some of the same attributes as the representation of fruit, but will have different values for them and will have different weights on both the attributes and the values.

To form the combined concept *red fruit* the adjective concept does three things: first, it selects the relevant attribute in the noun (colour, in this example); second, it places the total weighting on the value red, and nothing on the values green or brown; and third, it increases the weighting of the colour attribute overall. The net effect is to increase the overall weighting for the colour red relative to its weighting in the concept *fruit*. This results in *apple* being more similar to *red fruit* than to *fruit*, a finding that is mirrored by typicality ratings. Thus, the model predicts that the typicality of an instance in the combined concept may be greater than the typicality of the instance in the simple concept, unlike the model based on fuzzy set theory.

It seems, therefore, that when adjectives and nouns are combined to form complex concepts, they result in predictable typicality. In most cases of everyday discourse, where such combinations must be comprehended rapidly and effortlessly, typicality relations that depend on the sort of attribute-value weights that are proposed by Smith et al., may be the norm. We are still left, though, with difficult cases, like *ocean drive*, which Murphy and Medin (1985) suggest may be more frequent than is supposed. Indeed, Cohen and Murphy (1984) argued that it is impossible to explain how people form these kinds of compound concepts using only knowledge-independent operations; that is, using only the meanings of the constituent concepts without any reference to knowledge of how instances of the concepts are used in the world. For example, *engine repair* is repair of an engine, but *expert repair* is probably not repair of an expert. Cohen and Murphy argue that only our knowledge of the world can indicate the meanings of these combined concepts, not just a knowledge of their constituent meanings. Thus, a knowledge of the use of vehicles, their parts and what they do, and things that can go wrong with them can lead to the combination of *engine* and *repair* to get repair of an engine. Knowledge about experts leads to a different combination of *expert* and *repair* to get repair done by an expert. These arguments suggest that the probabilistic view cannot provide a complete account of conceptual combinations and that probabilistic representations need to be supplemented by theories.

Does Feature Similarity Explain why People Form the Concepts that They Do?

Objects seem to fall into natural clusters of similar kinds that are dissimilar to other clusters, and our concepts map on to these clusters. So perhaps similarity is the glue that makes categories cohere and that makes them learnable and useful. Many people have disputed this view, both philosophers (e.g. Quine, 1977) and psychologists (e.g. Murphy and Medin, 1985; Nelson, 1974).

Murphy and Medin argue that not only have approaches to conceptual coherence based on similarity been unsuccessful, they are insufficient in principle. For example, an exclusive focus on feature similarity leads to the assumption that concept membership is based solely on attribute matching. It also ignores the problem of how to decide what counts as an attribute. Finally, it engenders a view that concepts are little more than the sum of their constituent attributes. Murphy and Medin argue that all of these problems derive from a failure to view concepts in terms of how people actually use them; that is, people form concepts on the basis of interests, needs, goals and theories, not on the basis of feature similarity.

Attribute matching

Attribute matching cannot be the sole basis for concept membership. Inferences may be used instead. To take an example from Murphy and Medin, jumping into a swimming pool fully clothed is unlikely to be associated with the concept intoxicated, yet that information might well be used to decide (or to infer) that a person is drunk. In other words, deciding that someone is intoxicated may explain his or her behaviour, even though that behaviour was not previously a component of the concept. Yet in another context the same behaviour may be regarded as an instance of bravery. So the inference concerning category membership is not a simple one and is obviously not a straightforward matter of attribute matching.

In addition, Rips (1989) has shown that people can decide concept membership even when the decision runs counter to rated similarity. He asked one group of subjects whether an object five inches in diameter was more likely to be a coin or a pizza. This was a categorization task.

He asked a second group of subjects to judge the similarity of an object to either a coin or a pizza. This was a similarity task. The results showed that subjects doing the categorization task classed the object as a pizza. But the similarity group said that it was more similar to a coin. Clearly more is involved in categorization than a simple computation of similarity. Rips argues that this something more is knowledge (or a theory) about the variability of the sizes of the objects in question. Coins have a size that is mandated by law, while pizzas can vary greatly in size.

What counts as an attribute?

Many people have pointed out that there is an indefinitely large number of features that any two objects might have in common. So the real question is how the particular attributes that are deemed to be relevant are chosen. What is needed is a set of criteria by which the relevant attributes are selected (e.g. Goodman, 1972; Murphy and Medin, 1985; Quine, 1977). A feature-based view assumes that the relevant criterion is similarity: an instance is a member of a concept if its features are similar to the features of the concept.

However, Murphy and Medin (1985) argue that underlying knowledge rather than feature similarity determines concept membership on at least some occasions. It is hard to see what might be the surface similarity shared by objects like children, jewellery, televisions, paintings, manuscripts, and photographs. But they do fit together into a concept like *things to rescue if the house is on fire* (Murphy and Medin, 1985). Context can affect judgements of category membership as well. Barsalou and Sewell (1984) found that for the concept *hobbies*, fishing was thought to be a highly typical example from the perspective of a red neck but not from the perspective of a housewife. Medin and Shoben (1988) found that the terms *white hair* and *grey hair* were judged to be more similar than *grey hair* and *black hair*, but that the terms *white clouds* and *grey clouds* were judged to be less similar than *grey clouds* and *black clouds*. These kinds of results suggest that certainly on some occasions, people class an instance as a member of a concept on the basis of theoretical knowledge and not on similarity.

Children, too, use knowledge to judge concept membership, even when this conflicts with feature similarity. Gelman and Markman (1987) found that if category membership was pitted against perceptual similarity, children's responses were based on the category information, not perceptual similarity. Gelman and Markman taught young children that different novel properties were true of two example animals, and then asked which property was also true of a new example. For example, children were shown pictures of a flamingo bird, a bat and an owl. They were told that the flamingo feeds its baby mashed-up food and that the bat feeds its baby milk. The children were then asked how the owl feeds its baby. The owl looked like the bat but was in the same category as the flamingo. Even four-year-olds said the owl fed its baby mashed-up food. That is, they made an inference on the basis of knowledge of concept membership and not on perceptual similarity. Thus, children as well as adults seem to form concepts on the basis of what they know and not on the basis of similarity.

Furthermore, correlated features in people's mental representations may not always reflect empirical correlations in the world (Chapman and Chapman, 1967, 1969). Chapman and Chapman showed that therapists, as well as non-professionals, perceived correlations between test results and psychological disorders when they did not even exist – or even when the opposite correlation was obtained. Chapman and Chapman determined the actual relationship between verbal responses on a diagnostic test, known as the Rorschach test, and homosexuality. Some of these responses contain sexual content, while others do not. None of the sexual responses is associated with homosexuality but some of the non-sexual ones are. For example, homosexuals tend to report seeing monsters on one of the cards. However, when asked, clinicians claimed that sexual responses were the most valid signs of homosexuality. In another study, Chapman and Chapman presented test results to non-clinical subjects along with a description of each patient. In the presented results, Chapman and Chapman were careful to ensure that there was absolutely no correlation between sexual responses and the description of a patient as homosexual. But the experimenters did vary the correlation between valid, non-sexual responses and homosexuality from 0.5 to a perfect correlation of 1.0. The results showed that the subjects failed to recognize the presence of a true association and continued to believe that sexual responses related to homosexuality. Thus, categorization seems to depend on something that goes beyond the matching of attributes. It seems instead to depend on an underlying theory as to which attributes are believed to be important.

Perhaps underlying knowledge constrains our choice of concepts, not similarity at all. If this is so, it may well provide an account of what is to count as an attribute. That is, it is determined by the theory that guides the concept formation in the first place.

Are concepts the sum of their constituent attributes?

Such a view seems to drastically underestimate what it is that people know when they have a concept. People seem to know about the relationship between attributes rather than just the attributes themselves. This point is emphasized by Armstrong, Gleitman and Gleitman (1983). They pointed out that the features normally associated with the concept *bird* are just a pile of bird features unless they are held together in a 'bird structure' in some way. For example, building nests is linked to laying eggs; building nests in trees poses strategic problems that can be solved by the presence of wings and flying. It is possible to say, therefore, that birds have wings and feathers in order to fly, even in the absence of elaborate biological knowledge.

A consideration of the above point also suggests that studies using attribute listing may seriously under-represent what we know about concepts. Thus, the typicality effects emerging from these studies need to be treated with caution. It is certainly the case that many obvious properties are not listed. Keil (1990) commented that instances like robin and squirrel share many important properties that almost never show up in attribute listings (for example, having a heart, breathing, sleeping, being an organism, being a physical object, capable of being thought about, and so on). There are a number of possible reasons for these sorts of omissions (see e.g. Murphy and Medin, 1985), but the main point here is that attribute listings represent a biased sample of what people know when they have a concept, thus casting doubt on one of the principle methods that is used to provide evidence for the probabilistic view.

Thus we can return to the question, what makes people form the concepts that they do? And it seems that an answer in terms of feature similarity is insufficient. Rather, it seems that knowledge causes people to form concepts.

Overall, then, the probabilistic view runs into a number of difficulties. One is the relationship between family resemblance and similarity, another is the issue of conceptual combination, and the third is the notion of feature similarity as a mechanism for forming concepts. Discussion of these problems makes it clear that something else, namely knowledge (or theory), is involved in concept formation not just sets of features.

THEORETICAL KNOWLEDGE IN CONCEPT FORMATION

The notion of a theory is hard to pin down precisely. For the moment let us think of it as a person's intuitive model of the social and physical world, something akin to a set of schemas (e.g. Murphy, 1990). Some people's models may be highly enriched with specific knowledge in one or another domain, but this is not necessary for an intuitive model. In general, a model of some situation hangs together by means of a causal structure, as in the example of a 'bird structure', which may contain a great deal of causal information about why some features and functions occur together. Many of the arguments for the importance of theories as representations of concepts were presented in the previous section. In this section we will review the empirical evidence.

EVIDENCE FOR THE KNOWLEDGE-BASED VIEW OF CONCEPTS

Conceptual Combination

Smith, Osherson, Rips and Keane's (1988) attribute weighting model accounts for typicality effects in adjective–noun combinations. For example, *red apple* refers to the same thing as *apple* but with a heavily weighted colour attribute, having the value *red*. This accounts for the strong intuition that redness is more important to the concept *red apple* than it is to *apple*, even though redness is already typical of *apple*. However, Murphy (1988) has queried whether Smith et al.'s model can account for all the typicality effects in adjective–noun combinations. He pointed out that the model would also predict that if a feature is atypical of both the adjective and the noun, then it should be atypical of the combined concept.

To test this prediction, Murphy asked subjects to judge the typicality of a feature for an adjective concept, a noun concept, and the combined adjective–noun concept, e.g. *round table*, where the feature in question was: *used at a conference*. He found that subjects judged the feature to be more typical of the combined concept than of either of the constituent concepts in isolation, a finding that contradicts the attribute weighting model. Murphy suggests that background knowledge, not feature clusters, underlies our ability to understand new concepts.

Murphy (1990) also argues that noun–noun concepts (e.g. *ocean drive*) cannot be understood simply by combining the features of the constituent concepts, *ocean* and *drive*. Indeed, noun–noun combinations are not explained by Smith et al.'s model at all. In an attempt to account for such combinations, therefore, Murphy formulated a knowledge-based account of the processes underlying conceptual combination. He suggests that with adjective–noun concepts such as *red apple*, people apply a single dimension, such as colour, to the noun concept. This can be regarded as filling the slot for *colour* in an apple schema. However, with noun–noun concepts, such as *ocean drive*, the first noun does not pick out a unique slot in the schema for the second noun. Instead, it is necessary to decide what aspect of the first noun is being applied to the second. The slot must be identified before it can be filled. Thus when a noun appears as a modifier, it is necessary to integrate it with the second noun in the best way possible for that pair of words. It is only by integrating the noun modifier with the main noun and evaluating the resulting plausibility that the noun phrase can be understood. This is the knowledge-based view, and it predicts that noun–noun combinations will take longer to understand than adjective-noun combinations, a prediction that Murphy (1990) confirmed.

The Role of Knowledge in Learning New Concepts

It has long been held that conjunctive concepts (e.g. *all red squares*) are easier to learn than disjunctive concepts (e.g. *objects that are either red or square*). There is a wealth of empirical data to support this view (e.g. Bruner, Goodnow and Austin, 1956). However, more recent work derived from the knowledge-based view of concepts suggests that prior knowledge may alter this basic finding. Pazzani (1991) gave subjects a concept learning task in which the concept to be learned was either conjunctive (*small, yellow balloons*), or disjunctive (*either an adult or stretching a balloon*). The instances that were encountered by the subjects were photographs of a person doing something with a balloon. The pictures differed in terms of the colour of the balloon (yellow or purple), the size of the balloon (small or large), the age of the person (adult or child), and the action the person was doing (stretching the balloon or dipping it in water).

All subjects saw exactly the same photographs and had to predict after seeing each one whether it was a member of the concept or not. The subjects were informed each time of whether or not they were correct. There were two groups of subjects, the only difference between them being the instructions they received. One group received standard instructions for a concept-learning task. They were asked to predict whether each photograph was an example of alpha. Existing knowledge of balloons is irrelevant for this group. The second group were instructed to predict whether the balloon will be inflated when the person blows into it. For this group, called the inflate group, the subject's prior knowledge may provide expectations about likely hypotheses in the disjunctive case, since adults are stronger than children and stretching a balloon makes it easier to inflate. The number of trials taken before all the predictions were correct was measured.

The results showed two main things. First, the alpha group took fewer trials for the conjunctive concept than for the disjunctive concept, a finding which replicates previous work. Second, subjects in the inflate group took fewer trials for the disjunctive concept than for the conjunctive concept. This finding contradicts previous work and indicates that prior knowledge can override effects due to the structure of the concept. The results support the view that concepts consistent with prior knowledge require fewer examples to learn accurately than concepts that are inconsistent with prior knowledge.

Developmental Evidence

There is now an overwhelming body of evidence to suggest that concept learning in young children is heavily constrained by knowledge, by theories about the nature of the world. Furthermore, many people believe that the evidence supports the view that these constraints are innate, that children are biologically constrained to construe the world in certain ways. It is not possible to review all the developmental issues here. Instead, I will present an overview of the findings and some of their implications.

From the age of three months, infants seem to perceive objects as whole units. To do this, they use the basic principles of motion, principles that reflect fundamental constraints on the motions of physical bodies. That is, they use an intuitive theory of motion to determine what things in the world are whole objects (e.g. Spelke, 1990). Spelke and her colleagues used a range of techniques to investigate object perception in infants. All the experiments showed that young infants between three and five months perceive object boundaries by detecting surface movements and surface arrangements. For example, infants perceived two objects as separate units when one moved relative to the other, even when the objects were touching throughout the movement.

Spelke suggests that the same principles of motion underlie object perception in adults. The only difference that development makes is that the initial mechanisms become enriched by the growth of knowledge. Adults, therefore, know that there are other ways to distinguish objects besides motion. Spelke suggests that children first perceive objects by means of their unlearned (innate) theory of motion and then discover other distinctions. That is, by perceiving objects according to the principles of motion, they can then observe other properties of the object, such as its texture and shape. In this way infants' perceptual abilities are enriched by knowledge of the objects and they come to perceive objects in the same way as adults. The learning process is made possible because of the original constraints which make sure that whole objects are perceived.

Evidence also suggests that children's understanding of living things is constrained by intuitive models of biology. Carey (1985) asked children questions like 'is a button alive?', 'does a person have a heart?', or 'does an orchid eat?' and asked them to justify their answers. Her results suggested a number of things about children's concepts. First, with respect to the question about being alive, 4–7-year-olds believe that only animals and not plants are alive. Thus the children do not have a concept with the same extension as the adult concept of living thing.

Second, with respect to questions about properties such as having a heart or eating, young children appear to classify animals on the basis of behaviour, whereas 10-year-olds and adults see them as biological beings as well. For young children the prototypical animal is a person and other animals are classified as animals to the extent that they resemble people in their needs, thoughts and desires and in their social behaviour. In addition, young children attribute virtually all animal properties to humans, but the attribution of these same properties to other animals declines as their similarity to humans declines. By the age of 10 years, children (like adults) attribute properties like eating to all animals, and properties like thinking only to humans. Carey suggests, therefore, that children aged 5 years have an intuitive psychological theory that is based on human behaviour, and that forms the basis of biological knowledge. Therefore fruit, plants, and animals are grouped together because they are not human.

Third, in support of the view that young children's basic category cut is between humans and non-humans, Carey found that when 4-year-olds were told that humans have omenta, they attributed the property only to animals that were similar to humans. When told that a dog had an omentum, the younger children were less likely to attribute it to humans and other mammals than were older children. From these and other observations, Carey argues that the young children had to resort to similarity judgements for animals other than humans, since they did not have the biological knowledge to make their inductions in any other way. Nevertheless, it seems that young children form their first concepts according to unlearned principles of biology, based on a distinction between humans and non-humans. Once the early concepts are acquired, children can make other observations about the instances to make more fine-grained distinctions between them.

Work on the acquisition of early word meanings (e.g. Markman, 1989) and concepts of number (e.g. Gelman and Gallistel, 1978) also supports the view that acquisition is subject to constraints. For example, consider the beginning language learner who sees someone point to three books and say 'one, two, three' on one occasion and 'book, book, book' on another. Adults know that on the first occasion the books are being counted, so a different word is used each time regardless of whether the items are of the same kind or not, while on the second occasion they are being named, and so the same name is used for instances of the same class. But suppose the language learner does not share our knowledge of the different constraints on counting and naming. In these circumstances the child should either mix up the count words and names or think they are free to use the same words for counting or different words for naming. Yet children do not behave as if these are options. Instead, it seems as if they follow principles that constrain their interpretation of strings of words that are used for counting (Gelman, 1990).

Overall, then, it appears that theories constrain the kinds of concept that children will learn. This contrasts with the feature similarity view which supposes that any set of similarities will be perceived and grouped together. Taken together with the findings of Murphy (1990) on conceptual combination and Pazzani (1991) on learning, these observations suggest that concepts are represented as causal theories. Murphy supposes that these theories are in the form of scripts. However, it is equally plausible to suppose that they are a consequence of a connectionist system, such as the one proposed by Kintsch (1988) in his model of text comprehension (see Chapter 5). A connectionist system may be better able to account for the ease with which different components of knowledge are rapidly retrieved in the comprehension of complex concepts, goal derived concepts, and contextually determined concepts. Nevertheless, regardless of the mode of representation, the notion that causal theories underlie our use of concepts raises the question of the role of features in conceptual behaviour and of the relationship between features and theories.

THE RELATIONSHIP BETWEEN FEATURES AND THEORIES

If theories underlie conceptual behaviour, what role do features play in that behaviour? One possibility is that features are used to classify objects when theories fail. That is, at the frontiers of knowledge, instances are assigned to categories, and new concepts formed, on the basis of feature similarity. Carey (1985) seems to have adopted this view when she says that young children resort to similarity judgements when making decisions about animals other than humans because of their lack of any theoretical differentiation between non-human animals.

However, assigning features such a last-resort role, suggests that there are two distinct representational systems, a theory-based system that is used under normal circumstances, and a feature-based system that is switched on when the theory-based system fails. A more satisfactory view is one that suggests how theories and features might be related. A view that has come to be known as psychological essentialism seems to fulfil this role. It claims that people believe concepts have a true nature that cannot be observed directly but which governs all acts of categorization.

Psychological Essentialism

Medin (1989) has suggested that psychological essentialism may be at the heart of people's conceptual behaviour. First, he argues that people act as if things had essences or underlying natures that make them the things that they are. This is part of the intension of a concept. But another component of intension consists of a prototype or set of exemplars. This second component, together with a similarity metric for determining the similarity between instances in the world and the prototype or exemplar enables us to pick out instances of the concept.

Medin gives the example of the belief, or theory, in our culture that membership of the concepts *male* and *female* is genetically determined. Yet when we pick someone out as male or female we rely on characteristics such as hair length, height, facial hair, and clothing that represent a mixture of secondary sexual characteristics and cultural conventions. Although these characteristics are not as reliable as genetic evidence, they are far from arbitrary. Not only do they have statistical validity, they are also tied to our biological and cultural conceptions of male and female. One of the things that theories do is to provide the causal links from underlying 'essences' to surface similarity. Thus Medin argues that people adopt an essentialist heuristic, namely, the hypothesis that things that look alike tend to share underlying principles. He argues that classifying on the basis of similarity will be relatively effective much of the time, but that similarity will yield to knowledge of deeper principles. Inductions based on features alone succeed only to the extent that the features are linked with an underlying causal structure.

This view is consistent with the developmental literature (e.g. Carey, 1985; Gelman, 1990; Keil, 1989, 1990; Markman, 1990; Spelke, 1990) on the use of theories by very young children to constrain the ways they see the world, since that work suggests that right from the start infants assume that some hidden principle defines a concept. What has to be learned is the precise set of objects that is defined by the principle, and in what other ways the objects may be similar or different.

Certainly young children will use taxonomic groupings when they are given a name for the concept (Markman and Hutchinson, 1984), suggesting a willingness to entertain a grouping on the basis of unknown principles. In addition, a body of work by Gelman and her colleagues strongly supports the view that young children are essentialists. For example, Massey and Gelman (1988) found that young children distinguish between animate and inanimate things based on the principle of whether or not they can move themselves. Three- and four-year-old children were shown photographs of animals (mammals and non-mammals), rigid complex objects (like an exercise bike), wheeled objects (like an old-fashioned two-wheeled bike), and statues. The children were asked whether the object in the picture could move itself up or down a hill. The children consistently said that the animals could go up and down the hill by themselves. They denied that statues had this ability, despite the fact that these items looked more like animals than did some of the non-mammals.

Gelman (1990) argues, therefore, that children rapidly distinguish between animate and inanimate objects because processing is constrained by causal principles of movement. Thus young children can classify animals as members of the concept *animal* without having to rely on perceptual similarity. Animate objects cause themselves to move or change; but the cause of inanimate motion is an external force. Gelman refers to these two causal mechanisms as the innards principle and the external-agent principle.

Gelman argues that the innards principle underlies children's understanding that animals have essences that define them; that is, the principle constrains children to assume that certain natural objects have something on the inside that governs their movement and change. Thus, if asked what is on the inside of different things, children give similar answers for things as diverse as elephant, mouse and people. By contrast, there is no a priori reason to think that the insides of inanimate objects are common across kinds of objects, nor even to be concerned about the insides of inanimates at all. Thus, children's answers to questions about the insides of inanimate things are more likely to indicate lack of knowledge or to be based on perceptual information, that the inside is the same as the outside (Gelman and Meck, reported in Gelman, 1990). Children appear to know, therefore, that animate objects have insides and they treat this characteristic as part of the essence of animacy. Of course, children still have to learn what is on the inside and why it matters, since these things vary considerably across cultures and periods of history.

What all this seems to suggest is that concepts may differ in their intensions and extensions. The intension of a concept, what brings out its relationship with other concepts, consists both of an underlying principle, knowledge of which may be intuitive and incomplete, and of a learned prototype or set of exemplars. However, the extension of a concept may be determined only by the prototype or set of exemplars, together with a similarity metric for determining the similarity between instances in the world and the prototype or exemplar. This is similar to a view espoused by Miller and Johnson-Laird (1976) in their study of word meanings and to the view espoused by Medin and Ortony (1989) in their distinction between the core of a concept and an identification procedure for identifying instances. Such views serve to unite the work on features with the work on theories.

SUMMARY

The classical view of concepts assumed that the definition of a concept was a set of necessary and sufficient features. Thus concepts were assumed to be arbitrary and all-or-none. This view was replaced by the probabilistic view, which claimed that the definition of a concept was a set of characteristic features. While there is much evidence to support the probabilistic view over the classical view, there is also much evidence to suggest that features alone cannot account for conceptual behaviour. In particular, the probabilistic view has difficulties with its explanation of typicality effects, and feature-based views in general have difficulties with complex concepts, and with the use of feature similarity as an explanation of what makes concepts cohere.

Consideration of these difficulties has led to the formulation of a theory-based view of concepts: the definition of a concept is an underlying causal theory, probably in the form of a schema. Evidence for theories comes from work on conceptual combination, work on learning, and work on constraints on the way young children form concepts. One way in which theories and features may be combined is through the use of an essentialist heuristic: people assume that things look alike because they share an underlying principle, even if knowledge of the underlying principle itself is incomplete and schematic. Thus, theories and features play distinct roles in conceptual behaviour: theories are necessary to form a concept at all, and features are necessary to enrich the concept in new ways and to facilitate the identification of instances.

CHAPTER 9   Problem solving

Problem solving is a fundamental and pervasive cognitive ability. The range of problems people encounter is vast: finding employment, arranging a birthday party, winning a game of chess, solving mathematical equations, getting a new computer to work and so on. The problems we are routinely faced with are so diverse that it seems reasonable to suppose that there is a small set of general purpose rules that are applied to each new problem that arises. This is the view that has been taken by the information processors (e.g. Newell and Simon, 1972) in their work on problem solving. However, individuals acquire considerable skill in particular domains, such as mathematics or psychology, and experts solve problems in their domains differently from novices. The information processors, therefore, also propose domain-specific rules that are used by experts.

The information processors have confined themselves to well-defined problems, such as mathematical problems, in which the component steps in the solution can be explicitly described. This has led them to emphasize the deliberate, strategic nature of problem solving. By contrast, the Gestalt psychologists examined ill-defined problems, such as writing an essay, in which the steps in the solution cannot be readily described. Consideration of ill-defined problems leads to an emphasis on the unconscious and intuitive nature of problem solving. Recently, some of the ideas of the Gestalt psychologists have been made explicit in theories of ana-logical problem solving (e.g. Gentner and Gentner, 1983; Holyoak and Thagard, 1990). This chapter will review the work in these two different traditions (concerned with well- and ill-defined problems respectively).

WELL-DEFINED PROBLEMS: INFORMATION PROCESSING

Shopping for groceries looks like a simple problem, but there are many different ways to solve it. One possible solution is a follows.

First, make a list of the things you need. You might do this by going through the cupboards to see what needs replenishing, making a list of the meals for the week, and checking whether or not you have the ingredients already. Once you have a list, you need to get to the shops, so you need to check that you have your car keys. Then you can leave the house, get into the car, decide which supermarket to go to and drive to it. At the supermarket, you must park the car, collect a trolley, find the things on your list, take them to the cash desk, decide how to pay for them, pay for them, pack them in bags, carry them to the car, pack them in the boot, drive home, carry them in, unpack them, and put everything away. Then you have reached your goal and the problem is solved. The goal seems very modest and easy to attain. But if you have lived in another country, where the culture and the language are unfamiliar you will appreciate the complexity involved, and the vast amount of knowledge about the world that is used to constrain each decision.

The steps in the shopping problem can be described as a goal and a series of sub-goals, together with a set of rules for achieving them. An example rule is shown below:

IF	the goal is to go shopping	Goal
	and there is a shopping list	precondition
	and I have my car keys	precondition
	and I am in the car	precondition
	and I know which supermarket to use	precondition
THEN	drive to the supermarket	Action

If the preconditions of a rule are not met, they can be used to call on other rules that treat each precondition as a new goal to be satisfied. The first precondition in the rule above is the goal in the example below:

IF	the goal is to have a shopping list	Goal
	and I know what ingredients are needed	precondition
	and I know what is missing from the cupboards	precondition
	and I have a paper and pen	precondition
THEN	write the ingredients on the paper	Action

The rules above are called production rules, and each one consists of a condition (or goal), any preconditions, and an action. The IF part of the rule consists of a set of clauses describing the goal and the pre-conditions for the action. The action is specified in the THEN clause. The rule is only considered when the situation in the world matches the conditions in the rule.

Problems have an initial state, a goal state, and a sequence of steps for getting from one to the other. The sequence that was described above was not the only possible sequence. It is not necessary to make a shopping list, for example, or to travel by car, or shop at a supermarket. Since the number of possible ways to get from an initial state to a goal state is enormous, the real skill in problem solving comes in selecting the best route to the goal. Working out how people find a good route lies at the heart of the information processing approach to problem solving (e.g. Newell and Simon, 1972).

The information processing view is grounded in a computer program called the General Problem Solver, or GPS (e.g. Newell and Simon, 1972; Simon, 1985). A major claim made by Newell and Simon is that the key features of GPS also characterize human problem solving. They supported this claim by asking human subjects to solve the same problems as those solved by GPS and to think aloud as they did so. Analysis of the resulting verbal protocols suggested that the human subjects were indeed performing in ways that were similar to GPS.

Newell and Simon concluded that some of the important characteristics of the human information processing system are that it is a serial system consisting of input (sensory) and output (motor) systems, an active processor, a long-term memory of infinite capacity, a short-term memory of limited capacity, a class of goal structures that are used to organize problem solving, and a set of production rules that characterize the way that the information is used. The active processor converts the input into a representation of the problem space that is held in short-term memory. Production rules are stored in long-term memory and the ones that are relevant to the problem are retrieved during comprehension and also form part of the representation in short-term memory. The production rules convert the representation of the initial state into the goal state so that a response can be made.

Problem solving is seen as consisting of a translation of the input into an internal representation of the problem. Problem solving methods are then applied to this representation to yield a solution.

Translation and representation

There is a large body of evidence that has emphasized the importance of the way a problem is interpreted for attaining a solution. The best-known example is chess (De Groot, 1965). De Groot asked what made a chess grandmaster a better player than other players. To answer that question he collected protocols from some of the best chess players in the world as they selected chess moves. He also tested their memories for chess positions. De Groot found that grandmasters do not spend time considering and discarding alternative moves until they find the best one, although this is what we might expect. Instead, they appear to choose the best move within five seconds or less of looking at the position for the first time. However, they then spend up to 15 minutes verifying the correctness of the move. This contrasts with weaker players who select their best move only after slow and painstaking thought. In particular, De Groot found that grandmasters selected fewer moves for verification than did weaker players, but the moves they selected were markedly better.

This suggests that grandmasters perceive chess positions differently from weaker players. It is as if the solution is contained in the interpretation of the problem. That this might be the case was suggested by the results of De Groot's memory investigations. He found that grandmasters were extremely accurate at reconstructing a chess position from memory after five seconds of study. De Groot also noticed that when reconstructing a position from memory, grandmasters did not put the pieces on the board at a constant rate. Instead, they placed pieces in bursts, putting four or five pieces on the board in quick succession and then pausing before putting down another four or five pieces, suggesting that grandmasters perceive patterns rather than isolated pieces. Chase and Simon (1973) confirmed that their superior performance was not simply because grandmasters have better memories than ordinary players: the memory of grandmasters was no better than that of weaker players when they had to recall non-legal configurations of chess pieces.

It appears, therefore, that the way a problem is interpreted contributes to its eventual solution. But how is this interpretation achieved? Hayes and Simon (1977); Simon and Hayes (1976) investigated this question by asking subjects to think aloud from the time of first reading the problem instructions to the time that they were ready to begin working on it. Hayes and Simon then analysed the resulting verbal protocols for information about the way the problem was interpreted.

Table 9.1. The monster problems (adapted from Hayes and Simon, 1977)

Monster problem 1 (Move)

Three five-handed extraterrestrial monsters were holding three crystal balls.

Because of the quantum-mechanical peculiarities of their neighbourhood, both monsters and globes come in exactly three sizes with no others permitted: small, medium and large.

The medium-sized monster was holding the small globe; the small monster was holding the large globe; and the large monster was holding the medium-sized globe.

Since this situation offended their sense of symmetry, they proceeded to transfer globes from one monster to another so that each monster would have a globe proportionate to his own size.

Monster etiquette complicated the problem since it requires:

- that only one globe may be transferred at a time;
- that if a monster is holding two globes, only the larger of the two may be transferred;
- that a globe may not be transferred to a monster who is holding a larger globe.

By what sequence of transfers could the monsters have solved this problem?

Monster problem 2 (Change)

The same three monsters from problem 1 found themselves in an identical situation: the medium-sized monster was holding the small globe; the small monster was holding the large globe; and the large monster was holding the medium-sized globe.

Since this situation offended their sense of symmetry, they proceeded to shrink and expand themselves so that each monster would hold a globe proportionate to his own size.

Monster etiquette complicated the problem since it requires:

- that only one monster may change at a time;
- that if two monsters are of the same size, only the monster holding the larger globe can change;
- that a monster may not change to the size of a monster who is holding a larger globe.

By what sequence of changes could the monsters have solved this problem?

The protocols revealed that subjects adopt the representation that derives in the most direct way from the language of the problem instructions. For instance, two structurally identical problems differed in their ease of solution, reflecting differences in the way that the two problems were represented. An easy problem and a difficult problem are shown in Table 9.1. These two problems are formally equivalent, the only difference between them is that in the first problem the globes must be moved, while in the second problem the monsters must change size.

Hayes and Simon found that a problem like monster problem 1 was translated into a representation that had 'move globe' operators, while a problem like monster problem 2 was translated into a representation that had 'change monster' operators. They therefore proposed that as each sentence is interpreted it is used to build a representation which consists of two parts: a description of the situation, and a set of operators. The description of the situation is called the problem space and it represents such things as the problem elements, the relations between the elements, and the initial and goal states of the problem. In the monster problems, the monsters and globes are the elements, and the relations include a monster holding a globe. The operators are encoded as production rules which change the representation of the initial state into a series of intermediate representations until a representation of the goal state is constructed.

Hayes and Simon also found that subjects had difficulty solving two problems if the second one involved a representation (that is, *move* versus *change*) different from the first problem. Similarly, Reed, Ernst and Banerji (1974) found that experience with a problem facilitated later attempts to solve a similar problem only if the second problem was simpler than the first (and only then if the relationship between the two problems was pointed out to the subject). This suggests that subjects construct a representation of a problem that is very similar to its wording. That is, they construct a propositional representation rather than a mental model. They are therefore unable to transfer what they have done with a previous, similar problem because the propositions in each case are different and so the similarity is not recognized. To recognize that two problems are similar requires going beyond propositional representations and realizing that the two problems describe similarly structured situations.

Problem solving methods

Newell and Simon propose that there is a small number of general purpose, domain-free strategies that can be used to solve any kind of problem. They called these strategies weak methods since they do not exploit the full range of domain-specific knowledge that might be available to an expert. The impetus for proposing these strategies is to indicate how people (and computers) can move through the problem space without having to search all possible states.

To return to the shopping example, one way to find a solution to the problem would be to select moves at random and so reach the solution by a process of trial and error. But the problem space for most problems, including going shopping, is enormous. If we used a random search, we may never reach the goal because it would be impossible to keep the complete problem space in memory as well as record all the moves that have been made so far. A typical game of chess, for example, involves about 60 moves, with an average of 30 alternative legal moves that could be chosen each time. This makes a total of 30^{60}, a number so astronomical that no computer, not even the fastest, can play chess by exploring every possible move sequence. For every problem, the size of the search space increases exponentially with the number of moves required for solution. This produces what is called a combinatorial explosion, a property that makes many problems impossible to solve by an exhaustive search of all possible paths.

This is the problem that Newell and Simon faced when developing their computer program. How could they constrain the size of the search set in ways that were comparable to those used by humans? They did this in GPS by proposing a number of strategies, or heuristics. Heuristics are rules of thumb which usually give the correct solution although this cannot be guaranteed. They are to be distinguished from algorithms, which guarantee that the correct solution to a problem will be found. For example, our knowledge of the rules of arithmetic provides us with algorithms or systematic means of solving problems, such as 265 multiplied by 542. However, in some circumstances, we may be satisfied to estimate the solution to a problem and decide for example, that 265 multiplied by 542 is in the region of 150,000. In this case we would be using a heuristic strategy. There are many instances where memory constraints or other processing limitations prohibit the use of algorithms, or where there is no algorithm available. In these instances, people make use of heuristics.

Means–ends analysis

Newell and Simon proposed a small number of general heuristic methods, the most important of which is means–ends analysis. This involves breaking a problem down into sub-problems and tackling each sub-problem using a difference reduction strategy. The general feature is that the current state is matched against the goal state and if there are differences between the two, a sub-goal is set up to eliminate the difference. As each sub-goal is met, the procedure is repeated until the current state matches the goal state.

In order to do this, GPS first finds a production rule where the goal state is encoded in the condition of the rule. Then GPS tries to find a production rule that will eliminate the difference between the current state and the goal state and create a new state. This becomes a sub-goal. GPS compares its current state to the condition of the new production rule, and if the two match, the action in the second part of the rule is carried out so that a new state is constructed. If the current state does not match a condition then a new sub-goal is set up that will make the conditions the same. Each sub-goal is stored in a push-down stack and once the current sub-goal has been satisfied, the next one on the stack is retrieved and pursued. (A push-down stack is like a spike for holding letters. Each new letter is added to the spike; the last letter to be put on is at the top of the stack and so is the first to be taken off.) Obviously, the more unsatisfied sub-goals that have to be held on the stack, the greater will be the memory load. However, a means–ends analysis ensures that the search through the problem space is directed rather than random because the requirement to eliminate the difference between the current state and the goal state renders a trial and error search unnecessary.

The use of means–ends analysis was illustrated at the beginning of this chapter with the production rule for shopping. In that example, if any of the preconditions of the rule do not hold in the current situation, then a sub-goal for achieving the missing precondition is set up. The second rule shown at the beginning of the chapter did this by taking the first precondition of the shopping rule and using it as a sub-goal in the new rule. If the achievement of the sub-goal results in all the preconditions in the shopping rule being met, the rule can be applied and the goal achieved. If, however, other preconditions of the shopping rule still have to be met, then other sub-goals are set up until all the preconditions are satisfied and the rule can be applied.

Means–ends analysis depends on knowledge of both the initial state and the goal state: it involves both working forwards from the initial state to the goal state and backwards from the goal state to the initial state. However, working forwards and working backwards can also be used independently when one of the two states is insufficiently specified in the problem. Forward search involves applying operators to the current state to generate a new state; backward search involves finding operators that could turn the goal state into the current state.

Human Problem Solving and GPS Compared

GPS shows a remarkable facility for solving problems. However, it embodies a number of assumptions about problem solving, which require consideration. First, it assumes that weak methods, such as means–ends analysis, are sufficient to solve a wide range of problems. Second, it assumes that problem solving is serial, each step occurring after the previous one has been completed. Third, it assumes that problem solving is a deliberate, conscious process that can be explicitly described by the problem solver. We can ask, therefore, how likely it is that these assumptions hold for human problem solving as well as for problem solving by machine.

Problem solving uses weak methods

The kinds of problems that have been studied by the information processors are not problems that people habitually encounter. Moreover, there is little in the way of background knowledge of such problems that someone can acquire to become an expert at them. Thus weak methods, as opposed to powerful domain-specific methods, are adequate for their solution. Indeed, when psychologists investigated the way that people solve such problems, their performance was remarkably similar to that of GPS. The differences that arose were mainly due to human memory limitations. In contrast to computers, people have increasing difficulty as the number of sub-goals to be held in memory increases (Egan and Greeno, 1974), and to the fact that people are loath to select correct moves that increase the difference between the current state and the goal state (e.g. Atwood and Polson, 1976; Thomas, 1974).

However, problems that require expertise are solved differently by experts and novices (and GPS). Simon and his colleagues (e.g. Simon and Gilmartin, 1973) proposed that people acquire domain-specific rules when they become experts and the use of these rules is what distinguishes them from experts. For example, Simon and Gilmartin (1973) used domain-specific production rules in a computer simulation of the performance of expert chess players. The program (called the Memory and Perceptual Processor or MAPP) includes production rules in which the condition part of a rule identifies a configuration of chess pieces on the board. If a configuration matches a condition, then the action part of the production is executed. The main features of the simulation that distinguish it from a simulation of novice chess playing are that the rules identify chess positions, not individual pieces, and that these positions automatically trigger the relevant actions in production rules.

Problem solving is a serial and conscious process

The performance of experts, as opposed to novices, also casts doubt on the serial and conscious assumptions of Newell and Simon. For example, chess masters select a move very quickly and fail to consider the range of moves that less strong players consider. The chess master seems to make an intuitive choice rather than a conscious one, and a choice that suggests that a serial search of plausible moves does not occur.

The assumptions of serial and conscious processes are reflected in the use of verbal protocols to investigate problem solving and these assumptions have been strongly contested in a critique of verbal protocols (Nisbett and Wilson, 1977). In a detailed reply to Nisbett and Wilson, Ericsson and Simon (1980) identified those aspects of problem solving that are conscious and those that are not. Ericsson and Simon suggest that the contents of short-term memory are amenable to conscious inspection while the contents of long-term memory and the processes of retrieving those contents are not. They also argue that it is short-term memory that is used for actively solving problems, thus defending the use of verbal protocols.

Nevertheless, the role of retrieval from long-term memory in problem solving also needs to be addressed. Newell and Simon do this in their discussion of domain-specific production rules. These are stored in long-term memory (and hence cannot be explicitly described), their conditions can be matched to the problem situation in parallel, and the corresponding action is then retrieved automatically without conscious reflection. Conscious and serial processes are only involved in evaluating the effects of the retrieved action. They are also involved in deciding between alternative actions when production rules are not retrieved and a declarative representation of the problem has been constructed instead.

To summarize, the information processors view problem solving as finding a route through the problem space. For problems like the Tower of Hanoi or the monster problem, the route is selected by using weak methods, such as means–ends analysis. For problems like playing chess, which involve knowledge of the problem domain, the problem is solved differently depending on the level of expertise of the problem solver. Novices use weak methods to select a route through the problem space. Experts use domain-specific production rules to yield a solution directly. For Newell and Simon the search through the problem space using weak methods lies at the heart of problem solving. It is this kind of problem solving that involves serial and conscious processing.

ILL-DEFINED PROBLEMS

With ill-defined problems, the importance of unconscious and parallel processes comes to the fore. Ill-defined problems are usually difficult, not because the problem space is large but because we have trouble thinking of a way to solve the problem at all. Consider the radiation problem used by the Gestalt psychologist Duncker (1945):

Suppose you were a doctor faced with a patient who has a malignant stomach tumour. It is impossible to operate on the patient, but unless the tumour is destroyed the patient will die. There is a kind of ray that at a sufficiently high intensity can destroy the tumour. Unfortunately, at this high intensity the healthy tissue that the rays pass through on the way to the tumour will also be destroyed. At lower intensities the rays are harmless to healthy tissues but will not affect the tumour either. How can the rays be used to destroy the tumour without injuring the healthy tissue?

Most solutions to this problem that people think of are impracticable, e.g. sending the rays down the oesophagus. The best solution seems to be to irradiate the tumour from multiple directions simultaneously with low intensity rays so that the rays converge on the tumour. However, people rarely think of this solution, although they recognize its merits as soon as they hear it. This suggests that people do not solve the radiation problem by finding a route through the problem space. What, then, is going on? One answer is that subjects fail to retrieve the relevant information from long-term memory. However, they can recognize the information in the solution even though they failed to recall it. This answer reflects Gestalt view of problem solving and current views of analogical thinking.

The Gestalt View of Problem Solving

The Gestalt psychologists distinguished between reproductive and productive thinking and argued that reproductive thinking relies on the rote application of past solutions to a problem, whereas productive thinking, or insight, involves a restructuring of the problem often in major ways (e.g. Wertheimer, 1959). An example of reproductive thinking is the blind application of meaningless formulae when first learning mathematics or physics, while an example of productive thinking is the realization that the formula 7/3 actually 'means' that seven things can be divided into three equal portions. In the language of information processing, these two types of thinking might be viewed as the application of stored production rules on the one hand, and the use of declarative knowledge to understand the problem on the other.

The application of previously learned rules in reproductive thinking may even inhibit the correct solution – a well-practised algorithm may be applied to an inappropriate problem. The Gestalt psychologists said that these 'blocks' to problem solving were due either to set (e.g. Luchins, 1942) or to functional fixedness (e.g. Duncker, 1945). Set is the rote application of learned rules to solve a problem that could be solved in other ways, while functional fixedness is stereotypical thinking due to focusing on the familiar function of an object to the exclusion of other less familiar functions. For example, a box is typically a container. Other possible functions of a box, such as acting as a support for other objects, may be ignored because they are less typical, even though the less typical function might be needed to solve a problem.

Insight

Insight refers to the sudden realization of the solution to the problem, which is brought about by a reorganization of the way in which the problem is interpreted. A stereotypical (though probably apocryphal) example is that of Archimedes suddenly realizing, while he was in the bath, that the volume of water displaced by a solid object was equal to the volume of the object. A more mundane example of an insight problem, from Kohler (1969), is shown in Figure 9.1.

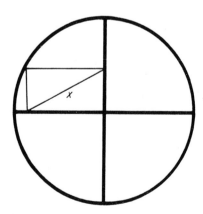

Line *x* is a side in a right angled triangle

Figure 9.1   The circle problem (adapted from Kohler, W. (1969); *The Task of Gestalt Psychology*. Copyright 1969 by PUP. Reproduced by permission of Princeton University Press)

In this problem, you are told that the radius of the circle is 5 inches, and you are asked to find the length of the line labelled x in the Figure 9.1. People generally puzzle over this problem for quite some time and attempt to solve it by retrieving learned rules of geometry and what is known about triangles. However, this application of learned rules will not solve the problem. What is needed is the insight that the problem concerns a rectangle whose diagonal is the radius of the circle, as can be seen by drawing in the second diagonal. This produces the solution: that the line x is 5 inches.

Insight seems to occur spontaneously without any conscious effort, a view that is supported by the results of a study by Maier (1933). He asked subjects to tie together two pieces of string that were hanging from the ceiling but too far apart to reach by hand. On the floor were a number of objects, such as pliers, that could be used to solve the problem. One solution is to use the pliers as a weight by tying it to the end of one of the pieces of string and so treat the string like a pendulum. After 10 minutes, a hint was given to the subjects who had not yet solved the problem. The experimenter walked past the string and set it swinging slightly by brushing against it with his shoulder. Some of the subjects solved the problem immediately after receiving this hint. However, they were unable to say how they had solved it. They did not seem to realize that the hint had helped them.

The sudden appearance of the solution through insight has been investigated by Metcalfe and Wiebe (1987). They presented subjects with either algebra problems or insight problems. An insight problem might be the following (from Metcalfe, 1986):

> A stranger approached a museum curator and offered him an ancient bronze coin. The coin had an authentic appearance and was marked with the date 544 BC. The curator had happily made acquisitions from suspicious sources before, but this time he promptly called the police and had the stranger arrested. Why?

While the subjects were solving the problems they gave ratings from 0 to 10 of how close they felt they were to the solution. If subjects were using means–ends analysis, or any heuristic search involving an account of the current state and the goal state, they should be able to report getting closer to the goal, since they would know that the difference between the current state and the goal state was being progressively reduced. The results showed that there was a gradual increase in the ratings for the algebra problems as the subjects approached the solution, consistent with the information processing view. But the ratings for the insight problems remained consistently low until just before the solution was reached, as if the solutions had suddenly appeared without prior warning. These results give empirical support to the view that insight is a real psychological phenomenon.

The problem with the Gestalt notion of insight is that there is no explicit account of the processes that underlie it. This contrasts with information processors who have provided an explicit account of the conscious serial search for a solution, and of the way that domain-specific production rules render explicit searching unnecessary. However, Holyoak and Thagard's (1990) model of analogical thinking does provide an explicit account of the way that knowledge is retrieved and used to solve a problem. Since both insight and analogical thinking involve the retrieval of relevant general knowledge from long-term memory, a theoretical account of analogical thinking may turn out to account for insight as well.

Analogical Thinking

An example

Gentner and Gentner (1983) were the first to show that analogies affect the way that people solve problems. They used two different analogies to teach groups of subjects, who were naïve about physical science, how electricity worked. One analogy was a water flow analogy while the other was a moving crowd analogy. In the water flow analogy, subjects were told that electricity flows through the wires of an electrical circuit in the same way that water flows through pipes. In the moving crowd analogy, subjects were told that electricity flows through the wires of an electrical circuit in the same way that a crowd of people moves through a passage. When subsequently tested on the effects of serial and parallel circuits, subjects who were taught the moving crowds analogy showed better understanding than those who were taught the water flow analogy. The group given the crowds analogy could treat a resistor as analogous to a turnstile and the electric current as analogous to the rate of movement of people. So the subjects could correctly infer that with a parallel circuit there would be an increase in current just as two parallel turnstiles in a passage would increase the rate of movement of people. Two serial resistors, on the other hand, reduce the current, just as two serial turnstiles would impede the flow of people. The group given the water analogy, however, would expect any resistance to the current, whether serial or parallel, to reduce it, just as any constrictions in a pipe would reduce the flow of water no matter how they were placed. Thus it appears that analogies influence our thought processes. The question is, therefore, how people use analogies to guide their thinking, even in the absence of explicit instructions.

Processes of Analogical Thinking

The processes of analogy involve four components:

1. interpretation and representation of the target problem,
2. the retrieval or selection of a plausibly useful source analogue,
3. mapping elements of the source analogue onto the target problem, and
4. the transfer of inferences from the source to the target domain.

Interpretation and representation concern language comprehension and are not specific to analogical thinking. In general analogy theorists assume that people construct a propositional representation of both the target problem and the source analogue, although they acknowledge that other forms of representation could also be used. The processes of retrieval and mapping are the key processes in analogical thinking. Retrieval occurs when a problem triggers the retrieval of a source analogue from long-term memory. Mapping occurs when the best set of correspondences is found between the source and the target. Mapping is necessary regardless of whether the source is spontaneously retrieved or is explicitly presented by a teacher. Once a source analogue has been mapped on to a target, all the novel information in the source is carried over to the target so that inferences can be made. This transfer of inferences is usually treated as part of the mapping process.

Models of analogical thinking have been proposed by Gentner (1983) and by Holyoak and Thagard (e.g. 1989, 1990). Gentner restricts her model to the mapping process, while Holyoak and Thagard's model has been developed to account for retrieval as well. The major difference between the two models is that Gentner claims that successful mapping will occur as long as the source is structurally similar to the target. Holyoak and Thagard, on the other hand, claim that the source must also be semantically and pragmatically similar to the target if successful mapping is to occur. In particular, Holyoak and Thagard emphasize the importance of pragmatic similarity.

THE PRAGMATIC MODEL OF ANALOGICAL THINKING

The pragmatic model has been developed over a number of years by Holyoak and his colleagues as part of a general model of induction (e.g. Gick and Holyoak, 1980, 1983; Holyoak, 1982, 1985; Holyoak and Koh, 1987; Holland, Holyoak, Nisbett and Thagard, 1986). More recent work (e.g. Holyoak and Thagard 1989, 1990) differs from the previous work by explicitly espousing a connectionist view of analogy.

Holyoak and Thagard's model is a constraint satisfaction model of analogue retrieval and mapping. They argue that both the retrieval of a suitable source analogue and completing a successful mapping are subject to the multiple, and parallel, constraints of syntax, semantics and pragmatics. These ensure that the source analogue that is retrieved and mapped on to the target is similar to the target in structure, content and overall goals. When all these constraints are satisfied, an analogy is retrieved and mapped onto the target problem.

Constraints on Analogical Processes

The major assertion of the model is that retrieval and mapping are governed by the constraints of structure, semantics and pragmatics. However, none of these constraints is absolute: they are regarded as pressures that guide processing, rather than requirements, and are the result of numerous local decisions about correspondences between propositions, predicates or arguments.

Structural constraints

Many people, particularly Gentner (1983) have emphasized the importance of structural constraints for successful mapping, and the evidence supports this emphasis. For example, Gick and Holyoak (1980) asked subjects to solve a problem about a general who wanted to capture a fortress. The fortress was situated in the middle of a country, surrounded by villages and with many roads radiating out from it. The general needed the strength of his entire army in order to take the fortress. However, the roads leading to the fortress were mined so that although a small group of men could pass across safely, a large group would set off the mines. Clearly, the general's situation was substantially parallel to that of the doctor in the radiation problem, described previously. When subjects were asked to use the fortress problem to help them solve the radiation problem, most of them did so successfully.

Gick and Holyoak used a number of different versions of the fortress story, each with a different solution. These included a solution where the general found an unguarded road that he sent his entire army along, and another where he divided the army into small groups and sent them simultaneously down the roads leading to the fortress so that they converged on it at the same time. The results showed that the different versions had clear effects on the solutions that subjects produced to the radiation problem. The subjects who heard the fortress story in which the general found an unguarded road were especially likely to suggest sending the rays down an 'open passage' such as the oesophagus to reach the tumour. By contrast, subjects who heard the fortress story in which the general had small groups converge on the fortress were likely to suggest the 'convergence' solution of directing multiple weak rays at the tumour from different directions. However, these results held only when subjects were explicitly told to use the first story as an analogy for solving the radiation problem. There was little spontaneous use of the analogy in the absence of specific instructions. Thus the analogy was successfully mapped on to the target problem, but was not spontaneously retrieved.

Gick and Holyoak argue that the structural similarity between the two problems facilitated successful mapping. For example, the goals of the radiation problem are that the rays destroy the tumour but do not destroy healthy tissue. These goals can be expressed as propositions thus:

DESTROY (ray,tumour)
NOT-DESTROYED (tissue)

The goals of the fortress problem are that the army capture the fortress without the troops being killed, expressed propositionally as follows:

CAPTURE (army,fortress)
NOT-KILLED (troops)

Although the contents of the two goals are different (they are dissimilar semantically), their structures are the same. They each consist of two propositions, the first containing two arguments, the second containing one.

Holyoak and Thagard propose two structural constraints. One says that mappings should be one-to-one. The other says that mappings should be structurally consistent. One-to-one mapping means that each proposition in the source domain maps on to exactly one proposition in the target domain. One-to-one mapping ensures that the first proposition of the fortress problem maps only on to the first proposition of the radiation problem and not to the second as well. If there is a one-to-one structural mapping between the propositions in two domains then the domains are said to be isomorphic (Holland, Holyoak, Nisbett and Thagard, 1986).

Structural consistency means that if a proposition in the target corresponds to a proposition in the source, then the constituent predicates and arguments of the paired propositions should also be paired. In the radiation and fortress problems, as well as the overall propositions being linked together, CAPTURE is mapped on to DESTROY, *army* on to *ray*, *fortress* onto *tumour* and so on, even though *army* and *fortress*, for example, are nothing like *ray* and *tumour* in their meanings.

However, structural similarity alone will overgenerate candidate analogies (Holyoak and Thagard, 1989, 1990). Holyoak and Thagard (1989) give the following example: *John is taller than Bill, and Bill is taller than Sam* is structurally analogous to *Mary is heavier than Susan, and Susan is heavier than Beth*. The propositions in each statement are isomorphic, with each statement consisting of two-place predicates. For example, TALLER THAN (John, Bill) is isomorphic with HEAVIER THAN (Mary, Susan). In this case, the propositions that are mapped are also semantically similar. Yet there is an equally valid isomorphism between the first analogy above and *Communism is more radical than socialism, and socialism is more radical than capitalism.* But here the analogy does not work because, despite the structural similarity, there is no semantic similarity between the two statements. Structural constraints alone allow the analogy between the *taller than* statement and the *communism* statement. The addition of semantic constraints would rule out the *communism* analogy but still allow the *heavier than* analogy, a situation which seems closer to the way that people use analogies.

Semantic constraints

Semantic constraints ensure that arguments and predicates in the target and source domain are semantically similar. For example, if an argument in the target domain is a synonym of an argument in the source domain then the two arguments are semantically similar.

An experiment by Gentner and Toupin (1986) supports the proposal that semantic constraints are used. They presented two groups of children with a series of simple stories about animals. After a child had acted out one version of the story (the source), the experimenter asked him or her to act out the same story but with different characters (the target). The children did not have to retrieve the analogy of the first story because they were told to use it, but the way that they acted out the stories revealed how well they could map the analogous story on to the new story. Semantic similarity was manipulated by varying the similarity of the animals in the various roles. High semantic similarity was achieved in the similar objects/similar roles condition: if the target story was about a dog, a seal, and a penguin, in particular roles, then a semantically similar source story involved a cat, a walrus, and a seagull in the same roles. Medium semantic similarity was achieved in the dissimilar objects condition: the source story involved a lion, camel and giraffe. Low semantic similarity was achieved in the similar objects/dissimilar roles condition: the source and target stories contained similar characters, as in the high similarity condition, but they played different roles in the two stories. The results showed that the semantically similar source stories consistently facilitated performance relative to the semantically dissimilar stories. Performance was uniformly good in the high similarity condition, but as the semantic transparency of the mapping decreased from high similarity to medium and low similarity, performance systematically declined.

Thus, semantic similarity is also used in mapping. However, a study by Holyoak and Koh (1987) varied both structural and semantic similarity. They used four versions of a light bulb problem as analogues of the radiation problem and found that both kinds of similarity were necessary for spontaneous retrieval (which includes mapping), but only structural similarity was necessary for mapping alone. On the basis of these findings, Holyoak and Koh argue that semantic similarity is the major constraint on retrieval, while syntactic similarity is more important for mapping.

Pragmatic constraints

Holyoak and Thagard argue that pragmatic goals are central to the mapping process. Pragmatic constraints ensure that the goals of the problem solver, such as solving the problem, answering a question, or arguing for a desired conclusion, help both retrieval and mapping. A number of different types of pragmatic constraints have been proposed. For example, Winston (1980) has emphasized the importance of causal knowledge, while others (e.g. Anderson and Thompson, 1989; Keane, 1990) have focused on the roles of high level plans and functional knowledge.

Pragmatic constraints favour correspondences that are pragmatically important to the problem solver. An element may be judged sufficiently important that some mapping for it should be found. Alternatively, a particular correspondence between two elements may be presumed to hold and so determine the inferences that are made. Consider the following example from Holyoak and Thagard (1989). Suppose someone is assessing the nature of the Contras' attempt to overthrow the government of Nicaragua in 1987 and is considering both Hungary and Israel as possible source analogues. All three analogues involve attempts to overthrow the government. But the two source analogues contain additional propositions that are therefore candidate inferences. The Hungary analogue categorizes the

Hungarians as freedom fighters and the United States support them. By contrast, the Israel analogue categorizes the PLO as terrorists and the United States do not support them. Now suppose that the problem solver is motivated to support the Contras. This is regarded in Holyoak and Thagard's model as a presumed correspondence, and hence will be treated as an additional mapping between the Contras target and the Hungary source relative to the Israel source. This additional mapping increases the likelihood that the mapping between the target and the Hungary source will be selected in preference to that between the target and the Israel source. Thus, the inference that, like the Hungarians, the Contras are freedom fighters will be carried over.

Keane (1990) provides empirical evidence for pragmatic constraints on analogies. He presented subjects with Maier's (1933) two-string problem.

Table 9.2. The higher order categories from the fire story

The fire

SETTING

A large number of people were trapped on the upper stories of a burning skyscraper. The authorities decided that the only way to save the people would be to use a helicopter. So, the air force were called and soon a helicopter arrived on the scene.

FAILED PLAN

At first the helicopter positioned itself near the burning building and a rope was lowered to where the people were. One of the people then grabbed hold of the rope by using a stick to bring it within reach. Then the helicopter carried this person to the ground. However, it soon became clear that this method was too slow and would not rescue all the people before the fire reached them. So, another method was tried.

SUCCESSFUL PLAN

The helicopter positioned itself between the burning building and another nearby building. The rope was thrown to the people in the burning building and one of them grabbed hold of it. Then, holding on to the rope this person swung from the burning building to the nearby building. Using this swinging method all the people were able to evacuate the burning building before the fire reached them.

Note: The categories shown in capitals were not included in the experiment
Source: Keane, 1990)

Two possible solutions are: (1) to use a stick to bring the furthermost string closer and then tie the two together, and (2) to swing the furthermost string like a pendulum, by attaching pliers to the end of it, and then, while holding the near string, catch hold of the other on the upswing. Before presenting the string problem, Keane presented his subjects with a story about a fire. In one version of the story an analogue to the pendulum solution is successful while an analogue to the stick solution is a failure. In another version of the story, the 'pendulum' plan failed and the 'stick' plan was successful. (See Table 9.2.)

Keane argued that a sensible pragmatic strategy would be to use the successful plan as the source analogue for the string problem, because the problem solver's goal is to find a successful solution. Thus, if pragmatic factors do play a role in problem solving, then subjects who read the version of the fire story shown in Table 9.2 should produce predominantly pendulum solutions to the string problem, while subjects who read the fire story with the failed and successful solutions reversed should produce predominantly stick solutions to the string problem. The results showed that subjects typically used the successful plan, irrespective of its specific content and ignored the failed plan, thus confirming the importance of pragmatic goals in problem solving.

Multiple Constraint Satisfaction

According to Holyoak and Thagard (1989, 1990) syntactic, semantic and pragmatic constraints are applied in parallel during problem solving. They each excite or inhibit a connectionist network which consists of concepts in long-term memory. The patterns of activation that result from encountering a problem lead to a number of concepts being activated. Once the overall activation level has settled to a stable state, the network of concepts with the highest activation level will be mapped.

Holyoak and Thagard have developed computer programs that use connectionist networks to simulate analogue mapping (Holyoak and Thagard, 1989) and analogue retrieval (Holyoak and Thagard, 1990). Structural constraints are central in the mapping process while semantic constraints are central in the retrieval process. Pragmatic constraints are important for both processes. These simulations are 'hybrid' symbolic connectionist models (see Chapter 2). They use parallel constraint satisfaction on symbolic (propositional) representations.

Simulations have been run on a range of different analogies and they accord well with the behaviour of subjects. For example, the mapping program successfully simulated the radiation problem and all four similarity versions of Holyoak and Koh's (1987) light bulb problem. The program finds the correct set of mappings for all four versions. In addition, cycles to success did not differ as a function of semantic similarity, but they did differ as a function of structural similarity, which was the major feature of Holyoak and Koh's results. The program also finds the appropriate mapping for the radiation problem in the convergence version of the fortress analogy (Gick and Holyoak, 1980), as well as successfully simulating a wide range of other analogical problems. (See Holyoak and Thagard, 1990.)

To summarize, Holyoak and Thagard's view the processes of retrieving and mapping a source analogue on to a target problem as being subject to syntactic, semantic and pragmatic constraints that operate in parallel. They suggest that syntactic constraints are most important for mapping and semantic constraints are most important for retrieval, while pragmatic constraints are important in both processes. By adopting a parallel, connectionist system, Holyoak and Thagard are able to account for seemingly intuitive processes that occur outside of conscious awareness.

SUMMARY

Two alternative views of problem solving have been presented in this chapter. The information processing view sees problem solving as a conscious and serial search through the problem space. Experts, however, retrieve domain-specific production rules, using unconscious and parallel processes. The application of production rules may yield a solution directly. The analogical view, on the other hand, concentrates on situations where rapid, unconscious, and intuitive solutions are produced, regardless of whether the problem solver is an expert or a novice. Rather than accounting for these unconscious, parallel processes by postulating the use of production rules, Holyoak and

Thagard argue that the information is retrieved from a connectionist network in which multiple constraints determine the final pattern of activation.

Thus, information processors try to account for both conscious and unconscious processes while the analogical theorists only account for unconscious processes. The question that arises is whether production rules or connectionist networks give the best account of unconscious processes. One answer to this question is to argue that both a rule-based and a connectionist system are necessary. Production systems seem to provide the best account of automatic actions, whether they are real actions such as driving a car or cognitive skills such as applying mathematical equations and they frequently depend upon extensive practice in a domain. Connectionist systems seem to provide the best account of the retrieval of conceptual (declarative) knowledge, a topic that seems to have been ignored by the information processors.

In addition, it seems likely that the conscious, strategic search proposed by the information processors operates on retrieved knowledge. Simply retrieving and mapping a source analogue may not be sufficient to solve a problem. A conscious search through the problem space is also necessary to pursue the implications of a retrieved analogy and to evaluate their validity (Holyoak, 1991). A conscious search may also be needed to evaluate the outcome of an action triggered by a production rule.

CHAPTER 10   Expertise, knowledge and creativity

This chapter examines Anderson's (1983) model of the acquisition of expertise that assumes that experts solve problems by using automatic procedures while novices use deliberate strategies that are applied to declarative knowledge. A review of the key characteristics of expertise indicates that the use of automatic procedures accounts for some but not all of the features of skilled performance, since the acquisition of declarative (or conceptual) knowledge is also important. The distinction between routine and adaptive expertise (Hatano, 1988; Holyoak (1991) distinguishes between these two components of skilled performance, automatic procedures and conceptual knowledge, and suggests that conceptual knowledge is crucial for ensuring that procedural knowledge can be transferred to new situations. However, the use of automatic procedures is important for freeing up capacity in short-term memory so that further learning can occur. Work on creative problem solving also emphasizes declarative rather than procedural knowledge. Traditional views see creativity as akin to insight, which is comparable to adaptive expertise, while the information processors see creativity as a serial search through the problem space.

THE ACQUISITION OF EXPERTISE

Anderson's (1983) model of the acquisition of cognitive skills embodies all the key assumptions of the information processing view of problem solving. In particular, it assumes that novices solve problems in the same way as GPS, using general purpose, domain-free strategies that operate on declarative knowledge. Experts, on the other hand, have complex production rules at their disposal that are domain-specific and that fire automatically when their conditions are met.

Anderson proposes that during the acquisition of expertise, declarative representations are turned into procedural representations. When problem solving is successful, the successful solution path is encoded as a new, specialized production rule that allows more efficient problem solving in the future. In addition, the production rules of experts encode large chunks of conditions and long sequences of actions that can be executed automatically.

Anderson's theory is called the adaptive control of thought and it has three major components: a working memory, a long-term declarative memory, and a long-term production memory. Representations of the environment are encoded in working memory and stored in long-term declarative memory. Working memory may subsequently retrieve this information in problem solving and if the information matches a condition in production memory, the production is executed. Declarative memory encodes facts which are represented as schemas, while production memory encodes actions which are represented as production rules. By including both declarative knowledge and productions, Anderson provides an account of how to move from thought to action. In addition, his model of learning is an attempt to account for how our initial groping attempts at solving a problem eventually become fast, automatic actions. In the model, learning consists of three stages: a declarative stage, a procedural stage, and a tuned procedures stage.

The Declarative Stage

Information about a new domain is normally provided by a teacher in declarative form and stored in declarative memory. General problem-solving methods are applied to the retrieved declarative knowledge to produce the appropriate action. Consider learning to drive. Initially, the new information, presented by an instructor, is explicitly stored in declarative memory. In order to carry out a sequence of actions, such as that needed for changing gear, each fact is retrieved and stored with other retrieved facts in short-term memory and used to work out what to do.

The Procedural Stage

Successful sequences of activity that are produced in the above manner are eventually compiled into productions. Compilation results from two effects of practice: composition and proceduralization.

Composition eliminates unnecessary steps from a sequence of productions, by constructing a single macroproduction from a pair of existing productions that have the same goal, and that frequently occur in succession during problem solving. The IF clauses and the THEN clauses of the two productions are combined to produce a single rule. Anderson (1983) gives the example of learning someone's telephone number, where the following two productions might be involved:

P1   IF   the goal is to dial X's telephone number
              and Xdigit1 is the first digit of X's telephone
                number
      THEN   dial Xdigit1

P2   IF   the goal is to dial X's telephone number
              and Xdigit1 has just been dialled
              and Xdigit2 is after Xdigit1
      THEN   dial Xdigit2

Composition combines these two productions into a single macroproduction like the following:

P1&P2 IF   the goal is to dial X's telephone number
              and Xdigit1 is the first digit of X's telephone
                number
              and Xdigit2 is after Xdigit1
      THEN   dial Xdigit1 and then Xdigit2

This composed macroproduction still requires that information, such as the telephone number itself, be retrieved from declarative long-term memory, and held in working memory so that it can be matched to the second and third clauses of P1&P2. To eliminate the involvement of long-term declarative memory altogether, proceduralization is necessary.

Proceduralization transforms declarative knowledge into procedures for actions. This means that specific actions can be retrieved directly. This not only has the effect of speeding up performance but also reduces the load on short-term memory, since there is no longer the need to keep all the declarative information in memory while the action is executed. Proceduralization occurs when variables in a production rule, such as X or Xdigit1, are replaced by specific values, such as the name of a person or the person's telephone number. For example, with repeated use, the rule P1&P2 above will be supplemented by a number of specific rules such as:

P*   IF   the goal is to dial Susan's telephone number
               and 3 is the first digit of Susan's telephone
                 number
               and 8 is after 3
      THEN   dial 3 and then 8

This second, more specific rule circumvents the need to find the telephone number and store it in declarative form in short-term memory until the procedure has been executed. It also makes the rule highly specific: the domain-specific declarative knowledge has been transformed into a procedure.

The Tuned Procedures Stage

The tuned procedures stage involves the strengthening, generalization, and discrimination of procedures (Anderson, Kline, and Beasley, 1977, 1980). Productions are strengthened every time they are used successfully. They are generalized by the replacement of some of their conditions with variables. Anderson (1983) gives the example of a person learning bridge who might have acquired the following pair of productions:

> IF   I am playing no trump
> and I have a king in the suit
> and I have a queen in that suit
> and my opponent leads a lower card in that suit
> THEN   I can play the queen

> IF   I am playing no trump
> and I have a queen in the suit
> and I have a jack in that suit
> and my opponent leads a lower card in that suit
> THEN   I can play the jack

Generalization replaces all the instances by variables, which results in:

> IF   I am playing no trump
> and I have Xcard1 in the suit
> and Xcard1 is an honour
> and I have Xcard2 in the suit
> and Xcard2 is an honour
> and Xcard1 follows Xcard2
> and my opponent leads a lower card in that suit
> THEN   I can play Xcard2

Discrimination occurs when a production cannot be executed. Suppose someone learning geometry has the following production:

> P1   IF   the goal is to prove that UVW and XYZ are
> congruent triangles
> THEN   try the method of side-angle-side and set as
> sub-goals:
> 1. To prove that UV and XY are congruent
> 2. To prove that angles UVW and XYZ are
> congruent
> 3. To prove that WU and ZX are congruent

This rule will work only if the angles of UVW and XYZ are given, otherwise the rule cannot be used successfully. Attempts to use the rule in the absence of the relevant information will result in the addition of the discriminating information in the IF part of the rule, as follows:

P2   IF   the goal is to prove that UVW and XYZ are congruent triangles
and the angles UVW and XYZ are mentioned
THEN   try the method of side-angle-side and set as sub-goals:
1. to prove that UV and XY are congruent
2. to prove that angles UVW and XYZ are congruent
3. to prove that WU and ZX are congruent

Anderson's theory of skill acquisition provides an explanation for the processes that underlie the change from being a novice to being an expert. The theory assumes that experts differ from novices in a number of specific ways that derive from their use of productions. However, investigations into the nature of skilled performance that have been carried out since Anderson's model was first proposed suggest that the picture is more complex than Anderson's model supposes. Some of the key characteristics of skilled performance that these investigations have uncovered are summarized below. They are each presented from the stand-point of Anderson's model after which the complications for the model are described. These complications suggest that the way in which auto-matic procedures are used needs to be more carefully specified. They also suggest that the use of procedures is not the only feature of expertise and that the acquisition of declarative knowledge is equally important. The characteristics that are listed have been culled from discussions by Anderson (1985), Chi, Glaser and Farr (1988), and Holyoak (1991).

CHARACTERISTICS OF EXPERTISE: THE INFORMATION PROCESSING VIEW AND ITS COMPLICATIONS

(1) Experts are Superior at Perceiving Patterns in the Environment

Ever since the early studies of chess grandmasters it has been supposed that experts perceive patterns rather than isolated elements.

This ability is captured in Anderson's model by the compilation and generalization of procedures. Computer simulations of expert performance also use production rules where the condition part of the rule identifies a configuration of information in the environment (e.g. Simon and Gilmartin's (1973) simulation of chess experts and Larkin's (1981) simulation of physics experts).

However, Holyoak (1991) argues that pattern perception does not invariably accompany expertise. He refers to the work of Allard and Starkes (1991) on expert volleyball players. Unlike experts in other sports, expert volleyball players do not show a superior ability to recall offensive volleyball patterns, although they do show a superior ability to detect the ball when presented with a slide of a position. Allard and Starkes argue that this is because offensive positions in volleyball are designed to deceive the defenders and so are not reliable predictors of the ball's positions. Thus, superior pattern perception seems to depend on its importance in the domain.

(2) Experts use Compiled Procedures

Anderson's model views expertise as the result of the automatic firing of compiled procedures. However, this suggests a rigidity of performance that is absent in truly skilled performance. A good example is the performance of expert radiologists (Lesgold, Rubinson, Feltovich, Glaser, Klopfer and Wang, 1988). Lesgold et al. showed both experts and novices an X-ray of a healthy person who had a lobe of her lung removed 20 years earlier. This caused the heart to shift its position so that it appeared to be wider than normal. Many of the subjects, both experts and novices, mistook the appearance for an enlarged heart, a sign of congestive heart failure, which is a very serious condition. When told to re-examine the film after learning that the patient had been found perfectly healthy in a recent physical examination and had undergone surgery a number of years before, the experts quickly revised their opinions. But the novices still insisted that the patient was dying. The experts, therefore, in contrast to the novices, seem to have acquired an understanding that allows them to be flexible in their use of pre-established routines and categories and that enables them to recognize and deal with novel problems.

(3) Expertise is Acquired through the Automatization of Conscious Declarative Knowledge

According to Anderson's model, automatic processes correspond to the use of procedures that have been acquired through practice. That is, learning results in explicit declarative knowledge becoming implicit procedural knowledge. However, Berry and Broadbent (1984) present evidence to suggest that, with complex tasks, implicit processes may be learned without ever having been explicit. They presented subjects with a computerized control task concerning output in a sugar factory. Over a series of trials, the subjects had to manipulate the size of the workforce so that a target level of sugar production was achieved. Subjects successfully learned to perform this task, but they were unable to answer questions about the relationship between the two variables when asked after the experiment. In a subsequent experiment, verbal instructions improved the answer to direct questions but had no effect on performance in the control task. Broadbent, Fitzgerald and Broadbent (1986) argue that successful actions and successful verbal responses can be manipulated independently, thus suggesting that implicit and explicit knowledge can be the result of separate processes. The acquisition of language can be seen as another example of the acquisition of implicit knowledge that was never explicit. These observations suggest that the acquisition of skills is more complex than Anderson supposed and does not invariably result from the proceduralization of declarative knowledge.

The above review of three characteristics of skilled performance suggest that Anderson's model of skill acquisition requires certain modifications. Procedures encode patterns in the environment only if perception of patterns is necessary for successful performance; experts show a greater flexibility in their use of procedures than is implied by Anderson's model; and the processes of learning may involve more than the conversion of explicit declarative knowledge into automatic procedures, since some implicit knowledge may never have been explicit. The following review of a further six characteristics suggests that declarative knowledge is also important in skilled performance. Specifically, declarative knowledge may be necessary to account for the transfer of knowledge across domains, for the continuing use of general purpose weak methods by experts, for the difficulties experts frequently encounter in skilled performance, for the learning differences between good and poor students, for the deep understanding of experts, and for experts' use of mental models as opposed to propositional representations.

(4) Expertise is Domain Specific

Domain specificity is a major feature of expertise and, according to Anderson, domain-specific knowledge does not transfer to other domains (e.g. Singley and Anderson, 1989), unless the domains share identical procedures. For instance, the superior memories of chess grandmasters are confined to legal chess positions and do not reflect a general advantage in memory ability (Chase and Simon, 1973). Similarly, Voss and Post (1988) have shown that experts in chemistry cannot transfer their expertise to other domains. Chemists solve political science problems much like novices, describing the causes for the problem at a very concrete and specific level, whereas domain experts describe more abstract causal categories.

However, other evidence disputes the idea that expertise does not transfer to other domains. Both Gentner (1983) and Holyoak (1985) have emphasized the use of analogical thinking as a means of transferring knowledge from one domain to another. More strikingly, Ericsson and Polson (1988) describe a headwaiter with an exceptional memory for restaurant orders. The waiter (JC) realized that customers noticed when he remembered their orders and gave him larger tips. Consequently JC made a greater effort to remember orders and was further rewarded with more large tips, which increased his motivation further. JC can remember complete dinner orders from over 20 people at several different tables without the use of any external memory aids.

Ericsson and Polson claim that JC's performance conforms to their model of skilled memory (Chase and Ericsson, 1981, 1982). This model holds that the effects of chunking in short-term memory cannot account for the effects of practice on increased memory span. Instead, skilled memory depends on a more efficient use of long-term memory: subjects generate long-term memory encodings of the presented information; the stored information is then rapidly accessed through retrieval cues associated with the encoding during initial storage. Investigations of JC supported this proposal. However, Ericsson and Polson also found that JC could use his memory skill to recall information from different domains and not just from meal orders. They suggest that JC has a sophisticated understanding of his own memory ability as well as a number of metacognitive skills that he exploits in memorizing any kind of material – as long as it is already encoded in his long-term memory. This ability to transfer memory skills to a new domain indicates that expertise is not always domain-specific.

(5) Experts use Productions, Novices use Declarative Knowledge

Anderson's model implies that experts have no use for general purpose heuristics operating on declarative knowledge. However, this does not seem to be the case. Experts do use general purpose heuristics, but the sophistication of their declarative knowledge leads to the heuristics being used differently by experts compared to novices.

In general, novices rely on a means-ends analysis which emphasizes a backward search from the goal while experts rely on a forward search from the given information in the problem. The clearest example of this comes from Larkin's (1981) investigations of expert and novice physicists. Larkin compared the performance of novices with that of experts on problems like the one below:

> An object dropped from a balloon descending at 4 metres per second lands on the ground 10 seconds later. What was the altitude of the balloon at the moment the object was dropped?

When novices solved this problem, they behaved like GPS (described in Chapter 9). They first formed a representation of the problem that consisted of the initial state and the final goal state. They then worked backwards from the goal state by retrieving an equation that contained the goal state, and then constructed sub-goals to find the values of other variables in the equation. The general strategy is illustrated in Table 10.1.

Table 10.1. A novice solution to the physics problem given in the text

1.   Set goal: Find distance travelled
      Distance = average velocity × time interval
      Known: time = 10 seconds
      Unknown: average velocity
      2.   Set sub-goal: Find average velocity
            Average velocity = (initial velocity + final velocity)/2
            Known: initial velocity = 4 m/s
            Unknown: final velocity
            3.   Set sub-goal: Find final velocity
                  Final velocity = initial velocity + (acceleration ×
                      distance)
                  Known: initial velocity = 4 m/s
                          acceleration = 9.8 m/s squared
                          time = 10 seconds
                  Unknown: none
                  Substitute: Final velocity = 4 m/s + 9.8 m/s
                      squared × 10 s
            4.   Pop sub-goals:
      5.   Average velocity = 4 m/s + 9.8 m/s squared + 10 s
                      = 102 m/s
6.   Distance = 53 m/s × 102 m/s/2
            = 530 m

Source: Adapted from Stillings et al., 1987.

There is a considerable memory load involved in holding the results of sub-goals until they can be used. However, the strategic differences between novices and experts can be seen most clearly by the excerpt from an expert's verbal protocol in Table 10.2.

Table 10.2. An expert solution to the problem given in the text

It's already got a velocity of 4 metres per second and it accelerates at 9.8 metres per second squared so its final velocity 10 seconds later, well, let's say its total additional velocity 10 seconds later would be 98 metres per second and that plus the 4 that it had to start with would be 102 metres per second

so its average velocity during that period would be 106 over 2 or 53 metres per second

and at 10 seconds that would mean it had dropped 530 metres.

Source: Stillings et al., 1987.

In the expert's protocol, the first paragraph corresponds to the sub-goal numbered 3 in the novice's solution, the second paragraph corresponds to the sub-goal numbered 2, and the last paragraph corresponds to the goal state, numbered 1 in the novice's solution. In other words, where a novice works backwards from the goal, an expert works forwards from the known variables without attending to the goal.

Experts' use of strategies differs according to both the nature of the problem and the domain itself. Expert physicists revert to a backwards search when faced with non-routine problems (Tweney, 1985). Computer programming experts always seem to use a backward search, probably because the initial state places few constraints on the solution path, while the goal state provides a clear statement of what needs to be done. However, expert computer programmers do use strategies that reflect their knowledge of the domain. Novices use a depth-first strategy, in which all the details of one sub-problem are worked out before the next sub-problem is identified. Experts use a breadth first strategy, in which all the sub-problems are identified at the top level before any of them is developed into a part of the program. Since the solution of one sub-problem may affect the solution of another, this strategy is clearly the most sensible and reflects domain-specific knowledge. Thus experts do use general-purpose heuristics to search the problem space. However, in contrast to novices, an expert's search is more severely constrained by knowledge of the specific domain.

Experts also use declarative knowledge differently from novices. Experts seem to flesh out their initial representation of the problem with additional background information, and spend more time in clarifying the initial problem (often drawing a diagram) than in solving equations. This contrasts with novices who apply the known formulae by rote and make less effort to understand the problem (Larkin, 1981). This is probably because experts have spare short-term memory capacity available for clarifying the problem.

(6) Experts Solve Problems more Rapidly than Novices

A key assumption of Anderson's model of expertise is that experts solve problems easily and quickly, through their use of productions.

This suggests that experts solve problems automatically, never have to puzzle things out, and never run into difficulties. Such a clear-cut picture is obviously untenable. Holyoak (1991) refers to the work of Scardamalia and Bereiter (1991) who point out that expert writers work longer and with more worry on the same assigned tasks as novices. Expert writers seem to work at the limits of their competence and so rarely rely simply on the automatic execution of well-learned procedures. Writing is not the only exception to Anderson's picture of expertise. The life histories of painters, composers, and poets are full of accounts of the difficulties of producing new works (see, e.g., Barron, 1969). Descriptions of scientific discoveries reveal that science too is fraught with difficulties. This can be seen in Tweney's (1985) analysis of Faraday's work, and in Watson's (1968) story of *The Double Helix*, an account of the race to discover the structure of DNA. Clement (1989) has also shown that expert physicists have difficulties with non-routine problems. Thus the picture emphasized by Anderson is only part of the story.

(7) Expertise is a Function of Practice

Anderson's model places a major emphasis on practice. However, the nature of the practice may be more important than its frequency. This is suggested by a study of the way that physics students learn new material (Chi, Bassok, Lewis, Reimann, and Glaser, 1989).

Chi et al. asked subjects to study four chapters of a physics text and to solve a series of problems after each chapter. Analysis of the students' verbal reports revealed that good students tended to study example problems by explaining and justifying each action, and by relating their explanations to the principles outlined in the text. This resulted in an increase in their knowledge of the principles concerned. By contrast, poor students rarely explained the example problems to themselves. When they did, their explanations did not seem to connect with their understanding of the principles in the text, and so the study of the examples did not result in any increase of their knowledge of these principles. In addition, good students successfully monitored their comprehension successes and failures, while studying the examples. Their ability to detect comprehension failures led them to attempt to understand the material. Poor students, on the other hand, were less accurate at detecting comprehension failures. Where they did, they occurred when mathematical expressions were manipulated, rather than at places where conceptual principles were instantiated.

Chi et al. suggest that the good students' explanations create inference rules that encode specific examples of the principles introduced in the text. Once these inference rules are constructed, then the process of compilation can take over and these declarative inference rules may be converted to procedures. Thus, the nature of the practice plays a crucial role in the acquisition of expertise. Practice and repetition need to be of the right kind.

(8) Experts have Superior Memories for Domain-specific Information

The superior memory performance of experts compared to novices has been undisputed since De Groot's (1965) and Chase and Simon's (1973) work on chess grandmasters. However, it appears that this distinction is not as clear-cut as has been supposed. Rather, it seems that experts remember different things from novices. For instance, Adelson (1984) examined the memory ability of computer programmers. She found that novices had better memory for details of code than did experts. The experts seemed to concentrate more on the overall goal structure of the programming task than on the details of the code. Hence their memory for the code was less good than that of the novices. However, the experts showed a greater ability than the novices to solve another programming task. These observations are compatible with work on language comprehension that suggests that comprehension results in a representation of the linguistic input (a propositional representation) that is then converted into a mental model of the text through the use of inferences based on non-linguistic knowledge. An expert will be better able to construct a mental model as a result of domain-specific knowledge than will a novice. This view is supported by evidence that shows that computing novices construct a propositional representation of a computing text while experts construct mental models (Kintsch, Welsch, Schmalhofer and Zimny (1990).

Experts See and Represent a Problem in their Domain at a Deeper Level than Novices; Novices Tend to Represent a Problem at a Superficial Level

Anderson (1985) lists this distinction between experts and novices, although it does not follow straightforwardly from his model of skill acquisition. Nevertheless, it is a well-documented distinction. Chi, Feltovich and Glaser (1981) asked expert and novice physicists to classify a large set of physics problems into similar categories. The novices used surface features of the problems to group them together. For example, they grouped together problems that dealt with inclined planes or rotations. By contrast, experts used the theoretical principles underlying the problems to group them together. For example, they grouped together problems that involved Newton's second law of conservation of energy, despite surface differences. Thus, experts go beyond the meanings of the words in the problem text and use their knowledge of physics to infer the theoretical status of the objects referred to in the problem, and they categorize problems in terms of their theoretical status rather than their surface meaning. Similar differences between experts and novices have been observed in radiology (Lesgold, 1988) and computer programming (Anderson, 1985). For example, the computing concepts of programming experts seem to be language independent, whereas novices seem to have concepts that are rooted in specific languages.

These observations emphasize both the flexibility with which experts use procedures and the importance of declarative or conceptual knowledge in expertise. Anderson's model gives an account of the acquisition of some components of skilled performance, such as those involved in reading, writing, and using mathematical equations. But it does not account for all aspects of expertise, which also involves an increase in the flexible use of procedures and in conceptual knowledge of the domain. The distinction between the use of automatic procedures and the use of domain-specific declarative knowledge has recently been described as a distinction between routine and adaptive expertise (Hatano, 1988; Holyoak, 1991).

ROUTINE AND ADAPTIVE EXPERTISE

Routine experts are able to solve familiar problems quickly and accurately, but they are less able to solve novel problems. By contrast, adaptive experts are able to use their declarative knowledge to find new solutions to novel problems. Hatano and Inagaki (1986) suggest that the flexibility in adaptive expertise is due to the acquisition of conceptual knowledge. They argue that the acquisition of procedures is not necessarily accompanied by an increase in conceptual knowledge, but that conceptual knowledge is necessary to find the meaning of each step in a procedure and of how it works.

A study by Mayer and Greeno (1972) shows how these two kinds of knowledge might be used in the solution of problems. They taught students elementary statistics concerning probabilities. One group (the concepts first group) was given conceptual instruction first: the concepts of probability were related to everyday notions such as batting averages or the probability of rain. Subsequently, they were introduced to the formulae. A second group (the formulae first group) was presented with the information the other way round. They learned the formulae first and then related the concepts to their everyday knowledge. The results showed that the formulae first group performed very well on subsequent problems that were very similar to those used during instruction, but they performed very poorly on questions about the formulae and on problems with no solution. With these latter problems, they simply tried to apply the formulae rather than thinking about the problem and realizing that the formulae would not work. The concepts first group showed the opposite pattern of results. They performed poorly when solving problems similar to those used in the instructions, but they performed very well on questions about the formulae and on problems with no solution. With these latter problems, they readily detected that the formulae would not work. The formula first group had been taught to use productions to solve the equations and were indulging in routine problem solving. By contrast, the concepts first group had been taught to see the links between their prior declarative knowledge and the new (declarative) knowledge about statistics and were indulging in adaptive problem solving.

Adaptive Expertise

Hatano (1988) illustrates the use of adaptive expertise with the 'street mathematics' of young Brazilian street vendors (Carraher, Carraher and Schliemann, 1985). These children acquire arithmetical skills while selling merchandise on the streets and they readily adapt their numerical operations to solve novel problems. For example, to find the price of twelve lemons of $5.00 each, a nine-year-old street vendor counted up by 10 (10, 20, 30, 40, 50, 60) while separating out two lemons at a time. According to Carraher et al., the mathematical abilities of the street vendors reveal a 'solid understanding of the decimal system', and their performance is equivalent to the use of decomposition and regrouping in formal mathematics.

Hatano suggests that these children are adaptive experts and that the reason they are so good at mathematics is because they are engaged in an interpersonal exchange that requires semantic transparancy to prevent the customer from becoming suspicious. Calculations are performed very quickly, through the use of meaning-rich declarative knowledge. However, there is no great premium on accuracy because errors will easily be spotted by either the vendor or the customer.

Carraher et al. tested the children on new problems in the laboratory. The children could solve word problems that involved the same operations they used on the street, even though word problems are normally found to be more difficult than number problems (Carpenter and Moser, 1982). Thus, the Brazilian children could use their street knowledge to solve equivalent equations in the laboratory. However, the children could not solve the equivalent problems if they were presented in numerical form (e.g. 5 times 35 = ?) rather than as a verbal description of the situation on the street. The unfamiliar numerical problem failed to activate the declarative knowledge that they typically used in their street transactions.

Routine Expertise

Hatano illustrates routine expertise by referring to abacus-using Japanese children. These children perform extremely rapid and accurate calculations. For example, Hatano reports a nine-year-child who solved 30 multiplication problems, such as e.g. 148 times 395, in less than a minute. He suggests that the children have acquired a vast store of specific rules that over time have become merged into general rules for solving equations, consistent with Anderson's model of skill acquisition. However, the abacus users were unable to solve paper and pencil problems of the same kind (Amaiwa, 1987). Amaiwa suggests that this is because they did not understand the meaning of the steps used on the abacus and so could not retrieve the relevant knowledge to help solve the pencil and paper problems. In other words, they had acquired a set of compiled procedures to solve equations, but had not acquired the declarative knowledge of mathematical concepts that shows how the procedures work.

Summary

Expertise involves the acquisition of both procedural and declarative knowledge. While Anderson's (1983) model of acquisition accounts for the automatic aspects of skilled performance, it does not address the question of how declarative knowledge is acquired. This requires a consideration of concept learning which was discussed in Chapter 8. These two aspects of expertise, the use of automatic procedures and the use of declarative knowledge, correspond to a distinction between routine and adaptive expertise. Evidence suggests that procedural knowledge alone is not sufficient to guarantee an understanding of the concepts of a domain. That requires declarative knowledge.

CREATIVITY

A traditional view of creativity is that it is a product of unconscious processes with the solution suddenly coming to mind when the problem solver least expects it. In order to place ideas of creativity within the general context of problem solving, Ericsson and Simon's (1980) distinction between conscious and unconscious processes is useful. They argue that people have conscious access to the contents of short-term memory, and it is short-term memory that is involved in the search for a solution. Hence their emphasis on conscious, serial processes. They also argue that there are two kinds of unconscious processes. There are those that are preconscious and inaccessible and which determine what will be the focus of our attention. Ericsson and Simon call these recognition processes. They are, by definition, unconscious, since they determine what will be consciously attended to. They correspond to the implicit noticing of either external sensory information or information retrieved from long-term memory. Then there are what Ericsson and Simon call automatic processes. These are processes that were once explicit but that have become automatic through learning. They correspond to the compiled procedures used by experts in Anderson's model of skill acquisition. (The work of Berry and Broadbent (1984) suggests that in some cases, these processes may never have been explicit.)

As far as creativity is concerned, it is recognition processes that are implicated when people propose that the solution comes to mind unexpectedly. This notion is contained in Wallas's (1926) account of the four stages of creative thinking, which he proposed after examining autobiographical accounts of creative thinkers. The four stages are: preparation, incubation, illumination and verification. Preparation involves active work on the problem, such as determining facts, and finding out what is already known. It is the patient work of the researcher. Incubation involves no active work on the problem. The ideas are left to lie fallow and other activities are pursued. Illumination is when an idea suggests itself out of the blue, like the Gestalt notion of insight, as if the incubation period was being used to solve the problem at a level beyond conscious awareness. Verification involves a deliberate and painstaking attempt to elaborate and confirm the solution, checking its consistency and following through its implications. The important stages, as far as creativity is concerned, are the stages of incubation and illumination and these are traditionally regarded as involving unconscious processes.

The postulation of unconscious processes invariably triggered a debate about whether or not they were necessary components of creativity. People with an information processing perspective (e.g. Ericsson and Simon, 1980; Posner, 1973; Simon, 1966, 1967) argued that there were a variety of ways in which notions like incubation and illumination could be explained that did not require the use of conscious and parallel processes.

For instance, Ericsson and Simon (1980) pointed out that reports of incubation have frequently been given many years after the supposed events occurred. It could be that the individuals did start to muse consciously on their problems but at the critical point rapidly solved the problem and then remembered only the solution and so reported the event as one of sudden insight that occurred without warning. Where claims of incubation are apparently well-founded, Simon (1966) has argued that it is not necessary to postulate the use of unconscious processes. He suggests that the occurrence of a rapid solution after several failures may be attributed to beneficial forgetting of misleading possibilities during a rest period, a break being a way of reducing set or functional fixedness.

Alternatively, illumination after a period of incubation may simply be due to a reduction in fatigue. It might also be that the rest period provides the occasion for additional practice. Finally, Simon (1967) queried the need for parallel processes to account for the way we notice the conditions that change our conscious thoughts. While he thought that parallel 'noticing' processes might be used to scan for danger signals, he also kept open the serialist option of time-sharing. Time-sharing is the ability to switch rapidly from one thought to another and so gives the appearance of doing two things at once without true simultaneity. Time-sharing is a way that serial computer systems allocate processing to various jobs that come in and queue for attention. So it is a serial method that can mimic parallel processes to some extent. Overall, the information processors prefer to account for the processes of problem solving – creative or otherwise – by reference to serial and conscious mechanisms.

However, the discussion in Chapter 9 indicated that problem solving involves both serial, conscious processes and parallel, unconscious ones. The revived interest in unconscious processing is due partly to the development of parallel distributed processing models of cognition (e.g. McClelland and Rumelhart, 1986) and in particular to Holyoak and Thagard's (1989, 1990) connectionist model of analogy. The use of multiple constraint satisfaction to determine which analogy will be retrieved and how it will be mapped takes much of the mystery out of the sudden retrieval of a solution in creative problem solving. Indeed, Holyoak and Thagard (1990) suggest that retrieval corresponds to insight – the sudden awareness that a potential solution is available.

Current views of creative thinking propose that two stages are involved rather than the four suggested by Wallas. The two stages have been variously described as: generation and selection (Johnson-Laird, 1988); discovery and verification (Langley, Simon, Bradshaw and Zytkow, 1987); or search and selection (Perkins, 1988). These two stages distinguish between producing a solution and subjecting that solution to further testing; that is, they distinguish between unconscious retrieval processes and a conscious, serial search. It can be seen as a distinction between originality on the one hand – generating a novel idea – and relevance on the other hand – verifying the idea's appropriateness.

Both originality (Guilford, 1966) and relevance (Perkins, 1988) are regarded as important criteria for creativity. However, knowledge is also a crucial ingredient, and domain-specific knowledge places constraints on what counts as a relevant solution (Johnson-Laird, 1988). Holyoak and Thagard's model of analogy indicates how such constraints might operate in a connectionist system and thus removes much of the mystery from the use of unconscious processes. Thus the likelihood of retrieving a powerful analogy will depend on the knowledge a person already has about a domain. The more knowledge you have about, say, physics, the more likely you are to find semantically similar analogies, to have high level pragmatic goals to constrain the final choice, and to have a rich set of structural constraints on the retrieved analogy. Holyoak and Thagard's model assumes that the precise pattern of excitation and inhibition in the knowledge network will determine what solution is finally retrieved.

The basic idea is that when a successful analogy is retrieved it yields a potential solution to the problem. Conscious thought is only involved in the verification stage, when the solution is checked for its relevance and its implications are pursued. This view is supported by a study (Novick and Holyoak, 1991) in which verbal protocols were recorded from some of the subjects required to solve mathematical problems by mapping the solutions of analogous problems. When the problems were conceptually analogous, the protocols revealed no signs of the mapping process, consistent with the use of a parallel and unconscious mapping mechanism. Instead, the protocols largely described laborious efforts to work out the implications of the correspondences between the two analogues, after the initial mapping process was apparently completed, consistent with the use of a serial verification procedure. However, it may be that the retrieved information does not yield a unique solution. In such circumstances, other problem-solving techniques are required. According to the information processors, these are general purpose heuristics that involve a serial and conscious search through the problem space.

THE INFORMATION PROCESSING VIEW OF SCIENTIFIC CREATIVITY

Simon and his colleagues (e.g. Langley, Simon, Bradshaw and Zytkow, 1987) claim that creativity and discovery can be explained by the same mechanisms that are used to account for other forms of problem solving. They dispute the importance of unconscious processes and argue that creativity is a result of general purpose search strategies. Creative thinking, like all thinking, is seen as a search through a problem space that is guided by the delineation of sub-goals and by the use of general heuristics such as means–ends analysis. Langley et al. do acknowledge the possibility that unconscious processes might be involved in the discovery (retrieval) of a potential solution, but they focus on the conscious processes involved in verification. It is the outcome of this second stage that results in the generation of a single solution.

They argue that we can distinguish between experts and novices in creativity as well as in other forms of problem solving. Expert thinking in a domain is characterized by the systematic application of powerful methods, powerful because they require specialized knowledge of the domain. Experts do not have to seek and search; they recognize and calculate. They use procedural, not declarative, knowledge. Problem solving by novices on the other hand is characterized by tentativeness and uncertainty. Novices often do not know what to do next, they search and test, and they use crude and cumbersome weak methods that do not depend on specialized knowledge, because novices are not familiar with the powerful tools of the expert. Langley et al. argue that everyone is a novice when it comes to being creative and discovering new truths at the frontiers of understanding. Consequently creativity is mainly characterized as novice problem solving: by trial-and-error search and the extensive use of weak methods.

Langley et al. assume that knowledge of the domain is used to constrain the generation of ideas. But they argue that at the frontiers of knowledge there will still be many acceptable solutions, so that the choice of one or other of these solutions is then determined by trial-and-error search. This idea is supported by Voss and Post (1988). Voss and Post presented economic problems such as:

> Imagine you are the Minister of Agriculture for the Soviet Union. Crop productivity has been too low for the past several years. What would you do to increase crop production?

About 24% of the experts' solution protocols (those of political scientists specializing in the Soviet Union) were elaborations of the initial state of the problem, as opposed to 1% of the novice's protocols. Elaborations of the initial state identified possible constraints, such as Soviet ideology and the amount of arable land. The authors argue that adding constraints amounted to a reduction in the search space. For example, introducing the constraint of the amount of arable land eliminated the solution of increased planting. Selecting a single solution from those that remained presumably required a serial search.

A study by Qin and Simon (1990) lends some support to the information processing view. Qin and Simon presented physics students with all the data that was available to Keppler when he discovered his third law of planetary motion and recorded the students' verbal reports while they inspected the data for obvious patterns. Many of the students 'rediscovered' Keppler's third law. Furthermore, they did so primarily through the use of means–ends analysis.

Perhaps the best support for Langley et al.'s position is that they have successfully simulated scientific discoveries on computer. Their best known program is called BACON (after Francis Bacon). BACON examines numerical data sets for systematic mathematical relations of various sorts through the use of four sets of production rules. These operate according to a means–ends analysis to achieve a top-level goal of incorporating the single independent term into one or more laws. The first set of productions lets the program gather data systematically. These operate by setting sub-goals that cause the conditions of other rules to match. For example, the first rule to be applied is INITIALIZE-INDEPENDENT, which initializes the values of the independent term, and creates a goal to iterate through these values. The second set of productions is responsible for noting regularities in the data collected by the first set of rules. The third set is responsible for defining new terms and for computing the values of terms once they have been defined, and the fourth set discards elements from memory that are no longer useful. Using these very simple tactics, BACON has redis-covered many important relationships in physics and chemistry, such as Boyle's law.

The first version of BACON generates solutions when all the relevant evidence has been examined. So it does not require separate produc-tions to test the laws it has found. It therefore uses a procedure where all possible constraints are applied at the discovery stage rather than having some apply at the verification stage. Such a model runs counter to the observation that in many creative achievements the ini-tial idea is subjected to a progressive series of revisions guided by con-straints. Other versions of BACON announce laws on the basis of partial evidence, and are capable of revising their conclusions after examining new evidence and of qualifying their generalizations by specifying the conditions under which they hold. Thus, the later ver-sions more closely model the creative process.

To emphasize the importance of prior knowledge, Langley et al. sug-gest that in the history of chemistry, the discovery of qualitative laws often precedes the discovery of quantitative relations. Another of their simulations (GLAUBER) rediscovered the theory of acids and alkalis, which is a qualitative law. On the other hand, Boyle's law and Dalton's law, which were discovered by BACON, are quantitative. Langley et al. suggest, therefore, that it is plausible to consider whether GLAUBER might contribute something to BACON's discov-ery process. They suggest, for example, that knowledge about com-pounds acquired by GLAUBER could be passed on to BACON and used to determine which experimental combinations to examine rather than examining all possible combinations. Such a proposal would more closely approximate the way knowledge constrains the choice of solution, although it has yet to be implemented in practice.

SUMMARY

Investigations of problem solving and of the nature of expertise have shown that thinking involves both conscious and unconscious processes. Conscious, serial thinking, which occupies short-term memory, can be characterized by the use of general purpose heuristics applied to retrieved declarative knowledge (Newell and Simon, 1972).

The unconscious, automatic performance of experts can be characterized by the use of compiled procedures embodied in production rules (Anderson, 1983). The unconscious, parallel and intuitive discovery of a potential solution can be characterized by the retrieval of an analogy from long-term memory, subject to multiple constraint satisfaction (e.g. Holyoak, 1990). The information processors argue that problem solving and creative thinking are mainly achieved by conscious, serial processes. However, the work on analogies and on adaptive expertise suggests that unconscious, parallel retrieval processes also play a major role in problem solving and creativity. Finally, the notion of adaptive expertise and the use of declarative knowledge in skilled performance indicates that Anderson's model of skill acquisition needs to be supplemented by an account of the acquisition of declarative, conceptual knowledge.

CHAPTER 11   Hypothesis testing, judgement and choice

This chapter is concerned with situations requiring complex decision making. Such situations can be thought of as involving both inductive and deductive processes. Take hypothesis testing for example. The initial formation of a hypothesis usually involves an inductive inference based on knowledge of the world; the hypothesis that if something is a bird, then it flies, for instance. This hypothesis can then be tested (or evaluated) using deductive inferences. A similar situation can be said to occur with judgement and choice, except that these situations usually trigger the consideration of more than one hypothesis and that the deductions are based on statistical rather than logical rules. However, the evidence suggests that these simple accounts may not be adequate. For example, we saw in Chapter 8 on concepts that hypotheses that are formed on the basis of experience are constrained by prior knowledge. This suggests that induction alone, in the absence of deductive processes, is insufficient to account for concept formation. The work reviewed in this chapter suggests that hypothesis testing is equally problematic, and that deductive processes may be overridden by error-prone inductive ones.

Hypothesis testing requires the use of logical rules of the kind discussed in Chapter 7. In this chapter, both non-logical and logical theories are discussed. Non-logical theories propose the use of pre-attentive heuristic processes involved in language comprehension or the retrieval of specific memories that contain the solution. Logical theories propose the use of domain-specific rules or the manipulation of mental models.

Judgement and choice involves complex situations in which the underlying competence, which represents a normative theory, is statistical. Utility theory is one such theory and it assumes that people make optimal judgements about the utility of different outcomes, based on what the person prefers. Probability theory is another and it assumes that people can make accurate decisions concerning the probability that different outcomes will occur. Decision theory is based on a combination of these two normative theories and it assumes that people can use the probability of an outcome together with its utility to estimate its expected utility. Research into this kind of reasoning has concentrated on the use of non-logical heuristics that lead to biases in performance. Kahneman and Tversky propose heuristics that operate on the representation of the problem, while Evans proposes heuristics that are involved in the construction of the representation as well as deductive (analytic) processes that operate on the resulting representation. All these views are discussed below.

HYPOTHESIS TESTING AND THE ROLE OF LOGIC

Suppose you have a hypothesis about the world such as, *if John visits Mary he takes her some flowers*, how do you go about trying to decide whether to believe this hypothesis or not? According to Piaget, you would make use of a mental logic, just as you would for purely deductive tasks of the kinds described in Chapter 7. In other words, for Piaget, the way in which we find out about the world involves the use of logic in much the same way as finding a valid conclusion from a set of premises involves the use of logic. Thus Piaget subscribed to the syntactic view of deduction discussed in Chapter 7.

In order to test this view, Piaget presented children and young adolescents with what might be called mini-scientific experiments and observed the way that they conducted these experiments. One example is the pendulum problem, in which the child was given all the necessary experimental materials and asked to find out what caused variations in the frequency of oscillation of the pendulum. According to Piaget, when children reach the final stage of development, the formal operational stage, they behave as if they were formulating a hypothesis about the pendulum of the form *if p then q* and then testing that hypothesis by manipulating the materials. Thus, children at the formal operational stage might postulate that the height from which the object falls is what causes the frequency of oscillation to change. That is, they have formulated a hypothesis of the form *if the height is changed then the frequency will change*. After this they systematically vary the height from which the object falls to check that the frequency changes, according to the rule of *modus ponens*. They also systematically vary the other potential influences, such as the force with which the object is pushed, to check that whenever the frequency does not change there has been no change in the height, according to the rule of *modus tollens*. (See Piaget and Inhelder, 1969.)

Piaget observed that children behaved in this way from the age of about 11 years and thus concluded that they had reached the adult stage of logical thinking in which content-free rules of logic are applied to problems. This view was first systematically put to the test by Wason (1968) when he devised what has come to be called the selection task. The task is a very close analogue to the kind of task that Piaget gave to children when investigating his developmental theory. Wason presented his subjects with four cards showing symbols such as the following:

E   K   4   7

The subjects were told that each card had a number on one side and a letter on the other. Their task was to turn over the minimum number of cards that they thought were necessary to find out whether the following rule was true or false: *If a card has a vowel on one side then it has an even number on the other side.* Subjects should select the E card to check, by *modus ponens*, that is has an even number on the back; and they should select the 7 card to check, by *modus tollens*, that is does *not* have a vowel on the back. This would parallel the performance of the children in Piaget's experiments when they were testing their hypotheses about the pendulum. However, Wason found that very few people got the right answer. Instead, the preferred solution was to select E, which is right, and 4, which is wrong. Choosing 4 is equivalent to choosing q in the rule *if p then q* and checking that p is present. That is, it is equivalent to affirming the consequent. Thus, contrary to the predictions of Piaget's theory, adults do not seem to use the rules of logic when trying to find out whether or not a hypothesis is correct. In particular, they fail to make use of *modus tollens* since they fail to select the *not q* card in the selection task.

Subsequent work by Wason and his colleagues (e.g. Johnson-Laird, Legrenzi and Legrenzi, 1972) suggested that the particular component of Piaget's theory that did not hold up was the notion that mental rules of logic are domain independent and general purpose. It transpired that if the task was changed from using abstract materials, as in the above example, to using concrete materials then performance improved dramatically. Thus, in their 'concrete' condition, Johnson-Laird, Legrenzi and Legrenzi gave subjects a version of the problem that used familiar, everyday materials. The four cards depicted four envelopes as shown in Figure 11.1.

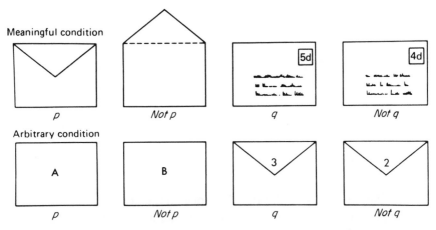

Figure 11.1   The postal worker problem (from Glass and Holyoak (1986); reproduced by permission of Random House)

The subjects were told to imagine that they were postal workers engaged in sorting letters. They were to decide if the following rule was being followed: *If a letter is sealed then it has a 5d stamp on it.* A rule such as this was in fact in force in England at that time although it has long since been discarded (as has the use of *d* to stand for penny). The choices were the four cards shown in Figure 11.1: a sealed and an unsealed envelope (*p* and *not p*), and a letter containing a 5d stamp or a 4d stamp (*q* and *not q*).

The results showed that 21 out of the 24 subjects gave the correct solution in this version of the task, which stood in stark contrast to the observation that only two of the 24 subjects gave the correct solution in a version of the task that used letters and numbers. This facilitation effect due to the familiarity of the materials has been the major focus of research in the 1970s and 1980s. And the debate has centred around the issue of how to explain the observed domain-specificity of performance that clearly runs counter to Piaget's notion of content-free syntactic rules.

Theoretical explanations fall into two main classes. One class proposes that people are not logical at all but instead rely on non-logical short cuts. These may be heuristic biases when the materials are abstract (e.g. Evans, 1984, 1989; Pollard, 1982), or direct retrieval of the original situation when the materials are familiar (e.g. Griggs and Cox, 1982). The other class proposes some form of domain-specificity to account for the facilitation with familiar materials. Two major variants within this general group are the use of domain-specific rules (e.g. Cheng and Holyoak, 1985; Cosmides, 1989)) and the use of mental models (e.g. Johnson-Laird, 1983; Johnson-Laird and Byrne, 1991; Manktelow and Over, 1990a, 1990b, 1991).

NON-LOGICAL THEORIES

Heuristic Biases

Evans (1989) points out that performance on the abstract selection task is extremely poor. He believes, therefore, that logical processes are not involved at all. (Of course, he does believe that logical performance is apparent in purely deductive tasks, such as those discussed in Chapter 7). Instead, people use heuristic processes when the materials are abstract and memory of the specific event when the materials are concrete. Evans first proposed the use of heuristic processes when he observed a matching bias in the selection task. Evans and Lynch (1973) found that when subjects were presented with a rule containing negatives, such as: *If there is an S on one side of the card then there is not a 9 on the other side,* they selected the cards that matched the elements explicitly mentioned in the rule. In the above example, they selected S and 9. This, of course, is the correct response but it is selected for the wrong reasons: the subjects seem unable to reason about the rule and merely pick cards that match the words in the rule.

A comparable effect occurs with: *If there is not a S on one side of the card then there is a 9 on the other side.* Most subjects selected the S and the 9. Thus, subjects seem to ignore the negation. Evans (1989) refers to this phenomenon as a matching bias and he suggests that it occurs during the automatic processes of comprehension that are required to understand the problem and that occur before any analytic reasoning processes are brought to bear. Evans refers to Sperber and Wilson's (1986) work on relevance and suggests that the instruction to investigate cards results in an assessment of the cards based on their exposed sides. That is, the instructions encourage subjects to make a relevance judgement about the cards. Such a judgement results in the matching bias.

Memory Retrieval

Logical processes may be bypassed if there are well-learned procedures that have replaced them. One such procedure seems to be the direct retrieval from memory of previous identical experiences that yield the correct solution. Evidence for this view comes from studies by Golding (1981) and by Griggs and Cox (1982). Golding tried to replicate Johnson-Laird, Legrenzi and Legrenzi (1972), and found that older subjects, who had experience of the postal rule, performed the task correctly, but that younger subjects, who had no experience of the postal rule, performed badly. Similarly, Griggs and Cox found that American students, who were also unfamiliar with the postal rule failed to show any facilitation in performance. By contrast, when the American subjects were presented with a rule concerning under-age drinking, based on the law in force in the State of Florida where they lived, they did show facilitation. Such findings are consistent with the view that specific memories are retrieved to solve the problem.

However, it soon became clear that direct retrieval of the solution from memory could not account for all cases of facilitation because it was also observed in contexts that the subjects could never have experienced themselves. The best-known example of this phenomenon is the Sears task devised by D'Andrade and originally reported by Rumelhart (1980). In this task, subjects had to imagine that they were store managers for Sears and that they had to inspect receipts at the end of the day to make sure that they had been properly filled out. The rule for filling out the forms was: *If any purchase exceeded $30, then the receipt must have the signature of the department manager on the back.* As in the usual procedure for the selection task, subjects saw four cards, in this case made to look like shop receipts, each with a price on one side and a space for a signature on the other side. One card showed a price of $75 (*p*), one a price of $25 (*not p*), one showed a signed receipt (*q*), and one showed an unsigned receipt (*not q*). The results showed that nearly 70% of the subjects selected the correct cards, yet few subjects would have directly experienced the problem domain. Rumelhart suggested that schemas, such as Schank and Abelson's (1977) scripts or Minsky's (1977) frames, that abstract general rules from experience can account for performance of this type in contrast to the memory-cueing hypothesis. The notion of schemas raises the possibility that domain-specific knowledge is required to evaluate a hypothesis, a possibility that is discussed in the next section.

DOMAIN-SPECIFIC THEORIES

Domain-specific Rules

Those who favour domain-specific rules argue that people reason logically only if they are familiar with the domain and if the relevant domain-specific rules are triggered by the situation. Cheng and Holyoak (1985) propose rules called pragmatic reasoning schemas that are based on notions like permission and obligation. By contrast, Cosmides (1985, 1989) proposes rules that are based on the notion of social exchange and are of the general form: *if you derive a benefit then you must pay a cost*. According to these rule-based views, there is no other way to produce logical behaviour except through the triggering of these domain-specific rules. Manktelow and Over (1990a, 1990b, 1991) query both of these accounts. They argue instead that the facilitation observed by Cheng and Holyoak and by Cosmides is confined to contexts of permission and obligation. That is, the concrete tasks require the use of deontic logic and not propositional logic.

Pragmatic Reasoning Schemas

Pragmatic reasoning schemas are clusters of generalized rules that are induced from ordinary life experience, and include schemas for permissions, obligations and causations. The best-known example is the set of abstracted rules for permissions, that is, situations in which some action may be taken only if some precondition is satisfied.

Cheng and Holyoak proposed that the permission schema contains the following four rules:

Rule 1: If the action is to be taken, then the precondition must be satisfied.

Rule 2: If the action is not to be taken, then the precondition need not be satisfied.

Rule 3: If the precondition is satisfied, then the action may be taken.

Rule 4: If the precondition is not satisfied, then the action must not be taken.

When a conditional is presented in a selection task, either the context or the content may evoke this permission schema, as in Johnson-Laird et al.'s (1972) study, where the content evokes the schema: *If a letter is sealed, then it has a 5d stamp on it.* Rule 4 of the schema then ensures that *not q* is selected since the 5d stamp is the precondition that must be satisfied. Thus, the rules of propositional logic are explicitly represented but only in a domain-specific way. There is no abstract system of rules that will apply in any domain.

Cheng and Holyoak (1985) supported their proposal by showing that an abstract task could be performed well as long as it triggered a pragmatic reasoning schema. They presented subjects with two abstract reasoning tasks that were logically identical. One task was like Wason's original selection task and referred to letters and numbers. The other task was an abstract description of a permission situation, that is: *If one is to take action A then one must first satisfy precondition P.* Performance on the letter/number task was poor, as expected. Only 20% of the solutions were correct. However, in the comparable abstract permission task, 60% of the responses were correct.

Violation of Social Contracts

Cosmides (1985) presents a different account of the role of domain-specific rules in the testing of hypotheses. According to Cosmides, knowledge is not the product of general inductive mechanisms. Instead, there are innate, highly modular mechanisms for reasoning in specific domains. Cosmides therefore takes issue with Cheng and

Holyoak over their notion of the inductive learning of pragmatic reasoning schemas and proposes instead that people possess, through evolution, innate schemas for reasoning about the specific domain of social exchange. Thus she suggests that facilitation occurs in the selection task because people have been selected, through evolution, to look for cheaters, that is, to look for people who get a benefit without paying a cost. It is as if people are conforming to a basic rule of the form: *If you take a benefit, then you pay a cost,* and are highly sensitive to violations of this rule.

According to Cosmides, this predilection to look for cheaters accounts for the observed facilitation effects in the selection task (including those found by Cheng and Holyoak in support of their pragmatic reasoning schemas). The way that the familiar tasks have been formulated (as in the Johnson-Laird et al (1972) study, for example) means that looking for the cheaters leads to the selection of the *not q* card. Cosmides (1989) tested this view by using a task where the predilection to look for cheaters would result in erroneous responses. She found that a background story eliciting ideas about cheaters can lead subjects into error. In the context of the story, concerning the need to have a tattoo before being allowed to eat cassava root, the rule: *If man has a tattoo on his face then he eats cassava root,* leads to selections of the cards corresponding to *not p* and *q;* that is to men who have no tattoo and who eat cassava root. According to Cosmides, these are the cheaters, since they do not pay the cost of the tattoo. She argues, therefore, for a specific inferential module concerned with violations of social contracts.

Deontic reasoning

Manktelow and Over (1990a, 1990b, 1991) argue that neither pragmatic reasoning schemas nor the predilection to look for cheaters is needed to account for the facilitation effect with concrete materials. They propose instead that the tasks that have been used trigger the construction of mental models according to a deontic semantics, not the semantics of propositional logic. They point out that the original Wason task, which required subjects to evaluate a conditional rule of the form: *If there is a letter on one side of the card then there is an even number on the other side,* was a clear example of an exercise in propositional logic. The subject's task was to determine whether or not the conditional rule was a true description of the state of affairs depicted by the cards. However, many of the tasks using familiar materials, including those used by Johnson-Laird, Legrenzi and Legrenzi (1972) and by D'Andrade (see Rumelhart, 1980) involve concepts of permission or obligation, a fact that is explicitly recognized by Cheng and Holyoak in their proposals concerning pragmatic reasoning schemas. However, rules of permission and obligation do not conform to the standard propositional logic. They conform instead to deontic logic, logic that is specifically concerned with permissions and obligations. Deontic logic differs from propositional logic in a number of ways. For one thing, it is not possible to determine whether or not a deontic rule is true or false simply by inspecting the state of affairs in the environment. Whether or not a rule of permission, such as *if you tidy your room then you may go to the cinema*, is true or false depends not just on the state of the world but on the goals and intentions of the speaker and the listener. So subjects in the tasks using familiar materials are not simply trying to see whether the rule is true or false. Rather they are trying to see whether or not people have violated the rule, and this is different from Wason's original task.

Manktelow and Over (1991) suggest, therefore, that Cosmides's proposal that people are predisposed to look for cheaters may reflect a more general predisposition to conform to the rules of deontic logic. They tested this proposal by varying the utilities associated with different courses of action. They pointed out that deontic rules invariably involve two parties: the person who makes the rule (whom they call the agent), and the person who is supposed to conform to the rule (dubbed the actor). Thus if a mother (the agent) says to her son (the actor): *if you tidy your room then I will let you out to play*, the cheating activity as far as the mother is concerned is if the son goes out to play without tidying his room. This is comparable to the cases examined by Cosmides and others. For example, it is comparable to sealing the envelope without paying 5d in the Johnson-Laird et al. task. But from the point of view of the son, the cheating activity is the case where he tidies his room but his mother does not let him go out to play. So what counts as violating the rule should be different in these two cases. Manktelow and Over present evidence to suggest that this is, in fact, the case. The selections people made conformed to deontic logic rather than to propositional logic.

Overall, evaluating the truth of deontic rules involves an evaluation of the intentions of both an agent and an actor, as well as a complex evaluation of the relative utilities associated with different courses of action for each person. Pragmatic reasoning schemas or social contract algorithms are unable to account for these abilities. Manktelow and

Over (1991) propose that the alternative domain-specific theory, mental models, may therefore provide a better account.

Mental Models

The problem with the proposals that have been considered so far is that each one accounts for only part of the total phenomenon. Thus, Piaget's original mental logic cannot account for performance failures with abstract tasks. The heuristics view accounts for errors but not for correct performance, and the memory view accounts for performance with familiar but not with unfamiliar materials. The views that people use domain-specific rules ignore the fact that people can make valid deductions that depend solely on the logical connectives (see Chapter 7). Content-specific rules cannot account for such general logical competence. The theory of mental models (Johnson-Laird, 1983; Johnson-Laird and Byrne, 1991) attempts to account for all these aspects of performance. It does so by proposing three stages of thought. First is the comprehension stage, in which people use their knowledge of language and knowledge of the world to construct a mental model of the situation described by the premises. Second is what can be called the inference stage, in which people try to formulate a description of the model they have constructed, a description that asserts something not explicitly stated in the premises. Third is what might be called the logical stage, in which people try to construct alternative models of the premises that refute their candidate conclusion. If there is no such model the conclusion is valid. If there is such a model, and a subsequent search reveals no conclusion that is consistent with all of the models, then the conclusion is invalid.

Johnson-Laird and Byrne (1991) argue that when the selection task is carried out, subjects consider only those cards that are explicitly represented in their models of the rule, and they then select those cards for which the hidden value on the other side could have a bearing on the truth or falsity of the rule. The facilitation effect is due to two things. First, certain contexts cause the state of affairs depicted by *not q* to be explicitly represented in the model. Second, familiar contents cause memories for the specific event to be retrieved. Thus, a rule used in Wason's original experiment, such as, *If there is an A on one side then there is a 2 on the other side,* yields models that represent A and 2.

Subjects only select the A card because that is the only card having a hidden value that could bear on the truth or falsity of the rule. If the interpretation of the rule is as a biconditional, that is, *If and only if there is an A on one side then there is a 2 on the other side*, then they will select both cards. This account accords with Wason's original findings.

Johnson-Laird and Byrne further suggest that rules with negated elements tend to elicit models that contain only positive items. That is, the rule, *If there is not an A on one side then there is a 2 on the other side*, elicits models which stand for *either* A or 2. A model that includes the negation is not constructed. Thus, subjects tend to make the same selections as those for the affirmative rule. In this way Johnson-Laird and Byrne account for Evans's matching bias. However, Evans's own account suggests *why* the matching bias may occur – it is a consequence of relevance judgements made during comprehension. These judgements probably lead to the construction of models suggested by Johnson-Laird and Byrne, but Johnson-Laird and Byrne give no reasons for why subjects should construct such models. A more precise account of the way that relevance and other aspects of discourse (see Chapter 6) constrain the use of inductive inferences in the construction of mental models might show more clearly how biases occur in reasoning.

Johnson-Laird and Byrne also assume that particular contents may trigger memories for violations (e.g. Johnson-Laird, Legrenzi and Legrenzi, 1972). In these circumstances, mental models are bypassed, and retrieved solutions are applied instead. They also suggest that particular contexts, such as deontic contexts (Cheng and Holyoak, 1985; Cosmides, 1989), lead to the explicit representation of the negative component of the rule, through the activation of deontic knowledge. For example, a rule of obligation such as *If we had promised then we would have had to go*, is counterfactual. Thus a model is constructed that contains the actual situation (we didn't promise and we didn't go) as well as the counterfactual situation (we did promise and we did go). Such an explicit model facilitates performance. This proposal suggests that the rules of deontic logic, like the rules of propositional logic, are simulated by a mental model, a view proposed by Manktelow and Over (1991). It receives some support from the work of Morrow, Bower and Greenspan (1989) who have shown that mental models are constructed from the perspective of a particular character in a text, and so the notion of different situations being associated with the different perspectives of the agent and the actor (Manktelow and Over, 1991) is plausible. However, Manktelow and Over suggest that what remains to be explained on a mental models account is the way that preferences among these different courses of action are established depending on their utilities.

The theory of mental models does not assume that logical behaviour is dependent on domain-specific rules. Instead, according to this view, logical behaviour is due to the manipulation of mental models: the search for alternative models that are consistent with the situation. Thus, the extent to which logical behaviour will emerge is determined by the number of models that have to be considered to derive a valid conclusion. The greater the number of models that are needed the greater the load on working memory and so the greater is the likelihood of error. According to the mental models account, then, there is a logical component that is distinct from domain-specific knowledge, but it is constrained by the limitations of working memory. On this view though, people *are* logical, just as Piaget proposed, but contrary to Piaget's view, people do not possess a mental logic.

Overall, the theory of mental models gives the best account of hypothesis testing, embodying as it does inductive and deductive processes. However, the theory requires greater specificity on a number of issues, such as the way that discourse notions, such as relevance, constrain inductive inferences during comprehension, the circumstances under which logic may be bypassed when specific memories are retrieved, and the way that people estimate and evaluate utilities.

DECISION MAKING AND THE ROLE OF STATISTICAL REASONING

In this section we are concerned with judgement and choice and with uncertain decisions. They might be uncertain because all the possible outcomes are not known, because the likelihood of each outcome is uncertain, or because there is no single correct decision or hypothesis anyway. Many of our most important decisions are of this latter kind, in which there are rewards and costs associated with the alternative courses of action. For example, when deciding on a future career, there may be a conflict between opting for a career that interests you but is poorly paid and one that is less interesting but very well paid. There may also be conflicts concerning what part of the country you prefer and where the jobs are, and so on. We cannot use logic to guide us in these kinds of situations because logic deals only with certain-ties: with necessary conclusions.

What kind of competence might underlie uncertain decisions if logic is not involved? What is needed is some kind of statistical reasoning that estimates the probability that one hypothesis or the other is the best choice. A normative theory of this kind, against which human performance can be evaluated, is known as decision theory and it assumes that people make optimal decisions based on the probability of each outcome and its utility to arrive at its expected utility. Thus, people need to be able to estimate probabilities, make a cost/benefit analysis of each possible outcome in order to arrive at its utility, and then make a decision based on the combination of the probabilities and the utilities, that is, based on the expected utilities.

Consider the following example, taken from the work on decision analysis, where normative theory is applied to real-world situations. The example is from medicine and is a case of a physician attempting to help a patient with cancer of the larynx who must choose between surgery and radiation therapy (McNeil, Weichselbaum and Pauker, 1981). The dilemma is that there is a longer life expectancy after surgery but normal speech is lost. However, given that the person sur-vives, there is little risk of long-term side effects with radiation ther-apy, although there are short-term side effects of nausea and hair loss. The physician or decision analyst elicits two utility functions from the patient, one representing the patient's preferences for surviving vary-ing numbers of years with artificial speech, as a consequence of surgery, the other representing the patient's preferences for surviving varying numbers of years with normal speech. The utilities are obtained by asking the patient to equate hypothetical situations offer-ing periods of guaranteed survival with gambles offering a 50/50 chance of survival for a specified period. From the answers to these questions, the analyst calculates the expected utility for each of the two alternatives to determine the optimal therapy for the patient.

Utility theory has a long history in economics and is the basis of most economic modelling and forecasting. Its history in the psychology of decision making began with the work of Ward Edwards in 1954, who was the first to investigate the possibility that people are 'rational' decision makers and follow the rules of utility theory. To cut a long story short, this turned out not to be the case (see Osherson (1990) and Slovic (1990) for reviews). After over a decade of research it became clear that people do not make decisions as predicted by decision theory. The ability to estimate probabilities, utilities and expected utilities is severely limited and highly labile, depending on such things as the wording of the problem, memory load, the nature of the required response (e.g. judging each option individually or choosing from two or more options), and the compatibility of the response and the task.

One reason why individuals have difficulty making optimal decisions has been emphasized by Simon (1959). He pointed out that the classical theory of utility optimization is a theory that assumes that all the individual has to do is to choose between fixed and known alternatives, to each of which is attached known consequences. But these assumptions take no account of the fact that, in the normal state of affairs, the alternatives are not given, many of the consequences are not known, and even if they were, the constraints on human cognitive processes would limit people's ability to evaluate each alternative and its consequences exhaustively.

Simon proposes the notion of bounded rationality to replace the optimization hypothesis. Bounded rationality asserts that cognitive limitations force people to construct simplified models of their problems. The key simplification, according to Simon is the replacement of the optimization goal by the satisficing principle: the first alternative that has a satisfactory (not optimal) outcome for each alternative is selected. In choosing somewhere to live, for example, a student may select the first flat that is satisfactory with respect to cost, size and distance from the lecture rooms.

One of the major outcomes of Simon's analysis was an increased interest in trying to spell out the nature of the cognitive processes that underlie human decision making. A large body of work by Kahneman and Tversky suggests that, instead of considering every possible alternative, people use a number of heuristics when making judgements, and these result in performance biases.

HEURISTICS AND BIASES

The leading researchers in this field, Kahneman and Tversky (Tversky and Kahneman, 1973) have claimed for many years that people do not use a normative statistical model for making statistical inferences.

Instead, they take short cuts, using strategic heuristics, such as representativeness and availability. While these heuristics are appropriate in some contexts, they frequently lead to errors and biases. Consequently Kahneman and Tversky have claimed that such biases are likely to be prevalent in real life and in expert decision making (e.g. Kahneman, Slovic and Tversky, 1982). However, after a decade of research, it has become increasingly clear that people can make sound statistical judgements when the circumstances allow. Thus, Kahneman and Tversky (1982) have modified their position to allow that subjects may have access to normatively appropriate 'rules', as well as to heuristics. They emphasize, though, that possession of a rule does not necessarily mean that it will be correctly applied. Kahneman and Tversky's heuristics are what might be called inferential heuristics, since they refer to methods of making inferences. Thus, Kahneman and Tversky now assume that people have access to two kinds of rules, heuristic rules and normative rules.

An alternative view holds that heuristic strategies refer not to deliberate inferences but to the automatic and preconscious processes of comprehension. This is the view of Evans (1984, 1989) that has already been discussed in relation to the matching bias in the selection task. Evans (1989) calls his heuristics representational heuristics, to distinguish them from the heuristic inference rules proposed by Kahneman and Tversky. These two views of heuristics are discussed below.

Inferential Heuristics

According to Kahneman and Tversky (1982), people generally use heuristic strategies when estimating probabilities and these strategies frequently lead to biases and errors. Their general thesis is that normative statistical reasoning coexists (Osherson, 1990) with non-statistical heuristic principles such as representativeness and availability.

Representativeness

If someone is given a description of an individual and asked if they think that the individual is an engineer (say) or a lawyer and they also know the proportions of engineers and lawyers in the population, people base their decisions solely on whether the description is more similar to an engineer or to a lawyer. They disregard the information about the proportion of engineers and lawyers in the population. Thus they base their decisions on how similar or representative is the individual to the group. This observation forms the basis of the representativeness heuristic, which is based on judgements of similarity rather than on statistical judgements based on the nature of the population.

To test the representativeness heuristic, Kahneman and Tversky (1973) asked subjects to judge whether a person picked at random from a sample of 100 was an engineer. One group (the engineer-high group) were told that the sample of 100 consisted of 70 engineers and 30 lawyers. A second group (the engineer-low group) were told that the sample consisted of 30 engineers and 70 lawyers. Subjects in both groups were asked to estimate the odds that the person picked at random from the sample of 100 was an engineer. Subjects in both groups were generally accurate. The engineer-high group correctly estimated that there was about a 70% chance that the person was an engineer, while the engineer-low group estimated that the chances were about 30%. The subjects were then told that another person had been picked at random from the sample, and they were given the following brief description of the person:

> Jack is a 45-year-old man. He is married and has four children. He is generally conservative, careful, and ambitious. He shows no interest in political and social issues and spends most of his free time on his many hobbies, which include home carpentry, sailing and mathematical puzzles.

Again, both groups were asked to estimate the chances that the person was an engineer. This time, both groups said that the chances that Jack was an engineer were greater than 90%. Thus, when given the description, subjects seem to ignore the base rate information completely. What seems to be happening is that in this second case, the subjects are basing their judgements on Jack's similarity or representativeness to the category engineer and not on the proportion of engineers in the sample. Since proportions do not enter into similarity judgements, the representativeness hypothesis predicts that both groups will give identical estimates of the likelihood that Jack is an engineer, a result that was obtained.

The solution to this problem depends on a statistical theory known as Bayes' Theorem, which gives an equation for estimating the relative likelihoods of two rival hypotheses after examining a piece of relevant evidence. In the above problem, the alternative hypotheses are that the person is either an engineer or a lawyer, and the evidence is the description of the person. Numerous experiments on such problems have shown that subjects' probability judgements will ignore the base rate information even if the presented evidence is totally uninformative and does not discriminate between the hypotheses at all.

Such results seem to support the non-logical view of Kahneman and Tversky very clearly. However, it is possible to argue that the inclusion of a description of the individual, in the example above, leads the subjects to weight that evidence more strongly than would normally be the case. Without that weighting, subjects show an ability to make probability judgements based on the proportion of engineers in the sample. Ever since the work of Grice (1975) and more recently Sperber and Wilson (1986) it has been well known that participants in a conversation assume that the speaker's contribution will be relevant to the topic. Thus, subjects are likely to assume that the addition of the description must be there for a reason and so might plausibly infer that its addition overrides the statistical information about the sample. This account is compatible with Evans's (1989) view that non-logical representational heuristics that occur during language comprehension are responsible for the biases in reasoning, since the pre-attentive stage is likely to include the relevance judgements and consequent inferences that form part of language comprehension. However, as long as the statistical nature of the task remains transparent to the subjects, then normative performance will be revealed.

This possibility was endorsed by Evans and Dusoir (1977) and by Bar-Hillel (1982). They replicated one of Kahneman and Tversky's findings but also showed that the original results may in fact reflect an underlying statistical competence that was overlooked in the original study. Kahneman and Tversky's (1972b) test was to present their subjects with the following problem:

A certain town is served by two hospitals. In the larger hospital about 45 babies are born each day, and in the smaller hospital about 15 babies are born each day. As you know, about 50% of all babies are boys. The exact percentage of baby boys, however, varies from day to day. Sometimes it may be higher than 50%, sometimes lower.

For a period of one year, each hospital recorded the days on which more than 60% of the babies born were boys. Which hospital do you think recorded more such days?

According to probability theory, the smaller hospital will more often experience deviant results, since the smaller a sample size, the greater will be the deviation from the mean of 50%. Put another way, the greater the sample size, the more accurate will be the estimate of the characteristics of the population. However, Kahneman and Tversky found that most subjects ignored the overall number of babies born in each hospital and said that there would be no difference between the two hospitals in the number of days where more boys than girls were born. Thus Kahneman and Tversky claimed that, yet again, the subjects were using the representativeness heuristic, since they ignored sample size and seem to focus instead on the similarities between the two hospitals.

Evans and Dusoir (1977) and Bar-Hillel (1982) replicated these results, but also included additional conditions in which the proportion of boys was changed from 60% to 70%, 80%, or 100%. In these circumstances, subjects correctly chose the smaller hospital significantly more often in the 70%, 80%, and 100% versions (with a majority of correct responses in the 100% version). Thus, when the variation from the mean of 50% is made more marked, subjects become more sensitive to the role of sample size.

Overall, the work on the representativeness heuristic suggests that it is employed when the statistical nature of the task is masked by the way the problem is described. When the descriptions and instructions are transparent, statistical reasoning is evident.

Availability

Availability is the second major heuristic that replaces statistical reasoning, according to Kahneman and Tversky. This heuristic is used to estimate frequencies or probabilities and it depends on the ease with which instances can be retrieved from long-term memory. For example, a doctor examining a patient with suspected food poisoning might recall a number of case histories of patients presenting similar symptoms in the doctor's past experience, and use this information to estimate the likelihood of rival diagnoses in the present case. Provided that the doctor's memory is accurate and that his or her experience encompasses a sufficiently large and unbiased sample of examples, this should provide a fairly accurate guide to probability. Unfortunately, memory does not work in such an error-proof way. People are more likely to remember vivid events than mundane ones

(Nisbett and Ross, 1980) and they are more likely to remember salient events to which attention has been directed than they are to remember non-salient ones (Taylor and Thompson, 1982). That is, some events in memory are more easily available than others.

The best-known example of availability effects comes from Tversky and Kahneman (1973). They asked subjects to estimate the proportion of words in English that begin with k and the proportion of words in which k is the third letter. Most people find it easier to think of words that start with k than words with k as their third letter, so they say that the former is the more probable. Actually, the latter is more probable. People think otherwise, according to Tversky and Kahneman, because memory of spellings tends to be organized by initial letters.

The notion of vividness or salience is given some support from a study by Lichtenstein, Slovic, Fischoff, Layman and Coombs (1978) who asked their subjects to estimate the likelihood for various occurrences. Their results showed that subjects tend to overestimate the frequencies of very low frequency events and underestimate the frequencies of high frequency events. For example, death from diabetes or strokes was underestimated while death from tornadoes and floods was overestimated. Apart from actual frequency, Lichtenstein et al. suggested that the estimates are also influenced by the frequency with which dangers were mentioned in the media. For example, tornadoes and floods were almost always reported in the papers, thus inflating their perceived frequency and salience, while deaths from common diseases such as diabetes and strokes were rarely reported.

Availability is also influenced by prior knowledge, expectancies and beliefs. Such is the case with what has become known as illusory correlation. Illusory correlation refers to the phenomenon that people tend to find in data what they think (before they look) will be there. The most dramatic example is a series of studies conducted by Chapman and Chapman (1967, 1969). These studies showed that clinicians provided with a series of case descriptions will perceive patterns of relations between clinical tests and diagnoses that conform with their prior beliefs, but are actually not present in the data presented. For example, Chapman and Chapman noted that when clinicians used the Draw-a-Person Test, they assumed that patients project aspects of their personalities into their drawings. Thus, atypical eyes were thought to be associated with suspiciousness and more likely to be drawn by paranoid patients.

Many studies have shown that these ideas are wrong. When drawings made by paranoid patients are compared with drawings by normal people, no differences are found in the eyes. Yet clinicians persisted in believing these ideas. It seems that this is because, as Chapman and Chapman showed, when presented with drawings by paranoid and non-paranoid people, clinicians will 'see' correlations that are consistent with their beliefs, even when such correlations do not exist in the presented sample. In this case, the bias arises from the selective encoding (and hence subsequent retrieval) of evidence that favours a prior belief and it parallels the effect of beliefs on logical reasoning that was discussed in Chapter 7.

Overall, Kahneman and Tversky have carried out extensive research on statistical reasoning, research that indicates that subjects appear to understand a statistical principle in one context and totally fail to apply it in another. They argue that when people fail to apply a statistical principle it is because they have used heuristic inference rules, such as representativeness and availability, instead. Thus both heuristic and statistical rules are available for use, but which type of rule is actually used depends on the specific problem. It was suggested in the discussion of representativeness, that performance might depend on the notion of relevance. Such a suggestion raises the possibility that on some occasions subjects are not using heuristic rules at all. Instead, erroneous performance may be due to processes of language comprehension. This is the representational heuristics view, and it is particularly plausible in those cases where performance is affected by the wording of the problem, which presumably influences comprehension.

Representational Heuristics

Evans (1984, 1989) distinguished between heuristic and analytic processes in reasoning. Heuristic processes are preconscious. They determine what will be the subject's representation of the problem information. These pre-attentive heuristics, therefore, affect the interpretation of the problem and result in an impoverished or distorted representation that then serves as the basis for subsequent analytic processing. Analytic processes are (sometimes) conscious. They refer to the processes involved in drawing inferences from mental representations rather than those involved in constructing representations. The distinction could be regarded as one between the inferences needed to construct a mental model (heuristic inferences) and the inferences derived from manipulating mental models (analytic inferences). Evans further suggests that errors in reasoning are due to heuristic processes rather than to analytic processes, a suggestion that makes sense when one considers that heuristic inferences are predominantly inductive (see Chapter 6), while the analytic processes are deductive. In particular, he proposes that pre-attentive relevance judgements are responsible for the biases in reasoning that have been observed.

We have already seen how judgements of relevance might account for results otherwise attributable to the representativeness heuristic. But what about availability? Perhaps the availability heuristic reflects the fact that as long as the information is available, salient for example, it will be perceived as relevant. Evans disputes this possibility and argues that availability is not sufficient for relevance. He refers to a task that illustrates the base rate fallacy (Kahneman and Tversky, 1972a). The task is one in which subjects are told that two cab companies run in a city, the Blue cab company, which has 85% of the city's cabs, and the Green cab company, which has 15%. A cab is involved in a hit-and-run accident and a witness later identified the cab as a green one. When tested under conditions similar to those at the time of the accident, the witness correctly identified each of the two colours 80% of the time and failed 20% of the time. Subjects are then asked whether it is more likely that the cab is, in fact, a green one or a blue one. Most subjects say green although the correct answer, which takes account of base rates as well as the witness's reliability, is blue.

In this example, as well as in other base rate tasks, the base rate information is available, but is clearly not perceived as relevant. Instead, the evidence, whatever its usefulness, is deemed by the subjects to be more relevant than the base rates. Thus, Evans argues that more is involved in the perception of relevance than simply having the information available. The base rate information is highly salient in the presentation but is still normally ignored. Evans favours, therefore, a view of relevance that is a function of pre-attentive language comprehension processes.

Bar-Hillel (1980) has also argued that the base rate information is ignored because it is not perceived as relevant. When it is made relevant, then base rate information is used. Thus, performance on the cabs problem is greatly improved if subjects are told that there are equal numbers of blue and green cabs but that 85% of the cabs involved in accidents are blue ones. In this changed, but statistically equivalent, example subjects are given a reason for seeing the base rate information as relevant. Thus, the way the problem is phrased, an important determinant of comprehension, has considerable effects of performance.

Comprehension effects are also apparent in another phenomenon observed by Tversky and Kahneman. This is the phenomenon known as framing, which is due to the wording of the problem. Framing refers to the way that a decision can be influenced by changing the emphasis of gains and losses. Tversky and Kahneman (1981) gave subjects problems like the following:

Imagine that the USA is preparing for the outbreak of an unusual Asian disease, which is expected to kill 600 people. Two alternative programmes to combat the disease have been proposed. Assume that the exact scientific estimates of the consequences of the programmes are as follows:

If Programme A is adopted, 200 people will be saved.

If Programme B is adopted, there is 1/3 probability that 600 people will be saved, and 2/3 probability that no people will be saved?

Which of the two programmes would you favour?

About 72% of the subjects chose Programme A. However, another group of subjects was given the following alternatives in place of the ones above:

If Programme C is adopted, 400 people will die.

If Programme D is adopted, there is 1/3 probability that nobody will die, and 2/3 probability that 600 people will die.

The subjects faced with these alternatives chose Programme D 78% of the time, although the two problems are formally identical. However, it is clear that the two problems are not pragmatically identical. Kahneman and Tversky account for these findings by suggesting that values are not fixed but are a function of the perception of gains and losses relative to some psychologically neutral reference point. Further, the function is steeper for losses than for gains so that a given change hurts more as a loss than it pleases as a gain. In the *people will be saved* frame, the reference point is the loss of 600 lives, so 200 people saved is seen as a gain, while 1/3 probability that 600 will be saved is not a large perceived gain. In the *people will die* frame, the reference point is that no lives are lost, so 400 people dying is seen as a severe loss, while the 1/3 probability that nobody will die is a large perceived improvement.

Kahneman and Tversky's analysis is an interesting account of how people's values may change as a function of a perceived reference point. However, these observations are also compatible with Evans's view that pre-attentive non-logical biases may result in an impoverished representation being available for making the judgements: what is perceived as relevant in the two cases above is markedly different and so the resulting representations that are used to evaluate the two choices are also different.

Overall, Evans's proposal concerning pre-attentive heuristic processes seems most applicable to cases where the wording of the problem affects performance. Furthermore, it opens the way for a more specific account of why errors occur in reasoning since it attributes errors to inductive inferences during comprehension, inferences that are receiving a good deal of attention in work on language comprehension (see Chapters 5 and 6). Evans's analytic processes are those processes that operate on the representation and they may include both deductive inferences as proposed by Johnson-Laird and inductive heuristics as proposed by Kahneman and Tversky.

SUMMARY

Work on hypothesis testing was inspired by Piaget's view that people possess a content-free mental logic. Experimental analogues on adults of Piaget's tests on children showed, however, that performance was strongly influenced by the content of the problem. To explain these results both logical and non-logical accounts have been proposed. Non-logical accounts include pre-attentive heuristic processes and the retrieval of specific memories of past solutions. Logical accounts include the use of domain-specific rules and the manipulation of mental models. Domain-specific rules that have been suggested are pragmatic reasoning schemas, and specific inferences concerning social contracts. Mental models implicate general knowledge in the construction of a model but assume that specific rules are unnecessary for deduction, arguing instead that deduction is the manipulation of mental models. In general, mental models provides the best account of hypothesis testing, although it needs to be supplemented by more precise accounts of the use of heuristics (inductions) in the construction of a model, by an account of the way that specific solutions to a problem may be retrieved from memory and by an account of how utilities are estimated.

Work on judgement and choice has been dominated by the heuristics and biases approach of Kahneman and Tversky. They propose that people use heuristic short cuts to reach a solution (consistent with Simon's notion of satisficing), and that these heuristics lead to biases in performance. However, Kahneman and Tversky now acknowledge that normative statistical knowledge may lead to correct performance in some situations. Kahneman and Tversky are concerned with inferential heuristics that operate on the representation of the problem. They therefore have difficulty accounting for evidence that shows that the way a problem is interpreted determines whether heuristic (inductive) processes or statistical (deductive) rules will be used.

Evans argues that errors are due to pre-attentive representational heuristics that are used during language comprehension to construct a representation. Thus he provides an account of how interpretation of the problem affects performance. Such a view is compatible with the work reviewed in Chapters 5 and 6 that showed the pervasive use of inductive inferences during comprehension. It is also compatible with the theory of mental models that supposes that models are constructed through the use of (mainly) inductive inferences applied to propositions. The inferences that operate on the resulting representation may be purely deductive as suggested by Johnson-Laird or they may also include inductive heuristics of the kind proposed by Kahneman and Tversky.

This book opened with a chapter that detailed the changing assumptions about the relationship between language and thinking in work in the two domains. The present chapter discussed work on thinking that heavily implicates language comprehension processes, processes that themselves involve both linguistic knowledge and inductive processes. It is time, therefore, in the next and final chapter, to consider again the relationship between language and thinking, this time in relation to the issues that have arisen in the book.

CHAPTER 12 Language, thought and representation

Chapter 1, presented a brief historical review of work on language and thinking to show how the two topics have come to be seen as increasingly interrelated. Prior to this perceived interrelatedness, psychological work on language concentrated on the psychological reality of linguistic rules on the one hand, and the use of inferences on the other. Subsequently the work led to a view of language use that emphasizes both linguistic and non-linguistic knowledge. Work on thinking, too, has increasingly recognized the need to consider the way in which a problem is comprehended in arriving at a conclusion, thus recognizing the influence of linguistic comprehension processes on thinking. Furthermore, a number of workers have proposed that people may construct two kinds of representations during language comprehension: a linguistic, propositional representation, from which is constructed a mental model of the situation described by the sentence. Discussion of these two types of representation (linguistic propositions and situational mental models) has also arisen in work on thinking to characterize the ways that people arrive at logically valid conclusions, solve problems, and test hypotheses, emphasizing yet again the influence of language on thinking.

Subsequent chapters of this book spelled out in more detail the nature of these developments and illustrated how inferences are used in conjunction with linguistic processing in language comprehension and how language comprehension influences thought. In this chapter we return to the relationship between language and thinking and consider it afresh in the light of issues discussed in the preceding chapters. We will discuss the similarities and differences between language and thought in terms of the processes that are used, the nature of the knowledge upon which those processes operate, the way that language is used to communicate ideas, and the way that knowledge might be represented to support those processes.

OVERVIEW OF THE CHAPTER

The processes of thought consist of inductive and deductive inferences, which are general purpose cognitive processes. These two kinds of inference operate jointly in thinking to derive a new conclusion. The same joint involvement of induction and deduction occurs in language comprehension when bridging and elaborative inferences are made. These inferential processes of induction and deduction serve two different functions. One is to recognize information in the environment and retrieve information from long-term memory so that the premises of an argument can be constructed. Such recognition and retrieval processes may be either inductive or deductive, although they ultimately derive from induction. A second function is to operate on the premises that have been generated to derive a conclusion. Deductive inferences are used for this purpose and the term *operational processes* is used to refer to them. These two functions are apparent in language as well as in thinking. Cognitive processes may also be conscious or unconscious. Recognition and retrieval are unconscious parallel processes while operational processes, operate serially and may be either conscious or unconscious (Ericsson and Simon, 1980, 1984). Both language and thought make use of comparable conscious and unconscious processes. Language and thought are therefore similar in their use of general purpose processes that serve comparable functions and operate in similar ways.

While induction and deduction are general purpose, knowledge is domain-specific. It is suggested therefore that language comprehension uses domain-specific linguistic knowledge and that this domain-specificity is what marks language off from thinking in other domains. Specific knowledge of a domain increases with increasing expertise and the major difference between novices and experts when solving the same problems is that novices use general purpose inductive and deductive processes to act upon simple concepts while experts use general purpose processes to act upon increasingly complex and interconnected concepts. In the normal course of events, adults are experts when it comes to language. They use highly complex domain-specific knowledge to parse sentences so that their meanings can be derived. However, adults may well be novices in the domain that is the topic of a text or discourse. Thus expertise in language is used to convey ideas from other domains. The degree of expertise in the domain under discussion determines the ease with which a non-linguistic representation (a mental model) of the sentences can be constructed. Language is distinct, therefore, in its use of domain-specific linguistic knowledge. But since it is also used to communicate concepts from other domains it involves non-linguistic knowledge as well.

The use of language to communicate ideas from other domains occurs during the construction of a propositional representation, which combines domain-specific linguistic information with the concepts underlying the words in the sentence. Thus the link between language and thought, which enables thoughts to be conveyed through language, is between words and their meanings. Activation of the concepts underlying the meanings of the words results in activation of the knowledge network in the domain under discussion. If a sentence is about horses, for example, the word *horse* will activate a concept in the knowledge domain that concerns horses.

A representational system that can support language and thought requires consideration of the above issues. First, a plausible representational system needs to allow the use of both parallel recognition and retrieval processes and serial operational processes. Second, a plausible system needs to allow these processes to retrieve and manipulate both domain-specific linguistic knowledge and knowledge from other domains. Neither symbolic nor connectionist systems on their own satisfy these constraints, since symbolic systems emphasize serial processes while connectionist systems emphasize parallel ones. Instead, a hybrid system is favoured, in which symbolic units are stored in a parallel (connectionist) network, thus allowing both parallel recognition and retrieval processes and serial operational processes to be applied to a common knowledge store. The use of a common knowledge store for the two kinds of processes also allows linguistic knowledge to be combined with knowledge from other domains when a representation of a sentence is constructed.

The discussion that follows contains examples of topics and theories that were discussed in preceding chapters. However, no attempt has been made to be exhaustive and only specific examples have been used. When discussing thinking, for example, the text concentrates primarily on reasoning, creativity and problem solving and only occasionally or in passing refers to other topics, such as concept formation or hypothesis testing. However, the ideas discussed can be applied to these other topics as well.

A number of arbitrary distinctions are made, such as those between conscious and unconscious processes and between propositional representations and mental models, both in this chapter and throughout the book. However, it needs to be borne in mind that the cognitive system is dynamic. That is, changes occur in the system over time. For example, the distinction between unconscious and conscious processes is hard to maintain in absolute terms. Language comprehension processes may be unconscious initially while processes occurring at a later point in time may be conscious. The distinction between propositional representations and mental models is equally blurred. At the extremes, propositional representations are distinct from mental models in that the former encode only information that is explicitly contained in the sentence while the latter includes inferences based on general knowledge as well. In reality though, the transition from one representation to the other is graded, with constructed representations ranging from the purely linguistic, as in propositional representations, through to increasingly rich mental models that depend on the ease with which additional information can be retrieved from long-term memory. Thus any distinctions that are made, such as those between unconscious and conscious processes or propositions and mental models, dissect a dynamic system by holding it static with respect to that distinction. The distinctions will break down when the dynamic nature of the system is emphasized.

Lastly, discussions of language in the chapter focus on comprehension. This is because the linguistic processes of comprehension differ from those of production and so they cannot be treated identically. Nor is there space to treat each individually. However, the general conclusions about the interplay between processes and knowledge and about the relation between language and thinking apply equally to comprehension and production.

GENERAL PURPOSE PROCESSES: INDUCTION AND DEDUCTION

In their work on problem solving, Newell and Simon (1972) highlighted the importance of general purpose processes. They argued that novice problem solvers (including experts solving novel problems) use general purpose heuristic strategies to find a solution. They thus emphasized the generality of inductive processes, such as means–ends analysis. Newell and Simon were not the first to argue that the processes of thought are general purpose and common to different knowledge domains. Piaget (e.g. 1950) made a similar case for deduction when he argued that cognitive development involved the acquisition of the rules of propositional logic. Thus, like Newell and Simon, Piaget believed that thought processes are general regardless of the domain. This view is maintained in this chapter except that, unlike Newell and Simon and Piaget, both induction and deduction are classed as the general purpose processes of thought, not one or the other in isolation.

Deductive inferences derive a conclusion from a set of premises according to the rules of logic. As long as these rules are followed, the conclusions will be valid. Propositional and syllogistic inferences are typical deductive inferences. Transitive inferences are also regarded as deductive, although they require the use of meaning postulates as well as standard rules of logic. Other logical operations include conjunction and disjunction. For example, recognition of a compound concept, such as *rural policeman*, involves the logical operation of conjunction. Recognition of a disjunctive concept (characterized by *or*), such as a server's loss of a point in tennis by *either* serving a double fault *or* failing to return the ball, requires the logical operation of disjunction.

Inductive inferences make a generalization, which may be unwarranted, on the basis of some evidence. For example, the statement that *Fido is a dog*, may be used as evidence to infer that Fido has four legs, since dogs usually have four legs. However, this is an inductive inference based on beliefs about dogs and may not be warranted. Unbeknownst to the reasoner, Fido might have been hit by a car and have only three legs as a result of the accident. Similarly, the identification of an object in the world, such as the identification of a plant as being a member of a particular species, is an inductive inference based on appearance and so may be mistaken. The 'weed' that has been discarded may have been a flower, for example.

We can distinguish between inductive and deductive inferences more precisely by saying that inductive inferences generate the premises for a deductive argument while deductive inferences derive a valid conclusion from the generated premises. (The conclusion itself may also form a premise in a new argument.) Consider again the Fido example. The information that *Fido is a dog* is recognized from the input. Activation of the concept of *dogs* during comprehension will lead to the retrieval of additional information about dogs, such as their four-leggedness. Recognition of information in the input and retrieval of information from long-term memory are inductive inferences that generate the premises of a deductive argument. Once the premises have been generated, deductive processes may operate on them to yield a valid conclusion as follows:

> Dogs have four legs   (12.1)
> Fido is a dog
>
> Therefore, Fido has four legs

Thus, we can distinguish recognition and retrieval processes from processes that operate on representations to derive new conclusions. These latter processes are called operational processes. Recognition and retrieval processes involve both induction and deduction, while operational processes are deductive. The retrieval of additional information about dogs having four legs in example (12.1) illustrates retrieval processes that are inductive. The retrieval of information to interpret a novel compound concept, such as *apartment dog*, illustrates retrieval processes that are deductive.

Recognition and retrieval do not require language for their implementation. Objects and events in the world, for example, can be recognized without the involvement of language. Similarly, information is retrieved from long-term memory without the involvement of language. However, language makes use of these processes in the course of generating representations of the linguistic input. By contrast, since operational processes manipulate the generated representations, they are dependent on the nature of those representations. Thus, when considering thought in relation to language, operational processes depend upon linguistic processes to construct the representations that are manipulated.

At heart recognition and retrieval are inductive, since the original premises to deductive arguments are always inductive. Thus, even though deductively derived conclusions may serve as premises, such conclusions depend initially upon inductively generated premises. Conversely, while operational processes are at heart deductive, they are still prone to error and seemingly inductive because they depend on induction to provide the content of the premises. Further, inductive inferences may influence thinking during a sequence of deductions and so increase the likelihood of error. For example, manipulating mental models when reasoning, verifying a potential solution in creative thinking, and reaching the solution in problem solving may all involve the retrieval of additional information during the sequence of operations. These examples are considered in more detail below.

Thinking

Logical reasoning is commonly thought of as a good example of 'pure' deduction. When presented with the following syllogism:

All A are B   (12.2)

All B are C

Therefore, All A are C

people have little difficulty in agreeing that the conclusion is valid. By contrast, creative thinking is commonly thought of as a good example of 'pure' induction. On the basis of what he or she already knows, an individual may produce (or infer) a novel idea that categorizes what is known in a new way and that leads to the recognition of new instances. However, the idea that there are 'pure' examples of deduction and induction does not square well with the discussion above, where it was suggested that the two processes are jointly involved in the derivation of a valid conclusion. Closer consideration of reasoning and creativity indicates that such pure cases of deduction and induction are indeed unlikely. Problem solving, too, involves an interplay between induction and deduction in the course of finding a solution.

Reasoning

The solution of logical problems depends on the form of the arguments, not on their content. Thus the following conclusion is logical:

If the moon is made of cheese   (12.3)
then it will soon be eaten.
The moon is made of cheese.

Therefore, The moon will soon be eaten.

No matter how much the truth of the premises and the resulting conclusions might be disputed, the inferences are logically impeccable. However, although people show that they are able to reason logically, they also have difficulty in ignoring the content of the problem. They therefore diverge from the dictates of logic in ways that indicate that they are seduced by the content rather than the form of the argument (Evans, 1989). Thus, people interpret premises in ways that are consistent with their own beliefs about the world and hence may construct representations of the premises that are different from the ones intended (e.g. Henle, 1962). People are also loath to accept a valid conclusion if the conclusion is unbelievable, while they more readily accept a valid conclusion if it conforms to beliefs about the world (e.g. Oakhill, Johnson-Laird and Garnham, 1989).

This influence of content is known as the belief bias effect and indicates the involvement of *induction* in what are traditionally regarded as formal logical tasks. Most major theories of reasoning acknowledge such influences of induction in supposedly deductive tasks, although they do so in different ways. Syntactic theorists (e.g. Braine, 1978; Rips, 1983) maintain a clear distinction between language and thought and attribute inductive inferences to processes occurring during language comprehension, so maintaining the view that thinking itself is purely deductive. By contrast the semantic view (e.g. Johnson-Laird and Byrne, 1991) eschews such a clear separation between language and thought. According to this view, inductive inferences are not confined to processes of comprehension. They are also used in the reasoning process itself, as well as providing a 'filter' on the acceptability of the final conclusion (Oakhill, Johnson-Laird and Garnham, 1989). Specifically, the semantic view assumes that reasoning involves a comprehension stage, an inference stage, and a logical stage. Inductive processes may lead to belief effects at any of these three stages. In the comprehension stage, the use of retrieved general knowledge along with the linguistic input to construct a mental model of the situation described by the premises requires inductive as well as deductive inferences. In the inference stage, where people try to formulate a candidate conclusion from the mental model, retrieved general knowledge may again be used to evaluate the conclusion. In the logical stage, where people try to construct alternative models of the premises that refute the candidate conclusion, retrieved general knowledge may be used yet again to construct the alternative models and to evaluate conclusions derived from them. However, despite their differences, both syntactic and semantic views assume that inductive processes contribute to the derivation of a logical conclusion while reasoning.

Creativity

Similar arguments can be made against the idea that creativity is an example of 'pure' induction. The retrieval of an idea that is novel for the thinker is normally regarded as a key feature of creativity and is largely inductive. However, induction alone cannot account for creative thinking, since novel ideas must also be seen to be relevant and lead to further insights (see Chapter 10). Operational processes are therefore needed to test the idea for its validity and to pursue its implications. These operational processes treat the retrieved ideas as premises from which new conclusions are derived. If more than one potential solution is retrieved, this second phase chooses between the alternatives. This second phase of thought is deliberate and constrained by short-term memory. In short, it is operational and occurs one step at a time in a serial manner. It is also a necessary component of creativity. It is not enough, for example, to have an original idea, since a creative solution will not be recognized as such unless its relevance to the problem has been verified and its implications spelled out. This is apparent, for example, when an idea is turned into a novel by a writer or a symphony by a composer or a theory by a scientist. In each case, the original idea or insight is followed by rigorous attempts to verify the idea and apply it in a systematic manner.

This distinction between a retrieval phase and an operational phase is consistent with the two-component view of creativity that was discussed in Chapter 10. For example, Langley, Simon, Bradshaw and Zytkow (1987) see creative thinking as consisting of discovery and verification. They thus distinguish between originality on the one hand – generating a novel idea – and relevance on the other hand – verifying the idea's appropriateness. While recognition and retrieval predominate in the first phase, operational processes predominate in the second. Perhaps the reason why creativity is thought to be less 'logical' than reasoning is because the premises are normally supplied in deductive reasoning so that retrieval processes are confined to interpreting the premises and evaluating the conclusion. In creative thinking, by contrast, the premises themselves are also retrieved from long-term memory so that idea generation as well as interpretation and evaluation requires retrieval processes.

Problem solving

The more mundane forms of problem solving also involve both induction and deduction. Unlike creativity, which focuses on ill-defined problems, problem solving focuses on well-defined problems for which there is a single correct solution. Means–ends analysis, which finds ways of reducing the difference between the initial state and the goal state, is often used in these circumstances (Newell and Simon, 1972).

Means–ends analysis uses operational processes to achieve the goal by transforming the initial state into an intermediate state and by successively transforming one intermediate state into another until the goal state is reached. This progressive transformation of one representation into another is brought about by deductive processes that are characterized by production rules. However, the particular route that is traversed using such production rules is dependent on the retrieval of background knowledge that determines what the contents of the problem states will be. Since retrieval is primarily inductive, the route to the solution is therefore prone to error.

It can be seen therefore that induction and deduction are jointly involved in thinking, through the use of recognition, retrieval and operational processes. We can now consider whether or not the same is true of language.

Language

In Chapter 5 a distinction was made between bridging inferences and elaborative inferences. Bridging inferences ensure that the sentences of a text or discourse cohere. Elaborative inferences, on the other hand, merely enrich the representation that is constructed and are not needed to establish coherence. Bridging inferences, therefore, are made during language comprehension but elaborative inferences may not be, or, if they are, may be made in only a very sketchy manner and very slowly. Both bridging and elaborative inferences involve inductive and deductive inferences.

Consider bridging inferences first. A bridging inference is needed to recognize that the person referred to by *she* in the second clause of (12.4) is the same as the person referred to by *Jane* in the first clause.

> Jane was late for her appointment with Sue   (12.4)
> and she hurried to get a taxi

Such an inference depends on the retrieval of a premise to the effect that if someone is late then they are likely to hurry. Retrieval of this premise is constrained by knowledge of shared assumptions about the nature of discourse and general principles of relevance and may of course be unwarranted (see Chapters 5 and 6). Nevertheless, the retrieved premise, together with premises constructed from the information in the sentence, then supports the deductive inference that *she* refers to *Jane*. Thus, bridging inferences use operational processes to derive a valid conclusion from premises generated by recognition of the input and retrieval from long-term memory.

Elaborative inferences also use operational processes on premises based on evidence in the input and on inferences retrieved from long-term memory. The inference that *the actress died* triggered by the sentence, *The actress fell from the 14th floor* (McKoon and Ratcliff, 1986) is an elaborative inference. It is a deductively valid conclusion derived from the evidence in the input (*The actress fell from the 14th floor*), and from retrieved information about buildings and the consequences of falling from a height.

The joint involvement of inductive and deductive processes in the two kinds of inference made during comprehension may account for the observation that the distinction between pragmatic and logical inferences does not seem to have any psychological consequences in comprehension (see, e.g. Singer, 1990). Sperber and Wilson (1986), have argued that the relevance of a discourse is established by deductive conclusions that are derived from inductively generated premises. The above discussion would support such a view except that the premises may be generated using deduction as well as induction.

In summary, therefore, language seems to make use of the general purpose cognitive processes of induction and deduction in the construction of a representation of a sentence. These processes also serve similar functions in language and thought, that is, they recognize and retrieve premises and operate on those premises. Language and thought, therefore, can be regarded as similar since they share these inductive and deductive inferential processes. Of course, there is more to language comprehension than the use of inferences. Syntactic information is also used to construct a linguistic representation of a sentence (see Chapter 3). Since syntactic processing is very fast and seems largely to occur outside of conscious awareness, consideration of it will be postponed until conscious and unconscious processes have been examined.

CONSCIOUS AND UNCONSCIOUS PROCESSES

Ericsson and Simon (1980, 1984) distinguished between what can and what cannot be verbally reported (roughly comparable to what can and what cannot be consciously accessed), and between two kinds of unreportable (unconscious) processes. Ericsson and Simon claim that the contents of short-term memory are what people describe when thinking aloud, while the processes responsible for reading information into short-term memory are not available for conscious inspection. In brief, we are conscious of the current contents of short-term memory, but of not much else. However, Ericsson and Simon also suggest that conscious processes may become automatic, and hence unconscious, with repeated practice over time. Ericsson and Simon, therefore, make a further distinction between two kinds of unconscious (or pre-conscious) processing: what they call recognition processes and automatic processes.

Conscious processes are characterized by production rules (Anderson, 1983; Newell and Simon, 1972). These rules are used by novices during the acquisition of expertise (Anderson, 1983). We are aware of their activity because they operate on the conscious contents of short-term memory. The application of production rules is serial: only one rule can operate at a time, thus reflecting the sequential nature of deliberate thought. With increasing expertise, the need to maintain information in short-term memory is eliminated and so conscious awareness of production rules is lost and they become automatic. The use of production rules corresponds to the use of operational processes that manipulate premises once they have been constructed.

One of the key features of production rules is that they describe a logical system. That is, they embody the principle of using a known rule (of the form *if p then q*), together with information about the truth of *p*, to infer that *q* follows. In this way the action described by *q* is carried out whenever the condition described by *p* is met. The derivation of *q* conforms to the rule of *modus ponens* in propositional logic.

In addition to the production rules identified by Ericsson and Simon, the manipulation of mental models also requires operational processes that may be conscious. Manipulation of mental models includes the ability to make inferences based on *modus tollens* as well *modus ponens*. *Modus tollens* is the inference *not p* from *if p then q* and *not q*. It is notoriously difficult (see Chapter 7), possibly because of the demands it makes on short-term memory as well as the need to make implicit information explicit in the mental model. However, with increasing expertise, as both kinds of inferences consistently lead to successful conclusions, the knowledge upon which they operate is encoded in production rules that become automatic. Thus, the once novel content becomes embedded in stored rules that fire automatically when the conditions encoded in the antecedents of the rules are met.

Performance based on mental models and on production rules is not purely deductive of course, since the processes depend on induction to provide their content. To take problem solving as an example, the initial state provides the content for *p*, the condition part of a production rule, while the goal (or sub-goal) state provides the content for *q*, the action part of the rule. Application of *modus ponens* when the production rule is used guarantees the successful conversion of the current state to the goal state. But the usefulness of reaching that goal state depends on the inductive processes that construct the initial state, the goal state and the intermediate states. Deductive production rules, therefore, cannot guarantee the validity of a conclusion because the content of the rules, what defines the problem states, depends upon recognition and retrieval processes that are largely inductive.

Unconscious automatic processes are production rules that may once have been conscious and have become inaccessible through learning and practice (Anderson, 1983; Ericsson and Simon, 1980, 1984). However, they may also be learned processes that have never been conscious at all. Such implicit learning seems to characterize skilled performance, such as learning to operate complex systems (e.g.

Broadbent, Fitzgerald and Broadbent, 1986) or learning a first language (e.g. Stevenson, 1988), rather than conceptual learning. When concepts are elaborated and ideas are developed they are more likely to be consciously manipulated. To modify an example from Johnson-Laird (1988) playing rugby is an automatic skill but a rugby trainer's knowledge of the rules of the game and the strategies that improve performance requires explicit understanding. Such explicit knowledge, unlike the automatic skill, has to be explicitly learned and so makes use of conscious processes. However, when production rules are automatic, the premises do not enter short-term memory and are instead manipulated outside of conscious awareness. Automatic production rules, like conscious ones, apply one at a time in a serial manner to transform one representation into another in the derivation of a conclusion.

Unconscious recognition processes are responsible for the retrieval of information from long-term memory and the recognition of information in the environment. To be consistent with previous terminology, the term retrieval will be used here when talking about retrieving information from long-term memory, and use of the term recognition will be confined to cases of recognizing environmental input. Nevertheless, in line with Ericsson and Simon, both retrieval and recognition can be regarded as unconscious processes that are responsible for generating the premises used by operational processes. As we have already seen, these unconscious processes may be either inductive or deductive depending, for example, on whether what is retrieved is a simple fact or a complex concept. Unconscious recognition and retrieval processes are very fast and occur in parallel. Thus many concepts in long-term memory may be activated during retrieval although only one of them can enter short-term memory and hence consciousness at any one time.

This tripartite distinction highlights further the complex yet intimate relationship between inductive and deductive inferences. Recognition and retrieval processes, which may be either inductive or deductive, are unconscious. They generate premises that are used by operational processes, such as those that manipulate mental models or apply production rules. Operational processes may be either conscious or automatic, depending on whether or not they operate on information that is held in short-term memory. This suggests that conscious and unconscious processes, like inductive and deductive processes, are jointly involved in both thinking and language.

Thinking

Thinking has traditionally been considered as a conscious, deliberate process, a view that is reflected in the information processing model of problem solving by Newell and Simon. However, if one thing is apparent from the discussion of thinking in this book, it is that much of human thinking goes on at an unconscious level. Indeed, it is likely that only a small part of thinking occurs at the level of conscious awareness. In conceptual behaviour, for example, the initial formation of a new concept may be largely unconscious, triggered as it is by the recognition of features in the environment and the retrieval of general knowledge from long-term memory (see Chapter 8). Furthermore, subsequent tests of whether or not the initial hypothesis is valid, using operational processes, may be either conscious or automatic (see Chapter 11), depending on whether or not short-term memory is involved. Short-term memory capacity is most likely to be used when novel information is manipulated (see Chapter 10).

Similar considerations apply to reasoning and creativity. We have already seen that both kinds of thinking involve unconscious recognition and retrieval processes for interpreting or generating premises. What we now need to add to this account is a delineation of conscious and automatic operational processes. Reasoning in a novel domain or at the boundaries of one's knowledge is often highly conscious and dependent on the deliberate rehearsal of novel information in short-term memory. Such conscious deliberations may be characterized as the manipulation of mental models (Johnson-Laird, 1983). With increasing expertise, these deliberations become embedded in production rules that fire automatically. Such expert behaviour may be characterized by the syntactic view of reasoning (e.g. Braine, 1978), a view that is supported by the results of the study by Wood (1969). (See also Stevenson, in press.)

Creativity relies on unconscious recognition and retrieval processes to generate the premises of a deductive argument, so that potential conclusions can be evaluated. With increasing expertise in a domain there are increasing constraints on retrieval, which makes it more likely that a successful solution will be retrieved. The hallmark of creative thinking may well be those rare occasions when the retrieved solution can be seen to fit the problem and to generate new insights almost immediately, thus reducing the contribution of conscious reflection. But in the normal course of events, such happy coincidences are probably rare, as Langley et al. (1987) have argued. Instead, generated ideas are normally subjected to intense conscious thought, which is operational, to establish their relevance and pursue their implications. In this case too, increasing familiarity with the ideas renders such conscious processes automatic. Thus reasoning and creativity involve conscious and automatic operational processes as well as unconscious recognition and retrieval processes.

Language

It has been said a number of times in this book that language comprehension is a fast, automatic process, much of which occurs outside of conscious awareness. In other words, we seem to be aware of an interpretation of a sentence, but we have no conscious access to the processes that led to this interpretation. Of course, the point at which we become aware of an interpretation is unclear. It is possible, for example, that we do not do so unless we engage in further reflective operational processes and manipulate alternative models of the state of affairs described by the text. Nevertheless, all three kinds of processes identified by Ericsson and Simon are implicated in the processes that result in an interpretation.

First, unconscious recognition and retrieval processes are involved in the construction of representations of text or discourse. Recognition of the input, together with retrieved concepts representing the meanings of the words in the sentence, contribute to a propositional representation. The retrieval of additional related concepts that are implicated by the sentence rather than explicitly stated contribute to a mental model of the situation described by the sentence. Second, automatic production rules use syntactic knowledge together with the retrieved concepts so that the relations between the concepts representing the words can be specified in the propositional representation. That is, production rules, which allow symbols to be lawfully combined in many different ways, seem best to characterize the linguistic processes that construct propositional representations (e.g. Kintsch, 1988). These automatic production rules may never have been conscious at all, since the processes of comprehension during language acquisition do not seem to be explicitly learned.

Production rules also compute bridging and (possibly) elaborative inferences to construct an integrated representation of the text that is based on the propositional representation in conjunction with implicated concepts. Such an integrated representation forms a mental model of the situation described by the sentence. Whether production rules that compute inferences during comprehension are automatic or conscious may depend on whether or not the comprehender deliberately attempts to make the conclusions explicit, and also on the level of expertise of the reader or listener in the knowledge domain under discussion. For example, when reading a text for the purposes of understanding and learning, the reader may explicitly attempt to establish the relevance of the derived inferences to the information in the text and to pursue the implications of conclusions derived from them. In addition, if the text is about an unfamiliar domain, then the inferences used to construct a mental model may also be conscious rather than automatic. However, increasing familiarity with the domain will lead to the inferences becoming automatically encoded in production rules so that they are no longer effortful and in need of short-term memory capacity.

In summary, like thinking, language comprehension involves both conscious and unconscious processes. The recognition of the linguistic input, the retrieval of concepts underlying the meanings of the words in the sentence, and the retrieval of related concepts all require the use of unconscious parallel processes. Operational processes of deduction also occur during comprehension. Syntactic parsing uses automatic production rules that are highly overlearned and that seem not to have been consciously learned. By contrast, bridging and elaborative inferences may use conscious processing if the information in the text or discourse is to be explicitly learned or if it is unfamiliar. Once such information has become familiar, the inferences can be encoded in production rules that are automatic.

The discussion suggests, therefore, that language and thought are similar in that they share a set of common processes that serve similar functions and are used in similar ways. However, it is also evident that the knowledge upon which these processes operate may influence their activity. We will, therefore, turn to a discussion of domain-specific knowledge that is acquired with increasing expertise and that is implicated in the use of general purpose cognitive processes in language and thinking.

DOMAIN-SPECIFIC KNOWLEDGE

Research on expertise has led to the notion of domain-specificity. Simon and his colleagues (e.g. Anderson, 1983; Simon and Gilmartin, 1973) argue that with increasing expertise, problem solvers replace weak general purpose rules with more powerful domain-specific rules. Of course, experts also use general purpose rules when they solve problems at the limits of their expertise (Langley et al., 1987). The term 'expert' is not meant to imply that experts know all there is to know of their domain. The efforts of experts to develop new ideas and to extend their knowledge are comparable to the efforts of absolute novices when first learning about a domain. Thus, the major differences between novices and experts are apparent only when they work on the same problems. Nevertheless, there is something that marks experts off from novices even when experts are struggling at the frontiers of their knowledge. This something, of course, is knowledge, which constrains the ways in which a novel problem is interpreted, and which is characterized by complex concepts and stored automatic production rules. Thus, the concepts in a domain that serve as the input to retrieval processes are richer, more complex and more interconnected in experts than in novices, and previously acquired knowledge has become embedded in production rules that can be retrieved and used automatically. The processes of induction and deduction, therefore, are general purpose processes but the knowledge that these processes retrieve and operate upon becomes more and more domain specific with increasing expertise. In other words, processes are general purpose; knowledge is domain specific. Linguistic knowledge is also domain specific and is not shared by other domains.

There is a great deal of evidence to support the idea that domain-specific principles are the mainstay of cognitive activity. Much of that evidence has been obtained by Newell and Simon and their colleagues in their work on problem solving. Although Newell and Simon started with the view that problem solving makes use of a small number of general purpose rules, they soon discovered that experts solve problems differently from novices in the same domain. Experts in many technical and academic domains show comparable differences to novices in the domain. For example, expert physicists (Larkin, 1981) radiographers (e.g. Lesgold et al., 1988), chess players (De Groot, 1965;

Chase and Simon, 1973) and computer programmers (e.g. Anderson, 1983) all make use of domain-specific knowledge to solve problems in their domains rapidly and without conscious effort. These same problems are solved only with great difficulty by novices. The rapid inferencing of experts seems to be due to the use of automatic production rules (Anderson, 1983). It is probably also due to the way that the knowledge network of an expert constrains the retrieval of relevant information while problem solving.

With extensive practice, deliberate processes that were originally needed to test the validity of a retrieved solution become converted into automatic production rules. Similarly, with increasing expertise, the knowledge base of a domain becomes more complex and more richly interconnected, thus increasing the likelihood that relevant information will be rapidly activated and retrieved. When chess grandmasters choose a move, for example, the perceived pattern on the chess-board triggers the retrieval of a specific move that has been used in similar situations before. However, since the retrieved move would not have been used in the identical situation before, it is then evaluated, using operational processes that may be conscious, before it is finally selected. The pattern on the board also activates a rich store of interconnected concepts that can be retrieved to aid interpretation of the current configuration of pieces. Chess novices, by contrast, have no such facility. They cannot retrieve a production rule that says that with a given configuration of pieces a particular move is probably the best, and they cannot retrieve a set of interconnected concepts that allow them to interpret the current pattern in terms of similar configurations. Instead, novices have to hold retrieved information about each individual piece in short-term memory and apply production rules to this information to generate possible moves. This leaves little spare capacity to evaluate potential moves and so mistakes are common. Novices, therefore, are hesitant in their problem solving and prone to error through the loss of information from short-term memory, and through lack of sufficient capacity to evaluate moves effectively.

Thus experts recognize and retrieve increasingly complex interconnected concepts and encode these complex concepts in the conditions and actions of production rules. The interconnections between the concepts act as constraints on recognition and retrieval since the concepts can activate each other once one of them has been activated.

Novices apply production rules to retrieved knowledge that is very simple, experts apply them to complex chunks of knowledge. Thus, experts have the advantage of automaticity acquired through practice, but they also have the advantage of retrieving complex knowledge that can be manipulated as mental models and encoded in production rules. This is the case even when they behave like novices and have to manipulate novel information in short-term memory when working at the frontiers of their knowledge.

Research on practical intelligence also shows how specific abilities enable people to retrieve information and so make inferences in their domain in a manner that is far superior to their normal mode of thinking. These studies have demonstrated impressive feats of cognition, including mathematical thinking in people doing supermarket shopping (Lave, Murtaugh and de la Rocha, 1984), statistical reasoning by tipsters when working out the odds for a bet on a horse-race (Ceci and Liker, 1988), three-dimensional mathematical and spatial reasoning by dairy workers skilled at stacking crates (Scribner, 1988), and complex navigational skills in pre-literate Polynesian islanders (Oatley, 1977). All of these studies attest to the importance of domain-specific knowledge.

The competent use of language by virtually every adult is a comparable complex feat. It has long been argued (e.g. Chomsky, 1959; Fodor, 1983) that one of the most important achievements of human development is the acquisition of language. Children as young as two and three years of age reveal sophisticated knowledge of complex linguistic concepts even in their earliest encounters with the domain. This linguistic knowledge may be seen as domain-specific knowledge that is employed by inductive and deductive processes in language use. Such a distinction between domain-specific linguistic knowledge and the use of that knowledge by general purpose cognitive processes characterizes the distinction between competence and performance (Chomsky, 1965). Linguistic competence is the domain-specific knowledge of language that everyone possesses. Linguistic performance depends upon the ways in which inductive and deductive processes retrieve, recognize and manipulate this knowledge and integrate it with concepts from other domains. Thus expertise in language involves the ability to retrieve and recognize increasingly complex linguistic knowledge and to embed it in automatic production rules through repeated practice. It also involves recognizing, retrieving and manipulating non-linguistic knowledge in the domain that is being communicated. The extent to which non-linguistic knowledge is manipulated automatically depends upon the goals of reading or listening and the level of expertise in the domain.

Barring accidents, all adults are domain-specific experts as far as language is concerned, but they may be only novices in the domain that provides the content of the message being conveyed. Thus, much of reading, listening, writing and speaking will be unconscious and effortless if the information that is communicated is familiar and does not need to be made explicit. In these circumstances there will be fast and efficient retrieval routes to additional relevant information in the form of stored production rules and a richly interconnected network of concepts. By contrast, reading, listening, writing and speaking will be conscious and effortful if the information that is communicated is unfamiliar or there is a need to for it to be explicitly learned. When reading an unfamiliar text, for example, there will be no fast or efficient retrieval routes to make inferencing automatic and so short-term memory must be used to derive the inferences explicitly. Underlying all this activity, however, is expertise in the domain of language that makes it possible to communicate and understand new ideas in both familiar and unfamiliar domains.

Language, therefore, can be regarded as a distinct skill, dependent on domain-specific knowledge that differs from knowledge in other domains. However, this specific linguistic knowledge is used to communicate ideas in other domains. In order for such communication to occur, there must be a link, or interface, between the processes that act upon domain-specific knowledge and those that act upon knowledge in other domains. The nature of this link is discussed in the next section.

Communicating Ideas: The Link between Language and other Knowledge Domains

During language comprehension, linguistic knowledge is combined with non-linguistic knowledge when a propositional representation is constructed. Automatic production rules that encode syntactic information are triggered by the words in the sentence to construct a representation that specifies the relations between the concepts underlying the words in the sentence. The concepts themselves are also activated by words in the sentence. These retrieved concepts activate other related concepts in the knowledge network of the domain that is the topic of the text or discourse. Thus, syntactic information from the linguistic domain is combined with information, in the form of concepts, from another domain to construct a propositional representation of the sentence. Additional related concepts are also retrieved from the non-linguistic domain through the activation of interconnecting links between the concepts and are used to construct a mental model of the sentence. The level of expertise of the comprehender will determine how many and how readily such additional concepts will be retrieved. If the comprehender is an expert in the domain and the knowledge network consists of highly interconnected concepts that are strongly linked, the related concepts will be numerous and readily retrieved. But if the comprehender is a novice in the domain and the knowledge network consists of relatively few concepts that have weak links to other concepts, then related concepts will be minimal and difficult to retrieve. Such an account is comparable to that proposed by Kintsch (1988).

The main point, though, concerns the way that common processes act on linguistic and non-linguistic knowledge to construct a propositional representation. This enables the non-linguistic information to be communicated to others. The non-linguistic knowledge is activated by the words in the sentence and represents the concepts underlying the meanings of the words. The link therefore between linguistic knowledge and knowledge in other domains is specified by the link between words and concepts. Words activate syntactic knowledge in the linguistic domain and concepts in non-linguistic domains. General purpose operational processes act on the retrieved knowledge to integrate the two domains in a propositional representation of the input. In this way, language can be used for communication.

It remains to consider how knowledge might be represented so that general purpose cognitive processes can operate on linguistic and non-linguistic knowledge to make communication possible.

Systems of Representation

Symbolic representational systems have symbols as units that are activated in a serial fashion. By serial it is meant that the activation of a unit depends upon the prior activation of another unit elsewhere in the semantic hierarchy. For example, in McClelland and Rumelhart's (1981) interactive model of word recognition (see Chapter 2), the activation of units that are high up in the hierarchy (e.g. word units) depends upon activation of units that are lower down in the hierarchy (e.g. letter units). Thus there is a sequential dependency between units at different levels. Another feature of symbolic representations is that they are logical (that is, deductive) systems. For example, the Collins and Quillian (1969) model of semantic memory is strictly logical, the system at any given point in time being in only one of two states, *true* or *false*. Thus an instance either is or is not a member of a category. There is no blurring at the edges and, contrary to the constraints of reality, no possibility of viewing instances as more or less typical of a category. Furthermore, knowledge about individuals that exist in the world, as opposed to conceptual knowledge about category membership, is hard to characterize in a semantic network.

Subsequent developments in symbolic systems have generally focused on attempts to modify such a strongly deductive model. That is, subsequent work has tried to develop serial symbolic systems that can accommodate inductive as well as deductive processes. The first step in these developments led to spreading activation models of semantic memory (e.g. Collins and Loftus, 1975), which allow for graded category membership based on typicality judgements. The second step led to scripts (e.g. Schank and Abelson, 1977) and frames (Minsky, 1977), which encode typical situations and events in the world as well as the more purely deductive conceptual knowledge. However, despite these developments, serial symbolic models, rooted as they are in sequential logical processes, have difficulty in giving a natural explanation of rapid and error-prone performance that is based on induction (see Chapter 2).

Parallel distributed processing (PDP) or connectionist systems were designed to overcome these problems. As the first name implies, PDP systems use distributed representations that are activated in parallel. By distributed it is meant that each unit is a simple element and that the activation of several of these units corresponds to the activation of a concept. In other words, the representation of a concept is distributed across several simple units. Activation occurs in parallel because many different units may be activated at the same time, as in the activation of the units corresponding to a specific concept. (McClelland and Rumelhart's (1981) interactive model of word recognition would be a parallel model if, on encountering a word such as RED, all the relevant units, including those at the feature level, the letter level and the word level, were activated directly by the stimulus.) Once activated, each unit will excite or inhibit other units with which it is connected, thus producing a pattern of activation that changes over time as new excitatory and inhibitory links become activated. When the system stabilizes, the final pattern of activation determines the current cognitive state of the system. If the final pattern of activation exceeds some threshold level, then it may enter short-term memory and hence conscious awareness.

This alternative to serial symbolic systems addresses the problem of induction directly. In PDP systems therefore, induction is primary because a parallel system supports recognition and retrieval processes that are ultimately inductive. Deduction, however, is a derivative notion that depends on the activation of the system. The extent to which PDP can explain all forms of deduction has yet to be established. However, it has proved difficult to simulate operational processes in a PDP system, since these processes are sequential, being dependent on the prior construction of representations that can be manipulated to derive a conclusion. A preoccupation with operational processes lies at the heart of a number of criticisms of PDP that point to the difficulties such systems have in interpreting relational information, such as that conveyed by language, and in explaining the serial and deliberate processes of thought that require the use of short-term memory (e.g. Fodor and Pylyshyn, 1988; Pinker and Prince, 1988). In addition, the PDP systems that have been used to explain cognitive processes are rarely distributed (see e.g. Holyoak, 1991; Kintsch, 1988). Instead, the units are symbolic units or simple concepts and the pattern of activation over a number of units defines a complex concept or proposition. This has the benefit of enabling both simple and complex concepts to be activated by similar processes. It also removes the element of PDP that makes it incompatible with a symbolic system.

Hybrid systems

Once the notion of distributed representations is removed from connectionist systems then the door is opened for a hybrid system that allows both parallel and serial processes to act on a common knowledge store. Thus, a parallel knowledge network, in which the units are concepts, can be used by both parallel processes of retrieval and serial operational processes that manipulate what has been retrieved. Operational processes may also be stored directly in the knowledge base in the form of automatic production rules that are retrieved in the same way as other stored knowledge, perhaps through the establishment of very strong links between the concepts encoded in the rules.

The essence of such a hybrid system is that the units are symbolic and that the links between the units are activated in parallel. In addition, the discussion of domain specificity implies that the knowledge network consists of sub-networks of highly interconnected concepts, corresponding to knowledge in specific domains. These sub-networks may have links to other sub-networks. In particular, the linguistic domain is connected to other domains through the links between words and the concepts that underlie them.

SUMMARY

Inductive and deductive inferences are general purpose processes of thought. Inductive inferences generate premises that form a deductive argument. Deductive inferences may also yield premises to form a new argument but in addition, deductive inferences derive valid conclusions from the generated premises. Both inductive and deductive inferences are used in the parallel and unconscious processes of recognition and retrieval, although inductive inferences are primary. Only deductive inferences are also used in serial processes that operate on the premises that have been recognized or retrieved. These operational processes may be conscious or automatic, depending on the goals of learning and on the familiarity of the subject matter. Language also makes use of these general purpose thought processes. Thus language and thought are similar in their use of common processes.

Deliberate attempts to learn new knowledge or to extend existing knowledge require the use of conscious operational processes that manipulate the knowledge to establish its relevance and pursue its implications. Such conscious processes become automatic with repeated use on the same material. If the learning is not deliberately undertaken, then the operational processes are always automatic, even during initial learning. The inferences that enrich mental models may be conscious if the contents of the text are novel and are being deliberately learned, becoming automatic with increasing familiarity. The use of production rules that encode syntactic information in parsing a sentence are automatic and are not the consequence of deliberate learning.

Knowledge of language is distinct from knowledge in other domains. However, language also communicates concepts from other domains. General purpose cognitive processes operate on both linguistic and non-linguistic knowledge during the communication of such concepts. This is made possible because the words of a language activate both concepts in non-linguistic domains and production rules that encode syntactic information in the linguistic domain.

A hybrid system of representation seems best placed to support both parallel processes of recognition and retrieval and serial operational processes. In such a system, the units are concepts connected together by links that are activated in parallel. A knowledge domain can be represented in the system by a sub-network of interconnected concepts that may have links to other sub-networks. Thus, words link the linguistic domain to other domains when the meanings of the words are activated.

Overall, therefore, we can say that language and thought share common processes of induction and deduction and use them for similar purposes of recognition, retrieval and the manipulation of premises. However, language can be said to be distinct from thought in that it depends on domain-specific linguistic knowledge. For language to be used in communication, however, linguistic knowledge must be linked to knowledge in other domains. Such a link can be found in the way that words activate both syntactic knowledge and concepts in other domains.

References

Adelson, B. (1984) When novices surpass experts: The difficulty of a task may increase with expertise, *Journal of Experimental Psychology: Learning, Memory and Cognition*, **10**, 483–495.

Allard, F. and Starkes, J.L. (1990) Expertise in sport (abstract) in *The Proceedings of the Twelfth Annual Conference of the Cognitive Science Society*, Lawrence Erlbaum Associates, Hillsdale, NJ.

Allard, F. and Starkes, J.L. (1991) Motor skill experts in sports, dance and other domains in *Towards a General Theory of Expertise: Prospects and Limits* (Eds K.A. Ericsson and J. Smith), Cambridge University Press, Cambridge.

Altmann, G. and Steedman, M. (1988) Interaction with context during human sentence processing, *Cognition*, **30**, 191–238.

Amaiwa, S. (1987) Transfer of subtraction procedures from abacus to paper and pencil, *Japanese Journal of Educational Psychology*, **35**, 41–48 (in Japanese with English summary).

Anderson, J.R. (1983) *The Architecture of Cognition*, Harvard University Press, Cambridge, Mass.

Anderson, J.R. (1985) *Cognitive Psychology and Its Implications*, 2nd edn, W.H. Freeman and Company, New York.

Anderson, J.R. and Bower, G.H. (1973) *Human Associative Memory*, John Wiley and Sons, New York.

Anderson, A., Garrod, S.C. and Sanford, A.J. (1983) The accessibility of pronominal antecedents as a function of episode shifts in narrative texts, *Quarterly Journal of Experimental Psychology*, **35A**, 427–440.

Anderson, J.R., Kline, P.J. and Beasley, C.M. (1977) A theory of the acquisition of cognitive skills, ONR Technical Report 77-1, Yale University. Cited by Anderson, J.R. (1983) *The Architecture of Cognition*, Harvard University Press, Cambridge, Mass.

Anderson, J.R., Kline, P.J. and Beasley, C.M. (1980) Complex learning processes, in *Aptitude, Learning, and Instruction*, Vol. 2 (Eds R.E. Snow, P.A. Ferderico and W.E. Montague), Lawrence Erlbaum Associates, Hillsdale, NJ.

Anderson, J.R. and Thompson, R. (1989) Use of analogy in a production system architecture, in *Similarity and Analogical Reasoning* (Eds S. Vosniadou and A. Ortony), Cambridge University Press, Cambridge.

Anderson, R.C. and Ortony, A. (1975) On putting apples into bottles: A problem of polysemy, *Cognitive Psychology*, **7**, 167–180.

Arkes, H.R. and Harkness, A.R. (1980) Effect of making a diagnosis on subsequent recognition of symptoms, *Journal of Experimental Psychology: Human Learning and Memory*, **6**, 568–575.

Armstrong, S.L., Gleitman, L.R. and Gleitman, H. (1983) What some concepts might not be, *Cognition*, **13**, 263–308.

Atwood, M.E. and Polson, P.G. (1976) A process model for water jug problems, *Cognitive Psychology*, **8**, 191–216.

Austin, J.L. (1962) *How To Do Things With Words*, Oxford University Press, Oxford.

Barclay, J.R. (1973) The role of comprehension in remembering sentences, *Cognitive Psychology*, **4**, 229–254.

Bar-Hillel, J.R. (1980) The base rate fallacy in probability judgements, *Acta Psychologica*, **44**, 211–233.

Bar-Hillel, M. (1982) Studies of representativeness, in *Judgement Under Uncertainty: Heuristics and Biases* (Eds D. Kahneman, P. Slovic, and A. Tversky), Cambridge University Press, Cambridge.

Barron, F. (1969) *Creative Person and Creative Process*, Holt, Rinehart and Winston, New York.

Barsalou, L.W. (1983) Ad hoc categories, *Memory and Cognition*, **11**, 211–227.

Barsalou, L.W. (1985) Ideals, central tendency, and frequency of instantiation as determinants of graded structure in categories, *Journal of Experimental Psychology: Learning, Memory and Cognition*, **11**, 629–654.

Barsalou, L.W. (1989) Intra-concept similarity and its implications for inter-concept similarity, in *Similarity and Analogical Reasoning* (Eds S. Vosniadou & A. Ortony), pp. 76–121, Cambridge University Press, Cambridge.

Barsalou, L.W. and Sewell, D.R. (1984) Constructing representations of categories from different points of view, Emory Cognition Project Technical Report No.2, Emory University, Atlanta, Ga.

Bartlett, F.C. (1932) *Remembering: A Study in Experimental and Social Psychology*, Cambridge University Press, Cambridge.

Barwise, J. and Perry, J. (1983) *Situations and Attitudes*, Bradford Books, MIT Press, Cambridge, Mass.

Begg, I. and Denny, P. (1969) Empirical reconciliation of atmosphere and conversion interpretations of syllogistic reasoning errors, *Journal of Experimental Psychology*, **81**, 351–354.

Berry, D.C. and Broadbent, D.E. (1984) On the relationship between task performance and associated verbalizable knowledge, *Quarterly Journal of Experimental Psychology*, **35A**, 39–49.

Bever, T.G. (1970) The cognitive basis for linguistic structures, in *Cognition and the Development of Language* (Ed. J.R. Hayes), John Wiley, New York.

Bower, G.H., Black, J.B. and Turner, T.J. (1979) Scripts in text comprehension and memory, *Cognitive Psychology*, **11**, 177–220.

Brachman, R.J. (1979) On the epistemological status of semantic nets, in *Associative Networks: Representation and Use of Knowledge by Computers*, Academic Press, New York.

Brachman, R.J. (1983) What IS-A is and isn't, *Computer*, **16**, 30–36.

Braine, M.D.S. (1978) On the relation between the natural logic of reasoning and standard logic, *Psychological Review*, **85**, 1–21.

Braine, M.D.S., Reiser, B.J. and Rumain, B. (1984) Some empirical justification for a theory of natural propositional logic, in *The Psychology of Learning and Motivation*, Vol. 18 (Ed. G.H. Bower), Academic Press, New York.

Braine, M.D.S. and Rumain, B. (1983) Logical reasoning, in *Handbook of Child Psychology, Vol. 3: Cognitive Development*, 4th edn, (Eds J.H. Flavell and E.H. Markman), John Wiley, New York.

Bransford, J.D., Barclay, J. and Franks, J. (1972) Sentence memory: a constructive versus interpretative approach, *Cognitive Psychology*, **3**, 193–209.

Bransford, J.D. and Franks, J.J. (1971) The abstraction of linguistic ideas, *Cognitive Psychology*, **2**, 331–350.

Bransford, J.D. and Johnson, M.K. (1972) Contextual prerequisites for understanding: some investigations of comprehension and recall, *Journal of Verbal Learning and Verbal Behaviour*, **11**, 717–726.

Broadbent, D.E., Fitzgerald, P. and Broadbent, M.H.P. (1986) Implicit and explicit knowledge in the control of complex systems, *British Journal of Psychology*, **77**, 33–50.

Bruner, J.S., Goodnow, J.J. and Austin, G.A. (1956) *A Study of Thinking*, John Wiley, New York.

Bruner, J.S., Olver, R.R., Greenfield, P.M. et al. (1966) *Studies in Cognitive Growth*. John Wiley, New York.

Byrne, R.M.J. and Johnson-Laird, P.N. (1990) Models and deductive reasoning, in *Lines of Thinking: Reflections on the Psychology of Thought, Vol. 1: Representation, Reasoning, Analogy and Decision Making* (Eds K.J. Gilhooly, M.T.G. Keane, R.H. Logie and G. Erdos), John Wiley, Chichester.

Cantor, N. and Mischel, W. (1977) Traits as prototypes: Effects on recognition memory, *Journal of Personality and Social Psychology*, **35**, 38–48.

Caramazza, A. and Zurif, E.B. (1976) Dissociation of algorithmic and heuristic processes in language comprehension: Evidence from aphasia, *Brain and Language*, **3**, 572–582.

Carey, S. (1985) *Conceptual Change in Childhood*, MIT Press, Cambridge, Mass.

Carnap, R. (1952) Meaning postulates, *Philosophical Studies*, **3**, 65–73.

Carpenter, T.P. and Moser, J.M. (1982) The development of addition and subtraction problem-solving skills, in *Addition and Subtraction: A Cognitive Perspective*, (Eds J.P. Carpenter, J.M. Moser and T. Romberg), Lawrence Erlbaum Associates, Hillsdale, NJ.

Carraher, T.N., Carraher, D.W. and Schliemannn, A.D. (1985) Mathematics in the streets and in schools, *British Journal of Experimental Psychology*, **3**, 21–29.

Carston, R. (1988) Implicature, explicature and truth-conditional semantics, in *Mental Representation and the Interface Between Language and Reality* (Ed. R. Kempson), Cambridge University Press, Cambridge.

Ceci, S.J. and Liker, J. (1988) Academic and non-academic intelligence: An experimental separation, in *Practical Intelligence: Nature and Origins of Competence in the Everyday World*, (Eds R.J. Sternberg and R.K. Wagner) Cambridge University Press, Cambridge.

Chafe, W.L. (1972) Discourse structure and human knowledge, in *Language Comprehension and the Acquisition of Knowledge* (Eds J.B. Carroll and R.O. Freedle), Winston, Washington.

Chapman, L.J. and Chapman, J.P. (1959) Atmosphere effect reexamined, *Journal of Experimental Psychology*, **58**, 220–226.

Chapman, L.J. and Chapman, J.P. (1967) Genesis of popular but erroneous diagnostic observations, *Journal of Abnormal Psychology*, **72**, 193–204.

Chapman, L.J. and Chapman, J.P. (1969) Illusory correlation as an obstacle to the use of valid psychodiagnostic signs, *Journal of Abnormal Psychology*, **74**, 272–280.

Chase, W.G. and Ericsson, K.A. (1981) Skilled memory, in *Cognitive Skills and Their Acquisition* (Ed. J.R. Anderson), pp. 141–189, Lawrence Erlbaum Associates, Hillsdale, NJ.

Chase, W.G. and Ericsson, K.A. (1982) Skill and working memory, in *The Psychology of Learning and Motivation*, Vol. 16 (Ed. G.H. Bower), pp. 1–58, Academic Press, New York.

Chase, W.G. and Simon, H.A. (1973) The mind's eye in chess, in *Visual Information Processing* (Ed. W.G. Chase), Academic Press, New York.

Cheng, P.W. and Holyoak, K.J. (1985) Pragmatic reasoning schemas, *Cognitive Psychology*, **17**, 391–416.

Chi, M.T.H., Bassok, M., Lewis, M.W., Reimann, P. and Glaser, R. (1989) Self-explanations: How students study and use examples in learning to solve problems, *Cognitive Science*, **13**, 145–182.

Chi, M.T.H., Feltovich, P. and Glaser, R. (1981) Categorization and representation of physics problems by experts and novices, *Cognitive Science*, **5**, 121–152.

Chi, M.T.H., Glaser, R. and Farr, M.J. (1988) *The Nature of Expertise*, Lawrence Erlbaum Associates, Hillsdale, NJ.

Chierchia, G. and McConnell-Ginet, S. (1990) *Meaning and Grammar: An Introduction to Semantics*, MIT Press, Cambridge, Mass.

Chomsky, N. (1957) *Syntactic Structures*, The Hague, Mouton.

Chomsky, N. (1959) Review of Skinner's Verbal Behaviour, *Language*, **35**, 26–58.

Chomsky, N. (1965) *Aspects of the Theory of Syntax*, MIT Press, Cambridge, Mass.

Chomsky, N. (1980) *Rules and Representations*, Blackwell, Oxford.

Chomsky, N. (1981) *Lectures on Government and Binding*, Foris, Dordrecht.

Clancy, P.M. (1980) Referential choice in English and Japanese narrative discourse, in *The Pear Stories, Volume III: Advances in Discourse Processes* (Ed. W.L. Chafe), Ablex Publishing Corporation Norwood, NJ.

Clark, H.H. (1969) Linguistic processes in deductive reasoning, *Psychological Review*, **76**, 387–404.

Clark, H.H. (1979) Responding to indirect speech acts, *Cognitive Psychology*, **11**, 430–477.

Clark, H.H. (1987) Four dimensions of language use, in *The Pragmatic Perspective: Proceedings of the 1985 International Pragmatics Conference* (Eds M.B. Papi and J. Verschueren), John Benjamins.

Clark, H.H. and Carlson, T.B. (1982) Speech acts and hearers' beliefs, in *Mutual Knowledge* (Ed. N.V. Smith), pp. 1–37, Academic Press, London.

Clark, H.H. and Clark, E.V. (1977) *Psychology and Language: An Introduction to Psycholinguistics*, Harcourt Brace Jovanovich, New York.

Clark, H.H. and Lucy, P. (1975) Understanding what is meant from what is said: A study in conversationally conveyed requests, *Journal of Verbal Learning and Verbal Behaviour*, **14**, 56–72.

Clark, H.H. and Marshall, C.R. (1981) Definite reference and mutual knowledge, in *Elements of Discourse Understanding* (Eds A. Joshi, B. Webber and I. Sag), Cambridge University Press, Cambridge.

Clark, H.H. and Wilkes-Gibbs, D. (1986) Referring as a collaborative process, *Cognition*, **22**, 1–39.

Clement, J. (1989) Learning via model construction and criticism: protocol evidence on sources of creativity in science, in *Handbook of Creativity: Assessment, Theory and Research* (Eds J. Glover, A. Ronning and C. Reynolds), Plenum Press, New York.

Clifton, C. (1990) The use of lexical information in sentence comprehension, Five College Cognitive Science Paper 90–1, University of Massachusetts.

Cohen, B. and Murphy, G.L. (1984) Models of concepts, *Cognitive Science*, **8**, 27–58.

Collins, A.M. and Loftus, E.F. (1975) A spreading activation theory of semantic processing, *Psychological Review*, **82**, 407–428.

Collins, A.M. and Quillian, R. (1969) Retrieval time from semantic memory, *Journal of Verbal Learning and Verbal Behaviour*, **8**, 240–247.

Conrad, C. (1972) Cognitive economy in semantic memory, *Journal of Experimental Psychology*, **92**, 149–154.

Cosmides, L. (1985) Deduction or Darwinian algorithms? An explanation of the 'elusive' content effect on the Wason selection task, unpublished Ph.D. thesis, Harvard University, Cambridge, Mass.

Cosmides, L. (1989) The logic of social exchange: Has natural selection shaped how humans reason? *Cognition*, **31**, 187–276.

Crain, S. and Steedman, M. (1985) On not being led up the garden path: The use of context by the psychological syntax processor, in *Natural Language Parsing* (Eds D. Dowty, L. Karttunen, and A. Zwicky), pp. 320–354, Cambridge University Press, Cambridge.

De Groot, A. (1965) *Thought and Choice in Chess*, Mouton, The Hague.

De Soto, C.B., London, M. and Handel, S. (1965) Social reasoning and spatial paralogic, *Journal of Personality and Social Psychology*, **2**, 513–521.

Dickstein, L.S. (1981) The meaning of conversion in syllogistic reasoning, *Bulletin of the Psychonomic Society*, **18**, 135–138.

Dijk, T.A. van and Kintsch, W. (1983) *Strategies of Discourse Comprehension*, Academic Press, New York.

Duncker, K. (1945) On problem solving, *Psychological Monographs*, **58** (5, Whole No. 270)

Egan, D.E. and Greeno, J.G. (1974) Theory of rule induction: Knowledge acquired in concept learning, serial pattern learning, and problem solving, in *Knowledge and Cognition* (Ed. L.W. Gregg), Lawrence Erlbaum Associates, Hillsdale, NJ.

Ehrlich, K. (1980) Comprehension of pronouns, *Quarterly Journal of Experimental Psychology*, **32**, 247–255.

Ehrlich, K. and Johnson-Laird, P.N. (1982) Spatial descriptions and referential continuity, *Journal of Verbal Learning and Verbal Behaviour*, **21**, 296–306.

Erickson, J.R. (1974) A set analysis theory of behaviour in formal syllogistic reasoning tasks, in *Theories of Cognitive Psychology: The Loyola Symposium* (Ed. R. Solso), Lawrence Erlbaum Associates, Hillsdale, NJ.

Erickson, J.R. (1978) Research in syllogistic reasoning, in *Human Reasoning* (Eds R. Revlin and R.E. Meyer), John Wiley, New York.

Ericsson, K.A. and Polson, P.G. (1988) A cognitive analysis of exceptional memory for restaurant orders, in *The Nature of Expertise* (Eds M.T.H. Chi, R. Glaser, and M.J. Farr), pp. 23–70, Lawrence Erlbaum Associates, Hillsdale, NJ.

Ericsson, K.A. and Simon, H.A. (1980) Verbal reports as data, *Psychological Review*, 87, 215–251.

Ericsson, K.A. and Simon, H.A. (1984) *Protocol Analysis: Verbal Reports as Data*, MIT Press, Cambridge, Mass.

Evans, J.St.B.T. (1972) Interpretation and matching bias in a reasoning task, *British Journal of Psychology*, **24**, 193–199.

Evans, J.St.B.T. (1982) *The Psychology of Deductive Reasoning*, Routledge & Kegan Paul, London.

Evans, J.St.B.T. (1984) Heuristic and analytic processes in reasoning, *British Journal of Psychology*, **75**, 457–68.

Evans, J.St.B.T. (1989) *Bias in Human Reasoning: Causes and Consequences*, Lawrence Erlbaum Associates, Hove and London.

Evans, J.St.B.T. and Dusoir, A.E. (1977) Proportionality and sample size as factors in intuitive statistical judgement, *Acta Psychologica*, **41**, 129–137.

Evans, J.St.B.T. and Lynch, J.S. (1973) Matching bias in the selection task, *British Journal of Psychology*, **64**, 391–397.

Fehr, B. (1988) Prototype analysis of the concepts of love and commitment, *Journal of Personality and Social Psychology*, **55**, 557–579.

Fehr, B. and Russell, J.A. (1984) Concept of emotion viewed from a prototype perspective, *Journal of Experimental Psychology: General*, **113**, 464–486.

Feldman, J.A. and Ballard, D.H. (1982) Connectionist models and their properties, *Cognitive Science*, **6**, 205–254.

Ferreira, F. and Clifton, C.Jnr. (1986) The independence of syntactic processing, *Journal of Memory and Language*, **25**, 348–368.

Fodor, J.A. (1983) *Modularity of Mind*, MIT Press, Cambridge, Mass.

Fodor, J.A., Bever, T.G. and Garrett, M.F. (1974) *The Psychology of Language: An Introduction to Psycholinguistics and Generative Grammar*, McGraw-Hill, New York.

Fodor, J.A., Fodor, J.D. and Garrett, M.F. (1975) The psychological unreality of semantic representations, *Linguistic Inquiry*, **VI**, 515–531.

Fodor, J.A., Garrett, M.F. and Bever, T.G. (1968) Some syntactic determinants of sentence complexity, II: Verb structure, *Perception and Psychophysics*, **3**, 453–461.

Fodor, J.A. and Pylyshyn, Z. (1988) Connectionism and cognitive architecture: a critical analysis, *Cognition*, **28**, 3–71.

Frazier, L. (1978) On comprehending sentences: syntactic parsing strategies, unpublished Ph.D. thesis, University of Connecticut, Storrs, Connecticut.

Frazier, L. (1987) Sentence processing: A tutorial review, in *Attention and Performance, XII: The Psychology of Reading* (Ed. M. Coltheart), pp. 559–586, Lawrence Erlbaum Associates, London.

Frazier, L. (1990) Parsing modifiers: Special purpose routines in the human sentence processing mechanism? In *Comprehension Processes in Reading* (Eds D.A. Balota, G.B. Flores d'Arcais and K. Rayner), Lawrence Erlbaum Associates, Hillsdale, NJ.

Frazier, L. and Fodor, J.D. (1978) The sausage machine: A new two-stage parsing model, *Cognition*, **6**, 291–325.

Frazier, L. and Rayner, K. (1982) Making and correcting errors during sentence comprehension: eye movements in analysis of structurally ambiguous sentences, *Cognitive Psychology*, **14**, 178–210.

Frege, G. (1879) Conceptual notation: A formula language of pure thought modelled upon the formula language of arithmetic, *Conceptual Language and Related Articles* (Ed. and trans. T.W. Bynum, 1972), Oxford University Press, Oxford.

Garnham, A. (1981) *Mental Models as Representations of Discourse and Text*, unpublished Ph.D. thesis, University of Sussex.

Garnham, A. (1985) *Psycholinguistic: Central Topics*, Methuen, London and New York.

Garnham, A. (1987) *Mental Models as Representations of Discourse and Text*, Ellis Horwood Limited, Chichester.

Garrod, D. and Anderson, A. (1987) Saying what you mean in dialogue: A study in conceptual and semantic coordination, *Cognition*, **27**, 181–218.

Garrod, S. and Sanford, A.J. (1985) On the real-time character of interpretation during reading, *Language and Cognitive Processes*, **1**, 43–59.

Gazdar, G. (1979) *Pragmatics: Implicature, Presupposition and Logical Form*, Academic Press, New York.

Geis, J.L. and Zwicky, A.M. (1971) On invited inferences, *Linguistic Inquiry*, **2**, 561–566.

Gelman, R. (1990) First principles organise attention to and learning about relevant data: Number and the animate-inanimate distinction as examples, *Cognitive Science*, **14**, 79–106.

Gelman, R. and Gallistel, C.R. (1978) *The Child's Understanding of Number*, Harvard University Press, Cambridge, Mass.

Gelman, S.A. and Markman, E. (1987) Young children's inductions from natural kinds: The role of categories and appearances, *Child Development*, **59**, 1532–1541.

Gentner, D. (1983) Structure-mapping: A theoretical framework for analogy, *Cognitive Science*, **7**, 155–170.

Gentner, D. and Clement, C. (1989) Evidence of relational selectivity in interpreting analogy and metaphor, in *The Psychology of Learning and Motivation* (Ed. G. Bower), Academic Press, New York.

Gentner, D. and Gentner, D.R. (1983) Flowing waters or teeming crowds: mental models of electricity, in *Mental Models* (Eds D. Gentner and A.L. Stevens), Lawrence Erlbaum Associates, Hillsdale, NJ.

Gentner, D. and Toupin, C. (1986) Systematicity and surface similarity in the development of analogy, *Cognitive Science*, **10**, 227–300.

Gernsbacher, M.A. and Hargreaves, D.J. (1989) Accessing sentence participants: The advantage of first mention, *Journal of Memory and Language*, **27**, 699–717.

Gerrig, R.J. (1987) Relevance theory, mutual knowledge and accidental relevance: Commentary on Sperber and Wilson's Precis of Relevance: Communication and Cognition, *Behavioural and Brain Sciences*, **10**, 717–718.

Gibbs, R.W. (1984) Literal meaning and psychological theory, *Cognitive Science*, **8**, 275–304.

Gick, M.L. and Holyoak, K.J. (1980) Analogical problem solving, *Cognitive Psychology*, **12**, 306–355.

Gick, M.L. and Holyoak, K.J. (1983) Schema induction in analogical transfer, *Cognitive Psychology*, **15**, 1–38.

Gildea, P. and Glucksberg, S. (1983) On understanding metaphor: The role of context, *Journal of Verbal Learning and Verbal Behaviour*, **22**, 577–590.

Gilhooly, K.J. (1982) *Thinking. Directed, Undirected and Creative*, Academic Press, London.

Glass, A.L. and Holyoak, K.J. (1986) *Cognition*, Random House, New York.

Glenberg, A., Meyer, M. and Lindem, K. (1987) Mental models contribute to foregrounding during text comprehension, *Journal of Memory and Language*, **26**, 69–83.

Glucksberg, S. (1991) When love is not a journey: what metaphors and idioms mean, paper presented at the Sylvia Beach Language Comprehension Conference, Newport, Oregon.

Glucksberg, S., Gildea, P. and Bookin, H. (1982) On understanding non-literal speech: Can people ignore metaphors? *Journal of Verbal Learning and Verbal Behaviour*, **21**, 85–98.

Glucksberg, S. and Keysar, B. (1990) Understanding metaphorical comparisons: Beyond similarity, *Psychological Review*, **97**, 3–18.

Goetz, E.T. Anderson, R.C. and Schallert, D.L. (1981) The representation of sentences in memory, *Journal of Verbal Learning and Verbal Behaviour*, **20**, 656–670.

Goldin, S.E. (1978) Memory for the ordinary: Typicality effects in chess memory, *Journal of Experimental Psychology: Human Learning and Memory*, **4**, 605–616.

Golding, E. (1981) The effect of past experience on problem solving. Paper presented to the British Psychological Society, Surrey University.

Goodman, N. (1972) Seven strictures on similarity, in *Problems and Projects* (Ed. N. Goodman), pp. 437–447, Bobbs-Merrill, Indianapolis.

Greene, J. (1986) *Language Understanding: A Cognitive Approach*, Open University Press, Milton Keynes.

Grice, H.P. (1975) Logic and conversation, in *Syntax and Semantics, Vol. 3: Speech Acts* (Eds P. Cole and J.L. Morgan), Seminar Press, New York.

Griggs, R.A. and Cox, J.R. (1982) The elusive thematic-materials effects in Wason's selection task, *British Journal of Psychology*, **73**, 407–420.

Guilford, J.P. (1966) Intelligence: 1965 Model, *American Psychologist*, **21**, 20–26.

Guyote, M.J. and Sternberg, R.J. (1981) A transitive-chain theory of syllogistic reasoning, *Cognitive Psychology*, **13**, 461–525.

Hampton, J.A. (1987) Inheritance of attributes in natural concept conjunctions, *Memory and Cognition*, **15**, 55–71.

Hampton, J.A. (1988) Overextension of conjunctive concepts: Evidence for a unitary model of concept typicality and class inclusion, *Journal of Experimental Psychology: Learning, Memory and Cognition*, **14**, 12–32.

Hartley, J. and Homa, D. (1981) Abstraction of stylistic concepts, *Journal of Experimental Psychology: Human Learning and Memory*, **7**, 33–46.

Hatano, G. (1988) Social and motivational bases for mathematical understanding, in *Children's Mathematics* (Eds G.B. Saxe and M. Gearhart), Jossey-Bass, San Francisco.

Hatano, G. and Inagaki, K. (1986) Two courses of expertise, in *Child Development and Education in Japan* (Eds H. Stevenson, H. Azuma and K. Hakuta), Freeman, San Francisco.

Haugeland, J. (1985) *Artificial Intelligence: The Very Idea*, MIT Press, Cambridge, Mass.

Haviland, S.E. and Clark, H.H. (1974) What's new? acquiring new information as a process in comprehension, *Journal of Verbal Learning and Verbal Behaviour*, **13**, 512–521.

Hayes, J.R. and Simon, H.A. (1974) Understanding written problem instructions, in *Knowledge and Cognition* (Ed. L.W. Gregg), Lawrence Erlbaum Associates, Hillsdale, NJ.

Hayes, J.R. and Simon, H.A. (1977) Psychological differences among problem isomorphs, in *Cognitive Theory*, Vol. 2 (Eds N.J. Castellan,

D.B. Pisoni and G.R. Potts), Lawrence Erlbaum Associates, Hillsdale, NJ.

Heim, I. (1983) The semantics of definite and indefinite noun phrases, Ph.D. thesis, University of Massachusetts, Amherst, Mass.

Henle, M. (1962) On the relation between logic and thinking, *Psychological Review*, **69**, 366–378.

Holland, J.H., Holyoak, K.J., Nisbett, R.E. and Thagard, P.R. (1986) *Induction: Processes of Inference, Learning and Discovery*, MIT Press, Cambridge, Mass.

Holyoak, K.J. (1982) An analogical framework for literary interpretation, *Poetics*, **11**, 105–126.

Holyoak, K.J. (1985) The pragmatics of analogical transfer, *The Psychology of Learning and Motivation*, **19**, 59–87.

Holyoak, K.J. (1990) Problem solving, in *An Invitation to Cognitive Science: Thinking, Vol. 3* (Eds D.N. Osherson and E.E. Smith), MIT Press, Cambridge, Mass.

Holyoak, K.J. (1991) Symbolic connectionism: toward third generation theories of expertise, in *Toward a General Theory of Expertise: Prospects and Limits*, (Eds K.A. Ericsson and J. Smith), Cambridge University Press, Cambridge.

Holyoak, K.J. and Koh, K. (1987) Surface and structural similarity in analogical transfer, *Memory and Cognition*, **15**, 332–340.

Holyoak, K.J. and Thagard, P.R. (1989) Analogical mapping by constraint satisfaction, *Cognitive Science*, **13**, 295–355.

Holyoak, K.J. and Thagard, P.R. (1990) A constraint-satisfaction approach to analogue retrieval and mapping, in *Lines of Thinking: Reflections on the Psychology of Thought, Vol. 1: Representation, Reasoning, Analogy and Decision Making* (Eds K.J. Gilhooly, M.T.G. Keane, R.H. Logie and G. Erdos), John Wiley, Chichester.

Huttenlocher, J. (1968) Constructing spatial images: A strategy in reasoning, *Psychological Review*, **75**, 550–560.

Inhelder, B. and Piaget, J. (1958) *The Growth of Logical Thinking*, Basic Books, New York.

Johnson, M.K., Bransford, J.D. and Solomon, S. (1973) Memory for tacit implications of sentences, *Journal of Experimental Psychology*, **98**, 203–205.

Johnson-Laird, P.N. (1977) Psycholinguistics without linguistics, in *Tutorial Essays in Psychology*, Vol. 1 (Ed. N.S. Sutherland), Lawrence Erlbaum Associates, Hillsdale, NJ.

Johnson-Laird, P.N. (1983) *Mental Models*, Harvard University Press, Cambridge, Mass.

Johnson-Laird, P.N. (1988) *The Computer and The Mind. An Introduction to Cognitive Science,* Fontana Press, London.

Johnson-Laird, P.N. and Bara, B.G. (1984) Syllogistic inference, *Cognition,* **16,** 1–61.

Johnson-Laird, P.N. and Byrne, R.M.J. (1989) Only reasoning, *Journal of Memory and Language,* **28,** 313–330.

Johnson-Laird, P.N. and Byrne, R.M.J. (1991) *Deduction,* Lawrence Erlbaum Associates, Hove and London.

Johnson-Laird, P.N., Byrne, R.M.J. and Tabossi, P. (1989) Reasoning by model: The case of multiple quantification, *Psychological Review,* **96,** 658–673.

Johnson-Laird, P.N. and Garnham, A. (1980) Descriptions and discourse models, *Linguistics and Philosophy,* **3,** 371–393.

Johnson-Laird, P.N., Herrman, D.J. and Chaffin, R. (1984) Only connections: A critique of semantic networks, *Psychological Review,* **96,** 292–315.

Johnson-Laird, P.N., Legrenzi, P. and Legrenzi, M.S. (1972) Reasoning and a sense of reality, *British Journal of Psychology,* **63,** 395–400.

Johnson-Laird, P.N. and Steedman, M.J. (1978) The psychology of syllogisms, *Cognitive Psychology,* **10,** 64–99.

Johnson-Laird, P.N. and Stevenson, R. (1970) Memory for syntax, *Nature,* **227,** 412.

Kahneman, D., Slovic, P. and Tversky, A. (1982) (Eds) *Judgement under Uncertainty: Heuristics and Biases,* Cambridge University Press, Cambridge.

Kahneman, D. and Tversky, A. (1972a) On prediction and judgement, ORI Research Monograph, 12(4).

Kahneman, D. and Tversky, A. (1972b) Subjective probability: A judgement of representativeness, *Cognitive Psychology,* **3,** 430–454.

Kahneman, D. and Tversky, A. (1973) On the psychology of prediction, *Psychological Review,* 80, 237–251.

Kahneman, D. and Tversky, A. (1982) On the study of statistical intuition, *Cognition,* **12,** 325–326.

Kamp, J.A.W. (1981) A theory of truth and semantic representation, in *Formal Methods in the Study of Language* (Eds J. Groendijk, T. Janssen and M. Stokhof), Mathematisch Centrum, Amsterdam.

Kay, M. (1973) The MIND system, in *Natural Language Processing* (Ed. R. Rustin), Prentice-Hall, Englewood Cliffs, NJ.

Keane, M.T.G. (1990) Incremental analogizing: Theory and model, in *Lines of Thinking: Reflections on the Psychology of Thought, Vol. 1:*

Representation, Reasoning, Analogy and Decision Making (Eds K.J. Gilhooly, M.T.G. Keane, R.H. Logie and G. Erdos), John Wiley, Chichester.

Keenan, J.M., Potts, G.R., Golding, J.M. and Jennings, T.M. (1990) Which elaborative inferences are drawn during reading? A question of methodologies, in *Comprehension Processes in Reading* (Eds D.A., Balota, G.B. Flores D'Arcais and K. Rayner), Lawrence Erlbaum Associates, Hillsdale, NJ.

Keil, F.C. (1989) *Concepts, Kinds, and Cognitive Development*, MIT Press, Cambridge, Mass.

Keil, F.C. (1990) Constraints on constraints: Surveying the epigenetic landscape, *Cognitive Science*, **14**, 135–168,

Kieras, D.E. (1981) Topicalization effects in cued recall of technical prose, *Memory and Cognition*, **9**, 541–549.

Kimball, J. (1973) Seven principles of surface structure parsing in natural language, *Cognition*, **2**, 15–47.

Kintsch, W. (1974) *The Representation of Meaning in Memory*, Lawrence Erlbaum Associates, Hillsdale, NJ.

Kintsch, W. (1988) The role of knowledge in discourse comprehension: A construction-integration model, *Psychological Review*, **95**, 163–182.

Kintsch, W. and Dijk, T.A. van (1978) Toward a model of text comprehension and production, *Psychological Review*, **85**, 363–394.

Kintsch, W. and Keenan, J.M. (1973) Reading rate and retention as a function of the number of propositions in the base structure of sentences, *Cognitive Psychology*, **5**, 257–274.

Kintsch, W., Welsch, D., Schmalhofer, F. and Zimny, S. (1990) Surface memory: A theoretical analysis, *Journal of Memory and Language*, **29**, 133–159.

Kohler, W. (1969) *The Task of Gestalt Psychology*, Princeton University Press, Princeton, NJ.

Lakoff, G. and Johnson, M. (1980) *Metaphors We Live By*, The University of Chicago Press, Chicago, Illinois.

Langley, P., Simon, H.A., Bradshaw, G.L. and Zytkow, J.M. (1987) *Scientific Discovery*, MIT Press, Cambridge, Mass.

Larkin, J.H. (1981) Enriching formal knowledge: A model for learning to solve textbook problems, in *Cognitive Skills and their Acquisition* (Ed. J.R. Anderson), Lawrence Erlbaum Associates, Hillsdale, NJ.

Larkin, J.H. (1983) The role of problem representation in physics, in *Mental Models* (Eds D. Gentner and A.L. Stevens), Lawrence Erlbaum Associates, Hillsdale, NJ.

Lave, J., Murtaugh, M. and de la Rocha, O. (1984) The dialectic of arithmetic in grocery shopping, *Everyday Cognition: Its Development in Social Context*, (Eds B. Rogoff and J. Lave), Harvard University Press, Cambridge, Mass.

Lefford, A. (1946) The influence of emotional subject matter on logical reasoning, *Journal of General Psychology*, **34**, 127–151.

Lesgold, A.M. (1988) Problem solving, in *The Psychology of Human Thought* (Eds R.J. Sternberg and E.E. Smith), Cambridge University Press, Cambridge, New York.

Lesgold, M., Rubinson, H., Feltovich, P., Glaser, R., Klopfer, D. and Wang,Y. (1988). Expertise in complex skill, in *The Nature of Expertise* (Eds M.T.H. Chi, R.Glaser and M.J. Farr), Lawrence Erlbaum Associates, Hillsdale, NJ.

Lewis, D.K. (1969) *Convention*, Harvard University Press, Cambridge, Mass.

Lichtenstein, S., Slovic, P., Fischoff, B., Layman, M. and Coombs, B. (1978) Judged frequency of lethal events, *Journal of Experimental Psychology: Human Learning and Memory*, **4**, 551–578.

Luchins, A.S. (1942) Mechanization in problem solving – The effect of Einstellung, *Psychological Monographs*, **54** (Whole No. 248), 1–95.

McClelland, J.L. (1981) Retrieving general and specific information from stored knowledge of specifics, Proceedings of the third Meeting of the *Cognitive Science* Society, pp. 170–172.

McClelland, J.L. and Rumelhart, D.E. (1981) An interactive activation model of context effects in letter perception: Part 1. An account of basic findings, *Psychological Review*, **88**, 375–407.

McClelland, J.L. and Rumelhart, D.E. (1986) A distributed model of human learning and memory, in *Parallel Distributed Processing: Explorations in the Microstructure of Cognition*, Vol. 2 (Eds J.L. McClelland, D.E. Rumelhart and the PDP Research Group), Bradford/MIT Press, Cambridge, Mass.

McClelland, J.L., Rumelhart, D.E. and Hinton, G.E. (1986) The appeal of parallel distributed processing, in *Parallel Distributed Processing: Explorations in the Microstructure of Cognition*, Vol. 2 (Eds J.L. McClelland, D.E. Rumelhart and the PDP Research Group), Bradford/MIT Press, Cambridge, Mass.

McKoon, G. and Ratcliff, R. (1980) The comprehension processes and memory structures involved in anaphoric reference, *Journal of Verbal Learning and Verbal Behaviour*, **19**, 668–682.

McKoon, G. and Ratcliff, R. (1986) Inferences about predictable events, *Journal of Experimental Psychology: Learning, Memory and Cognition*, **12**, 82–91

McKoon, G. and Ratcliff, R. (1990) Textual inferences: models and measures, in *Comprehension Processes in Reading* (Eds D.A. Balota, G.B. Flores d'Arcais and K. Rayner), Lawrence Erlbaum Associates, Hillsdale, NJ.

McKoon, G., Ratcliff, R. and Siefert, C. (1989) Making the connection: Generalized knowledge structures in story understanding, *Journal of Memory and Language*, **28**, 711–734.

McNeil, B.J., Weichselbaum, R. and Pauker, S.G. (1981) Speech and Survival: Tradeoffs between quality and quantity of life in laryngeal cancer, *The New England Journal of Medicine*, **305**, 982–987.

Maier, N.R.F. (1933) Reasoning in humans II: The solution of a problem and its appearance in consciousness, *Journal of Comparative Psychology*, **12**, 181–194.

Mani, K. and Johnson-Laird, P.N. (1982) The mental representation of spatial descriptions, *Memory and Cognition*, **10**, 181–187.

Manktelow, K.I. and Over, D.E. (1990a) Deontic thought and the selection task, in *Lines of Thinking: Reflections on the Psychology of Thought*, Vol. 1 (Eds K.J. Gilhooly, M.T.G. Keane, R.H. Logie and G. Erdos), John Wiley, Chichester.

Manktelow, K.I. and Over, D.E. (1990b) *Inference and Understanding. A Philosophical Perspective*, Routledge, London.

Manktelow, K.I. and Over, D. (1991) Social roles and utilities in reasoning with deontic conditionals, *Cognition*, **39**, 85–105.

Marcus, M. (1980) *A Theory of Syntactic Recognition for Natural Language*, MIT Press, Cambridge, Mass.

Markman, E.M. (1989) *Categorization and Naming in Children: Problems of Induction*, Bradford/MIT Press, Cambridge, Mass.

Markman, E.M. (1990) Constraints children place on word meanings, *Cognitive Science*, **14**, 57–78.

Markman, E.M. and Hutchinson, J.E. (1984) Children's sensitivity to constraints on word meaning: Taxonomic vs. thematic relations, *Cognitive Psychology*, **16**, 1–27.

Massey, C. and Gelman, R. (1988) Preschoolers' ability to decide whether pictured unfamiliar objects can move themselves, *Developmental Psychology*, **24**, 307–317.

Mayer, R.E. and Greeno, J.G. (1972) Structural differences between learning outcomes produced by different instructional methods, *Journal of Educational Psychology*, **63**, 165–173.

Medin, D.L. (1986) Commentary on 'Memory storage and retrieval processes in category learning', *Journal of Experimental Psychology: General*, **115**, 373–381.

Medin, D.L. (1989) Concepts and Conceptual Structure, *American Psychologist*, **4**, 1469–1481.

Medin, D.L. and Ortony, A. (1989) Psychological essentialism, in *Similarity and Analogical Reasoning* (Eds S. Vosniadou and A. Ortony), pp. 179–195, Cambridge University Press, Cambridge.

Medin, D.L. and Shoben, E.J. (1988) Context and structure in conceptual combination, *Cognitive Psychology*, **20**, 158–190.

Medin, D.L. and Smith, E.E. (1984) Concepts and concept formation, *Annual Review of Psychology*, **35**, 113–138.

Mervis, C.B. and Pani, J.R. (1980) Acquisition of basic object categories, *Cognitive Psychology*, **12**, 496–522.

Metcalfe, J. (1986) Premonitions of insight predict impending error, *Journal of Experimental Psychology: Learning, Memory, and Cognition*, **12**, 623–634.

Metcalfe, J. and Wiebe, D. (1987) Intuition in insight and non-insight problem solving, *Memory and Cognition*, **15**, 238–246.

Miller, G.A. (1962) Some psychological studies of grammar, *American Psychologist*, **17**, 748–762.

Miller, G.A. and Johnson-Laird, P.N. (1976) *Language and Perception*, Cambridge University Press, Cambridge.

Minsky, M. (1977) Frame system theory, in *Thinking: Readings in Cognitive Science* (Eds P.N. Johnson-Laird and P.C. Wason), Cambridge University Press, Cambridge.

Montague, R. (1968) Pragmatics, in *Contemporary Philosophy: A Survey* (Ed. R. Klibansky), Florence, La Nuova Italia Editrice (reprinted in Thomason, 1974).

Montague, R. (1974) *Formal Philosophy: Selected Papers*, Yale University Press, New Haven, Connecticut.

Morrow, D.G., Bower, G.H. and Greenspan, S.L. (1989) Updating situation models during narrative comprehension, *Journal of Memory and Language*, **28**, 292–312.

Murphy, G.L. (1988) Comprehending complex concepts, *Cognitive Science*, **12**, 529–562.

Murphy, G.L. (1990) Noun phrase interpretation and conceptual combination, *Journal of Memory and Language*, **29**, 259–288.

Murphy, G.L. and Medin, D.L. (1985) The role of theories in conceptual coherence, *Psychological Review*, **92**, 289–316.

Nelson, K. (1974) Concept, word and sentence: Interrelationships in acquisition and development, *Psychological Review*, **81**, 267–285.

Newell, A. (1981) Reasoning, problem solving and decision processes: The problem space as a fundamental category, in *Attention and Performance*, Vol. 8 (Ed. R. Nickerson), Lawrence Erlbaum Associates, Hillsdale, NJ.

Newell, A., Shaw, J.C. and Simon, H.A. (1958) Elements of a theory of human problem solving, *Psychological Review*, **65**, 151–66.

Newell, A. and Simon, H.A. (1972) *Human Problem Solving*, Prentice-Hall, Engelwood Cliffs, NJ.

Newstead, S.E. (1989) Interpretational errors in syllogistic reasoning, *Journal of Memory and Language*, **28**, 78–91.

Newstead, S.E. (1990) Conversion in syllogistic reasoning, in *Lines of Thinking: Reflections on the Psychology of Thought, Vol.1: Representation, Reasoning, Analogy and Decision Making* (Eds K.J. Gilhooly, M.T.G. Keane, R.H. Logie and G. Erdos), John Wiley, Chichester.

Nicol, J. (1988) Coreference Processing During Sentence Comprehension, Doctoral Dissertation, MIT (cited in Nicol and Swinney, 1989).

Nicol, J. and Swinney, D. (1989) The role of structure in coreference assignment during sentence comprehension, *Journal of Psycholinguistic Research*, **18**, 5–20.

Nisbett, R.E. and Ross, L. (1980) *Human inference: Strategies and Shortcomings of Social Judgement*, Prentice-Hall, Englewood Cliffs, NJ.

Nisbett, R.E. and Wilson, T.D. (1977) Telling more than we can know: verbal reports on mental processes, *Psychological Review*, **84**(3), 231–259.

Norris, D. (1987) Syntax, semantics and garden paths, in *Progress in the Psychology of Language*, Vol. 3 (Ed. A. Ellis), Lawrence Erlbaum Associates, London.

Novick, L.R. and Holyoak, K.J. (1991) Mathematical problem solving by analogy, *Journal of Experimental Psychology: Learning, Memory and Cognition*, **17**, 398–415.

Oakhill, J., Johnson-Laird, P.N. and Garnham, A. (1989) Believability and syllogistic reasoning, *Cognition*, **31**, 117–140.

Oatley, K.G. (1977) Inference, navigation and cognitive maps, in *Thinking: Readings in Cognitive Science* (Eds P.N. Johnson-Laird and P.C. Wason), Cambridge University Press, Cambridge.

Oden, C.G. (1987) Concept, knowledge and thought, in *Annual Review of Psychology* (Eds M.R. Rosenzweig and L.W. Porter), **38**, 203–227.

Ortony, A. (1979) Beyond literal similarity, *Psychological Review*, **86**, 161–180.

Ortony, A., Schallert, I., Reynolds, R. and Antos, S. (1978) Interpreting metaphors and idioms: Some effects of context on comprehension, *Journal of Verbal Learning and Verbal Behaviour*, **17**, 465–477.

Osherson, D.N. (1990) Judgement, in *An Invitation to Cognitive Science: Thinking*, Vol. 3 (Eds D.N. Osherson and E.E. Smith), MIT Press, Cambridge, Mass.

Osherson, D.N. and Smith, E.E. (1981) On the adequacy of prototype theory as a theory of concepts, *Cognition*, **9**, 35–58.

Pazzani, M.J. (1991) Influence of prior knowledge on concept acquisition: Experimental and computational results, *Journal of Experimental Psychology: Learning, Memory and Cognition*, **17**, 416–432.

Perkins, D.N. (1988) Creativity and the quest for mechanism, in *The Psychology of Human Thought* (Eds R.J. Sternberg and E.E. Smith), Cambridge University Press, Cambridge.

Piaget, J. (1926) *The Language and Thought of the Child*, Routledge and Kegan Paul, London.

Piaget, J. (1950) *The Psychology of Intelligence*, Routledge and Kegan Paul, London.

Piaget, J. and Inhelder, B. (1969) Intellectual operations and their development, in *Experimental Psychology: Its Scope and Method* (Eds P. Fraisse and J. Piaget), Routledge and Kegan Paul, London.

Pinker, S. and Prince, A. (1988) On language and connectionism: Analysis of a parallel distributed processing model of language acquisition, *Cognition*, **28**, 73–193.

Pollard, P. (1982) Human reasoning: Some possible effects of availability, *Cognition*, **12**, 65–96.

Posner, M.I. (1973) *Cognition: An Introduction,* Scott, Foresman, Glenview, Ill.

Qin, Y. and Simon, H.A. (1990) Laboratory replication of scientific discovery procedures, *Cognitive Science,* **14,** 281–312.

Quillian, M. R. (1968) Semantic memory, in *Semantic Information Processing* (Ed. M. Minsky), MIT Press, Cambridge, Mass.

Quine, W.V.O. (1977) Natural kinds, in *Naming, Necessity and Natural Kinds* (Ed. S.P. Schwartz), Cornell University Press, Ithaca, New York.

Rayner, K., Carlson, M. and Frazier, L. (1983) The interaction of syntax and semantics during sentence processing: Eye movements in the analysis of semantically biased sentences, *Journal of Verbal Learning and Verbal Behaviour,* **22,** 358–374.

Reed, S.K., Ernst, G.W. and Banerji, R. (1974) The role of analogy in transfer between similar problem states, *Cognitive Psychology,* **6,** 436–450.

Revlin, R. and Leirer, V.O. (1978) The effects of personal biases on syllogistic reasoning: Rational decision from personalized representations, in *Human Reasoning* (Eds R. Revlin and R.E. Mayer), Holt, New York.

Revlis, R. (1975) Two models of syllogistic reasoning: Feature selection and conversion, *Journal of Verbal Learning and Verbal Behaviour,* **14,** 180–195.

Richards, I.A. (1936) *The Philosophy of Rhetoric,* Oxford University Press, Oxford.

Rips, L.J. (1983) Cognitive processes in propositional reasoning, *Psychological Review,* **90,** 38–71.

Rips, L.J. (1989) Similarity, typicality and categorization, in *Similarity and Analogical Reasoning* (Eds S. Vosniadou and A. Ortony), Cambridge University Press, Cambridge.

Rips, L.J. and Marcus, S.L. (1977) Suppositions and the analysis of conditional sentences, in *Cognitive Processes in Comprehension* (Eds M.A. Just and P.A. Carpenter), Lawrence Erlbaum Associates, Hillsdale, NJ.

Rosch, E. (1973) On the internal structure of perceptual and semantic categories, in *Cognitive Development and the Acquisition of Language* (Ed. T.E. Moore), Academic Press, New York.

Rosch, E.H. (1975) Cognitive representations of semantic categories, *Journal of Experimental Psychology: General,* **104,** 192–233.

Rosch, E. and Mervis, C.B. (1975) Family resemblances: Studies in the internal structure of categories, *Cognitive Psychology*, **7**, 573–605.

Rumelhart, D.E. (1980) Schemata, the building blocks of cognition, in *Theoretical Issues in Reading Comprehension* (Eds R.J. Spiro, B.C. Bruce and W.F. Brewer), Lawrence Erlbaum Associates, Hillsdale, NJ.

Rumelhart, D.E., Smolensky, P., McClelland, J.L. and Hinton, G.E. (1986) Schemata and sequential thought processes in PDP models, in *Parallel Distributed Processing: Explorations in the Microstructure of Cognition, Vol. 2: Psychological and Biological Models*, Bradford/MIT Press, Cambridge, Mass.

Sachs, J.S. (1967) Recognition memory for syntactic and semantic aspects of connected discourse, *Perception and Psychophysics*, **2**, 437–442.

Sanford, A.J. (1987) *The Mind of Man*, Yale University Press, Yale.

Sanford, A.J. (1989) Component processes of reference resolution in discourse, in *Advances in Cognitive Science* (Ed. N. Sharkey), Ablex Publishing Corporation, New York.

Sanford, A.J. (1990) On the nature of text driven inference, in *Comprehension Processes and Reading* (Eds D.A. Balota, G.B. Flores D'Arcais and K. Rayner), Lawrence Erlbaum Associates, Hillsdale, NJ.

Sanford, A.J. and Garrod, S.C. (1981) *Understanding Written Language*, John Wiley, Chichester.

Sapir, E. (1944) Grading: A study in semantics, *Philosophy of Science*, **11**, 93–116.

Savin, H.B. and Perchonock, E. (1965) Grammatical structure and the immediate recall of English sentences, *Journal of Verbal Learning and Verbal Behaviour*, **4**, 348–353.

Scardamalia, M. and Bereiter, C. (1991) Literate expertise, in *Toward a General Theory of Expertise: Prospects and Limits* (Eds K.A. Ericsson and J. Smith), Cambridge University Press, Cambridge.

Schank, R.C. (1982) Reminding and memory organisation: an introduction to MOPs, in *Strategies for Natural Language Processing* (Eds W.G. Lehnert and M.H. Ringle), Lawrence Erlbaum Associates, Hillsdale, NJ.

Schank, R.C. and Abelson, R.P. (1977) *Scripts, Plans, Goals and Understanding*, Lawrence Erlbaum Associates, Hillsdale, NJ.

Schank, R.C., Lebowitz, M. and Birnbaum, L. (1978), *Integrated Partial Parsing*, Computer Science Department, Yale University.

Schiffer, S.R. (1972) *Meaning*, Clarendon Press, Oxford.

Schmalhofer, F. and Glavanov, D. (1986) Three components of understanding a programmer's manual: Verbatim, propositional and situation representations, *Journal of Memory and Language*, **25**, 279–294.

Scribner, S. (1988) Thinking in action: some characteristics of practical thought,. in *Practical Intelligence: Nature and Origins of Competence in the Everyday World* (Eds R.J. Sternberg and R.K. Wagner), Cambridge University Press, Cambridge.

Searle, J. (1969) *Speech Acts*, Cambridge University Press, Cambridge.

Shaver, P., Pierson, L. and Lang, S. (1975) Converging evidence for the functional significance of imagery in problem solving, *Cognition*, **3**, 359–375.

Sidner, C.L. (1983) Focusing in the comprehension of definite anaphora, in *Computational Models of Discourse* (Eds M. Brady and R.C. Berwick), MIT Press, Cambridge, Mass.

Simon, H.A. (1959) Theories of decision making in economics and behavioural science, *American Economic Review*, **49**, 253–283.

Simon, H.A. (1966) Scientific discovery and the psychology of problem solving, in *Mind and Cosmos: Essays in Contemporary Science and Philosophy* (Ed. R.G. Colodny), University of Pittsburgh Press, Pittsburgh.

Simon, H.A. (1967) Motivational and emotional controls of cognition, *Psychological Review*, **74**, 29–39.

Simon, H.A. (1985) Information-processing theory of human problem solving, in *Issues in Cognitive Modeling* (Eds A.M. Aitkenhead and J.M. Slack), Lawrence Erlbaum Associates, Hillsdale, NJ.

Simon, H.A. and Gilmartin, K.A. (1973) A simulation of memory for chess positions, *Cognitive Psychology*, **5**, 29–46.

Simon, H.A. and Hayes, J.R. (1976) The understanding process: Problem isomorphs, *Cognitive Psychology*, **8**, 165–190.

Singer, M. (1979) Processes of inference in sentence encoding, *Memory and Cognition*, **7**, 192–200.

Singer, M. (1980) The role of case-filling inferences in the coherence of brief passages, *Discourse Processes*, **3**, 185–201.

Singer, M. (1990) *Psychology of Language: An Introduction to Sentence and Discourse Processes*, Lawrence Erlbaum Associates, Hillsdale, NJ.

Singley, M.K. and Anderson, J.R. (1989) *The Transfer of Cognitive Skill*, Harvard University Press, Cambridge, Mass.

Skinner, B.F. (1957) *Verbal Behaviour*, Appleton-Century Crofts, New York.

Slovic, P. (1990) Choice, in *An Invitation to Cognitive Science*: Thinking, Vol. 3 (Eds D.N. Osherson and E.E. Smith), MIT Press, Cambridge, Mass.

Smith, E.E. and Medin, D.L. (1981) *Categories and Concepts*, Harvard University Press, Cambridge, Mass.

Smith, E.E. and Osherson, D.A. (1984) Conceptual combination with prototype concepts, *Cognitive Science*, 8, 337–361.

Smith, E.E., Osherson, D.A., Rips, L.J. and Keane, M. (1988) Combining prototypes: A selective modification model, *Cognitive Science*, **12**, 485–527.

Smith, E.E., Shoben, E.J. and Rips, L.J. (1974) Structure and process in semantic memory: a featural model for semantic decisions, *Psychological Review*, **81**, 214–241.

Speelman, C.P. and Kirsner, K. (1990) The representation of text-based and situation-based information in discourse comprehension, *Journal of Memory and Language*, **29**, 119–132.

Spelke, E.S. (1990) Principles of object perception, *Cognitive Science*, **14**, 29–56.

Sperber, D. and Wilson, D. (1982) Mutual knowledge and relevance in theories of comprehension, in *Mutual Knowledge* (Ed. N.V. Smith), Academic Press, London.

Sperber, D. and Wilson, D. (1986) *Relevance: Communication and Cognition*, Basil Blackwell, Oxford.

Sperber, D. and Wilson, D. (1987) Precis of relevance: communication and cognition, *Behavioural and Brain Sciences*, **10**, 697–710.

Stevenson, R.J. (1986) The time course of pronoun comprehension, in *Proceedings of the Eighth Annual Conference of the Cognitive Science Society* (Ed. C. Clifton), pp. 102–109, Lawrence Erlbaum Associates, Hillsdale, NJ.

Stevenson, R.J. (1988) *Models of Language Development*, Open University Press, Milton Keynes.

Stevenson, R.J. (in press) Rationality and Reality, in *Rationality* (Eds K.I. Manktelow and D. Over), Routledge, London.

Stevenson, R.J. (to appear) Models rules and expertise: Commentary on 'Deduction' by P.N. Johnson-Laird and R.M.J. Byrne (1991), *Behaviourial and Brain Sciences*.

Stillings, N.A., Feinstein, M.H., Garfield, J.L., Rissland, E.L., Rosenbaum, D.A., Weisler, S.E. and Baker-Ward, L. (1987) *Cognitive Science: An Introduction*, MIT Press, Cambridge, Mass.

Taraban, R. and McClelland, J.L. (1988) Constituent attachment and thematic role assignment in sentence processing: influences of content-based expectations, *Journal of Memory and Language*, **27**, 597–632.

Tarski, A. (1931) The concept of truth in formalised languages, in *Logic, Semantics, Metamathematics: Papers from 1923 to 1938*, (Trans. J.H. Woodger), Oxford University Press, Oxford.

Taylor, S.E. and Thompson, S.C. (1982) Stalking the elusive vividness effect, *Psychological Review*, **89**, 155–181.

Thomas, J.C., Jr (1974) An analysis of behaviour in the hobbits-orcs problem, *Cognitive Psychology*, **6**, 257–269.

Till, R., Mross, E.F. and Kintsch, W. (1988) Time course of priming for associate and inference words in a discourse context, *Memory and Cognition*, **16**, 283–298.

Tourangeau, R. and Rips, L. (1991) Interpreting and evaluating metaphors, *Journal of Memory and Language*, **30**, 452–472.

Tversky, A. (1972) Elimination by aspects: a theory of choice, *Psychological Review*, **79**, 281–299.

Tversky, A. and Kahneman, D. (1973) Availability: a heuristic for judging frequency and probability, *Cognitive Psychology*, **5**, 207–232.

Tversky, A. and Kahneman, D. (1981) The framing of decisions and the psychology of choice, *Science*, **211**, 453–458.

Tweney, R. (1985) Faraday's discovery of induction: A cognitive approach, in *Faraday Rediscovered: Essays on the Life and Work of Michael Faraday* (Eds D. Goodling and F. James), Stockton Press: New York.

Voss, J.F. and Post, T.A. (1988) On the solving of ill-structured problems, in *The Nature of Expertise* (Eds M.T.H. Chi, R. Glaser and M.J. Farr), pp. 261–286, Lawrence Erlbaum Associates, Hillsdale, NJ.

Vygotsky, L.S. (1934/1962) *Thought and Language*, MIT Press, Cambridge, Mass.

Wallas, G. (1926) *The Art of Thought*, Jonathan Cape, London.

Waltz, D.L. and Pollack, J.B. (1985) Massively parallel parsing: a strongly interactive model of natural language interpretation, *Cognitive Science*, **9**, 51–74.

Wanner, E. and Maratsos, M.P. (1978) An ATN approach to comprehension, in *Linguistic Theory and Psychological Reality* (Eds M. Halle, J.W. Bresnan and G.A. Miller), MIT Press, Cambridge, Mass.

Wason, P.C. (1960) On the failure to eliminate hypotheses in a conceptual tasks, *British Journal of Psychology*, **11**, 92–107.

Wason, P.C. (1968) Reasoning about a rule, *Quarterly Journal of Experimental Psychology*, **20**, 273–281.

Wason, P.C. and Johnson-Laird, P.N. (1972) *Psychology of Reasoning: Structure and Content*, Batsford, London.

Wason, P.C. and Shapiro, D. (1971) Natural and contrived experience in a reasoning problem, *Quarterly Journal of Experimental Psychology*, **23**, 63–71.

Watson, J.B. (1925) *Behaviourism*, New York, Norton.

Watson, J.D. (1968) *The Double Helix*, New American Library, New York.

Wertheimer, M. (1959) *Productive Thinking*, Harper and Row, New York.

Wheeler, D. (1970) Processes in word recognition, *Cognitive Psychology*, **1**, 59–85.

Whitehead, A.N. and Russell, B. (1910–13) *Principia Mathematica*, Cambridge University Press, Cambridge.

Whorf, B.L. (1941) The relation of habitual thought and behaviour to language, in *Language, Culture and Personality* (Ed. L. Spier), University of Utah Press, Salt Lake City, Utah.

Wilson, D. and Sperber, D. (1981) On Grice's theory of conversation, in *Conversation and Discourse* (Ed. P. Werth), London, Croom Helm.

Winograd, T. (1972) Understanding natural language, *Cognitive Psychology*, **3**, 1–191.

Winston, P.H. (1980) Learning and reasoning by analogy, *Communications of the ACM*, **23**, 689–703.

Wittgenstein, L. (1953) *Philosophical Investigations*, Basil Blackwell, Oxford.

Wood, D.J. (1969) The nature and development of problem-solving strategies, unpublished Ph.D. thesis, University of Nottingham.

Woods, W.A. (1970) Transition network grammars for natural language analysis, *Communications of the Association for Computing Machinery*, 13, 591–606.

Woods, W.A. (1975) What's in a link? Foundations for semantic networks, in *Representation and Understanding* (Eds D.G. Bobrow and A.M. Collins), Academic Press, New York.

Woodworth, R.S. and Sells, S.B. (1935) An atmosphere effect in formal syllogistic reasoning, *Journal of Experimental Psychology*, 18, 451–460.

INDEX

syntactic constraints, 52, 117–18,
228–9
syntactic knowledge, 129, 301–2,
306
syntactic processing, 22, 55–6,
58–60, 62, 65, 71, 73, 80, 81, 292
serial, 24, 60, 79
syntactic representation, 60–1, 79,
80, 97
of texts, 105, 108
syntactic system, 158
syntactic theories, 164, 166, 167
and reasoning, 156, 158–60, 162,
169, 172, 178–9, 181, 288–9
syntax, 1–3, 4, 9–10, 12, 61, 73, 89,
90, 105, 116, 127, 158
ambiguous, 55, 56, 58–9, 61, 64–6,
74
rules of, 7, 27
structure, 3, 4, 7, 10–13, 17, 51, 55,
63, 66

Taraban, R., 62, 72, 80
experiments, 74–8
target problems, 221, 222, 224
target sentences, 113
Tarski, A., 86
taxonomic groupings, 203
taxonomy, 100–1
text base, 125–6, 128
text comprehension, 104–5, 129–30
models of, 106–11, 201
text processing, 124–5
texts, 99, 116, 131, 282
representations of, 105, 107–8,
109–11, 125, 126, 129, 297
memory of, 108–11, 115–16, 120
textual constraints, 117, 119–20,
129
Thagard, P.R., 51, 52, 220, 222, 224,
226–7, 228–30, 250, 251
thematic processor, 66, 74, 77, 80
thought, 1, 22, 27, 53, 217–18, 232,
252, 281, 282, 294, 300
analogical, 24
combined with language, 23, 25

conscious, 54, 59, 251, 254–5,
295–6
creative, 249, 252
deductive, 16–17, 20, 54, 282, 288
independence from language, 1,
7, 9, 12, 16, 18, 21–2, 23, 228,
288, 306
inductive, 16, 54, 282
logical, 8, 23
process of, 8, 19, 20, 21, 26, 221,
282, 285, 295
relationship with language, 1–2,
6–9, 16–18, 19, 24–5, 228,
280–1, 283, 288, 292, 297,
305–6
rule-governed nature of, 49
sequential nature of, 292
stages of, 266
Till, R., 128
time-sharing, 250
topics, 119, 125–6, 148, 150, 151, 154,
282
Toupin, C., 225
Tourangeau, R., 154
Tower of Hanoi problem, 20, 216
transitive inference, 17, 18, 19, 20,
23, 159, 160, 285
transformations, 7, 10
trial-and-error search, 253
truth conditional theories, 83, 136–7
tuned procedural learning, 232,
234–6
Tversky, A., 19, 270–6, 278–80
typicality, in concepts 186, 187,
188–9, 190–1, 196–7, 204

unconscious processes, 24, 216, 229,
248–50, 252, 254–5, 282, 284,
292–4
language comprehension, 297, 301
of thought, 295–6
underlying principles, 202–3, 204,
205
universal statements, 27
utility, 269
theory, 256, 269–70

Index compiled by Noa Kleinman